FORGOTTEN SCOTTISH VOICES FROM THE GREAT WAR

DEREK YOUNG

TEMPUS

First published 2005

Tempus Publishing Limited
The Mill, Brimscombe Port,
Stroud, Gloucestershire, GL5 2QG

British Library Cataloguing in Publication Data.
A catalogue record for this book is available from the British Library.

ISBN 0 7524 3326 1

Typesetting and origination by Tempus Publishing Limited
Printed in Great Britain

Contents

Preface

I have tried for some time now to think of an introduction to this book. Something witty, contemporary, controversial or even, God forbid, philosophical. I have failed miserably at every attempt, and yet in a strange perverse way for once I am content with my failure. It is not for me to tell the story of events, but for those who served. My role is only to tie events together, join the dots if you like. It is for others to recall the events which had an impact upon all sections of Scottish society. What has been assembled is a picture of the war as seen by those who were there, telling of the dull and the mundane, giving a picture of everyday life in the trenches as well as the excitement of combat. The war brought out the best and worst in people and affected Scots of all ages and from all walks of life – the young and the not so young, single men and those leaving behind families, the unemployed and those giving up the luxury of full-time, stable employment.

William Begbie joined the 7th Battalion Royal Scots in the summer of 1914, aged just fifteen years. When Private Begbie came home from the local drill hall and broke the news of his enlistment to his parents they had differing views:

> When I arrived home, my mother said 'Take your uniform back – you are too young to be a soldier', but my father only laughed and said to my mother, 'This will do him no harm – Territorials don't go to war'.

On 4 August 1914 Begbie was mobilised with the rest of his battalion, one of the youngest members of the British army to go to war. In 1915 at the age of sixteen he was wounded twice in the hell that was Gallipoli. He subsequently served in Egypt and was gassed in France during the last German offensive of the war in 1918. Territorials don't go to war!

The First World War was costly for Scotland. Even now, ninety years after the event, the number of Scottish dead varies depending on where the information is obtained, but the Scottish National War Memorial at Edinburgh Castle records over 147,000 Scottish deaths in the Great War. Second Lieutenant Alan Macgregor Wilson, serving in France with the 8th Battalion Black Watch, spoke for all of us when he wrote:

> I do not hear the guns today. Yesterday and today they have been quiet. The lull before the storm. But still the ambulances pass with their freight of sadness. The eternal stream. But how much more sad is the thought of those who have been left. Finding their last resting place in foreign soil. The luxury of a coffin is denied. They are too many these fallen heroes. I wonder sometimes how long will it take for these sons of Britain to be forgotten. Never, I hope, and least when judgement calls.

The Armistice did not signal an end to unnecessary suffering. In the early hours of New Year's Day 1919 the Admiralty yacht *Iolaire* ran aground off the island of Lewis. With lifeboats for 100 and lifejackets for only eighty, the vessel had nevertheless been deemed safe to carry 260 servicemen returning to the island after four years of war. Out of 284 passengers and crew only seventy-nine survived. Men who had suffered four years of the bloodiest conflict the world had ever known drowned within sight and sound of their homes. These men were among the 690,235 Scots who served, not only with Scottish regiments but in every branch of the armed service and in every theatre of war.

In recent years it has become obligatory to attack as naive or idealistic those whose writings in any way imply that there is a futility in war. Naive! Idealistic! I can live with that.

In an age when Scottish regiments are once again facing the threat of amalgamation I would encourage readers to take the time to visit some of the numerous regimental museums scattered across the country. Staffed by dedicated individuals and desperately underfunded, they are part of our heritage. I have always found the staff of these museums to be both helpful and informative. Thomas Smyth, archivist at the Black Watch Museum, Perth, rates a special thank you, as does Lt Colonel Fairrie at the Queen's Own Highlanders Museum, Fort George, who was kind enough to assist with photographs. At the regimental museum of the King's Own Scottish Borderers, Ian Martin also took time to help with photographs and deserves a special mention, while at the Royal Scots Museum, Edinburgh Castle, David Murphy similarly went out of his way to assist.

My thanks also go to the staff of the University of Dundee Archives and especially the staff of the Special Collections, University of Leeds, who, it seems, can never do enough to help.

Finally, I would like to take this opportunity to thank all those who contributed letters, diaries and photographs for inclusion in this book. There are too many to list here but my heartfelt thanks go out to them all.

Derek Rutherford Young

You always walk with your head held high
In quiet innocence you cry
No quarter given, none was asked
All that's left are the memories of a distant past.

You've known despair, you've known sorrow
Suffered heartache, but you know it's going to take
Something soft and gentle to brush away the tears
All that's left are the memories of those distant years.

In silence and in pain you wait patient for the end
Your life's been full, you've lost old friends
Still, in the autumn of your days, in your old familiar ways
The memories keep flooding back every time that old familiar music plays.

Ruth Ford

1

Mobilise for War

Led by the pipes, the 1st Battalion Cameron Highlanders marched out through the gates of Edinburgh Castle, crossed the esplanade filled with cheering onlookers, and trooped down to the train station to embark for France. As they left to take their place with the British Expeditionary Force, crowds of friends and well-wishers gathered at the station to give them a send-off. The battalion was once more going to war. No one on that day realised that few of those leaving would ever return. Across the country, similar scenes were being played out as Scotland's regular and Territorial battalions went through the process of mobilising for war.

On 4 August 1914 Great Britain had once again entered into a war in continental Europe. Troops were mobilised and Territorial units were sent to their war stations to protect bridges, aqueducts, railway lines and reservoirs. In an effort to bring the battalions up to strength, reservists were called back to the colours and issued with the necessary equipment while any shortfalls in men and equipment were quickly made good. Officers and men on leave were hurriedly recalled and returned to find regimental depots in the throes of organised chaos as battalions prepared to leave and new recruits flooded in, adding to the confusion. Trains, wagons and horses were commandeered. Trains were not only required to transport the men – the battalion transport train had also to be transported by rail. Horses and general service wagons had to be transported to ports of embarkation.

In stark contrast to the very public departure of the Camerons from Edinburgh, and of the equally public display of support, in Glasgow the 1st Battalion Cameronians (Scottish Rifles) mobilised with less fanfare. R.C. Money recalled that the battalion mobilised in five days, collecting reservists and spare equipment, then departed for Southampton without the fanfare and cheering crowds of well-wishers seen elsewhere:

> Our send of[f] from Glasgow was singularly quiet because it took place in the middle of the night and we just slipped quietly out of the gates of Maryhill barracks and very few of us ever saw them again.

His diary also recalled that their departure clearly suffered from a lack of preparation. The battalion 'left Glasgow in 4 trains, with cattle trucks. Cattle trucks "hopelessly inadequate" for the draft horses; several died.' The roofs of the cattle trucks were too low for the heavy draft horses, and on arrival at Southampton a great number were found dead in the trucks. His fellow officer Captain R.H.W. Rose recorded that the battalion crossed the Channel on 14 August. We are told the battalion 'embarked on SS *Caledonia*. Fine Anchor Line ship, very lucky, as many in pig boats, not told where going.' Elsewhere, H.D. Clark noted that by 8 August the 2nd Battalion Argyll & Sutherland Highlanders had absorbed 600 reservists and was up to complement. The battalion left Fort George on 9 August and arrived at Southampton on the morning of 10 August. Mobilisation itself was not without incident. Clark recalled the chaos when the battalion left Fort George:

> There was a scheme whereby horse owners in the area were subsidised throughout the years, in order that they would provide horses for transport of the battalion when required on mobilisation being ordered. Of course the horses were new to each other

> and had to be made up into teams and fitted with harness from the quartermasters store which was brand new and very stiff. As one can imagine it was very difficult to make up a happy team of horses to pull the various wagons and when we did eventually move down to entrain to go to war, our progress from Fort George to the station was like a rodeo which entertained the local inhabitants to a great extent.

It was clearly not expected that they would get up to strength so quickly, and when the battalion reached Southampton there was not enough room on the vessel allocated. One company had to remain behind for later onward travel. Clark also recalled that when the battalion landed in France 'the great difficulty was to prevent the troops enjoying the hospitality of the villagers as we passed along because they put out buckets of red wine and so on for the troops to drink as they passed.' Second Lieutenant J.C. Cunningham, serving alongside Clark, recalled one of the major difficulties associated with mustering Highland regiments:

> We had a company of MacLean's complete and 2 companies of Campbell's and the others were mixed but at that time [outbreak of war] if you were in those companies you had to know the last three numbers of everybody in your company and the roll call was called by the last 3 numbers of the man's number. We were all Campbell's. So it was no good calling Campbell, Campbell, Campbell and they used to be called 591, 724.

The scene at Dingwall station when the Seaforth Highlanders entrained was one of calm efficiency as relatives and ex-soldiers gathered on the platform in an atmosphere of reflection to wish them a safe return, while the King's Own Scottish Borderers, embarking from Dublin, also did so in an unhurried manner, reminiscent of a peacetime mobilisation exercise. War was declared in the atmosphere of a Bank Holiday weekend.

Scotland was in the throes of the Trades Holidays – the annual summer holiday period – and in many cases the Scottish Territorial battalions had just completed their annual summer camp and were prepared, if not ready, to mobilise. The 6th Battalion Black Watch contained an Irish company, raised and based in Ireland:

> These Irishmen formed a self-contained company and journeyed over to attend the annual training camps in Scotland. The company managed to assemble, make the journey from Ireland, and present itself at the Perth barracks only two days after war was declared.

Streets lined with cheering crowds were a common sight in the early days as troops, both regular and Territorial, were mobilised and dispatched to their war station. Friends, family and workmates would turn out to give the departing troops a rousing send-off with popular songs and stirring speeches. In many instances a party atmosphere developed at railway stations as departing troops were sent off to war with presents of food, and in many cases drink, for the long journey south.

Scotland's Territorial battalions expected to play their part from the start. While regular Scottish battalions were mobilised for war in Europe, the Territorial Force was mobilised for home defence and increased training:

> In August 1914 the Territorial Force in Scotland was in the process of completing its annual camp and was ideally positioned to respond to the mobilisation. There was a feeling at large that the army would soon be in action.

The unforeseen ability to mobilise and absorb the extra manpower necessary to come up to full establishment was not confined to the regular army. The 7th Battalion Black Watch, which was based and recruited in Fife, had gained some 332 recruits by the time it reached its war station on 7 August:

> Recruiting was extremely brisk. Men flocked from all parts of the country to join their local battalion, with the result that while the marching-out state, on breaking camp at Monzie, showed a total strength of 570, the corresponding state on the morning after arrival at the war station was 902.

The 7th Battalion Royal Scots was mobilised on 4 August and, after spending the night quartered in the local drill hall, entrained on the morning of 5 August to the sound of the battalion band. Private William Begbie remembered the event:

> In our company we had a few Reservists [men who had served with the army in peace time and were not liable to be called up]. Many of us who were just recruits had to listen when they were telling us what to do and what to expect. After the train started, one of the reservists said it was a long journey to the South of England and when on active service we would not get much sleep so we should take a nap when we could. To prove his point he took off his tunic, boots and trousers to have a nap. To our surprise the train stopped and a bugler sounded the fall-in. We had all taken off our equipment and put it under the seat so it was a real scramble when an NCO shouted, 'Put your equipment on the platform and fall in with your rifles'. We had a quiet giggle when the man who had taken his trousers off had to parade without them. About 20 yards away was a bridge across the railway and some people, mostly women, started to laugh when they saw what was happening.

Lieutenant Alexander Nicol of the 5th Battalion Argyll & Sutherland Highlanders was mobilised and sent to his war station at the Western Barracks, Dundee, a converted poorhouse. Nicol spent his time guarding the Tay Bridge and conducting road patrols, and slept in a commandeered bobbin factory. In a letter to his mother he described the town as 'a funny mixture of a place. Winding streets, slums all mixed up together. It is not bad when taken all together.' Having moved to Dunfermline in early May 1915 in preparation for posting overseas, Lieutenant Nicol wrote:

> It seems settled that we are going to the Dardanelles but whether we go to Egypt first for some more training or to the seat of war, nobody knows. Everyone really wanted to go to France where the Army has been putting up such a splendid fight against great odds, but this move is much better than remaining here so we don't grumble. All we hope is that we are not put on garrison duty anywhere.

Nicol's desire to avoid any form of garrison duty reflected the general desperation to get involved in the 'real' action.

'SCOTS WHA HAE'

The Shirker's Version

We're Scots wha ne'er for Britain bled,
Scots wha'm French has never led,
An' care mair for oor cosy bed,
Than ony victory.

This is no the day nor hour;
Wait till winters storms are owre,
We'll aiblins then smash Wilhelm's power,
And show our bravery.

It's graund to read o' foemen brave,
An' glorious fechtin' by the lave,
But lists o' wounded mak' us grave,
An sweer to cross the sea.

We're unco prood o' King and law'
But nothing moves us like fitba',
Sae ither men the sword may draw,
And keep us safe and free.

Lay the Prussian Junkers low,
An' we'll see'd a' in a picter show,
Hoo oor brave billies struck their blow,
An' dared to do or die.

Sae let puir Belgium thole her pains,
An' mourn for murdered wives and weans,
We dinna care to risk oor banes,
Or fecht to set her free.

2

'Awa' for a Sodjer'

As war was declared, men rushed to enlist. Eager volunteers flocked to the colours, their reasons as complex and varied as their backgrounds. Nowhere was this more evident than in Scotland, a country which, although small in size and population, nevertheless managed to provide 690,235 recruits during the war; a figure which included a higher proportion of volunteers than any other home country. Some enlisted out of a sense of patriotism or duty; others saw it as an opportunity for adventure, with memories of short-term service in the Boer War still fresh in their mind. Others saw it as relief from unemployment or the chance of escape, however temporary, from a life of drudgery. Whatever the reason, men came forward in unprecedented numbers. The demand for manpower was immediate, with Lord Kitchener making a direct appeal to the people of Scotland:

> I feel certain that Scotsmen have only to know that the country urgently needs their services to offer them with the same splendid patriotism as they have always shown in the past... their services were never more needed than they are today... I rely confidently on a splendid response to the national appeal.

Scotland responded enthusiastically to this call for manpower, with crowds of eager volunteers filling the recruiting offices and overflowing into the streets outside. Edinburgh's Cockburn Street recruiting office remained open day and night processing crowds of volunteers. Working-class men, eager to support their country, rubbed shoulders with members of the Faculty of Advocates – the recruiting office in Cockburn Street was a short stone's throw from the High Courts. In Dundee, where smaller but no less enthusiastic crowds gathered, the city's Nethergate recruiting office was 'practically invaded by men of all classes offering their services'. William Linton Andrews, a journalist in Dundee, used his literary skills to describe the sight that greeted his arrival at the local drill hall:

> Men were pouring in, overwhelming the ordinary staffs. Men were ready to sign anything, and say anything. They gave false names, false addresses, false ages. They suppressed their previous military service, or exaggerated it, just as seemed to promise them best. (W.L. Andrews, *The Haunting Years*, p.13)

There were similar scenes in Glasgow, where large crowds gathered outside the city's Gallowgate recruiting office. It was quickly reported that the Gallowgate office had been unable to cope with the rush of recruits and 'the police had difficulty in getting hundreds of intending soldiers to wait in the queues till their turn came'. Men who had come forward to enlist found that they were expected to wait in the street while the recruiting staff, unable to grasp the urgency of the moment, continued to follow the slow, laborious, pre-war procedure, including a cold bath for every volunteer prior to medical examination. L.B. Oatts, in his work *Proud Heritage: The Story of the Highland Light Infantry*, describes the scene at Hamilton in the early days of the war:

> The HLI Depot at Hamilton, already worked off its feet dealing with the reservists, was thrown into a complete state of chaos lasting four days, by 'a howling rabble arriving from Glasgow to enlist.' These stout hearts declined to leave, and the majority slept in the open in and around the barracks until they could be dealt

with – when two of them were found to have only one leg apiece, one tried to get away with 'a wooden foot', and several others had glass eyes.

Further north, in Aberdeen, Alexander Cheyne, who had graduated in Classics from Aberdeen University, worked his passage across the Atlantic and rode the Canadian prairie for a year before returning to Aberdeen to train for the ministry. When the war broke out, one of his professors set the class an essay on the subject 'My duty in the present national crisis', and when they had finished writing the entire class marched down to the nearest recruiting office and enlisted. Cheyne, Second Lieutenant 5th Battalion Gordon Highlanders, was the sole survivor of this enthusiastic young group.

It was not only in Scotland that Scots were coming forward. C.N. Barclay enlisted in London and highlighted his reasons for coming forward:

> With three or four friends I decided to join the London Scottish, and one day during the second half of August I visited their headquarters in Buckingham Gate, London, was medically examined and enlisted. My real reason for doing this was a simple one – at my age and in my circumstances, and in the atmosphere of patriotic enthusiasm at the time, I would have been ashamed not to do so, and my parents would have been ashamed of me if I had not done so. Secondary reasons were that several of my friends were joining the same regiment; also I had already decided that I did not want to be a Civil Engineer. It seemed likely to be a dull sort of profession. [He subsequently served in the army for thirty-two years.]

Joseph Brotherton MacLean, who was born in Glasgow on 30 March 1889, had emigrated to New York in 1911 but returned to Scotland in 1914 shortly after the outbreak of war, sailing from New York on 28 October. He was commissioned as a second lieutenant in the 7th Battalion Cameronians. H.E. May was working as a London policeman when war began. He travelled north to Scotland and enlisted in the Cameron Highlanders, rising to the rank of sergeant and in the process winning the Military Medal. In some parts of Scotland it was an adventure merely to reach the recruiting depot. Robert M. Craig, Corporal, 5th Battalion Cameron Highlanders, had to travel south from Shetland by ferry as far as Aberdeen and then by train on the notorious Highland Railway. He recalled his feelings on arrival in his diary:

> In due course I arrived at Fort George – a very dismal place, right on the seashore – and entered barracks, which looked to me exactly like a prison. I should not have been surprised to see the 'Abandon hope' inscription over the door, and I certainly felt very small and forlorn, and not at all military-like.

In Glasgow, William Nelson's initial attempt to enlist met with failure:

> He was initially rejected on medical grounds and his ill-health was attributed to poor dental health. To improve the position all of his teeth were extracted. The operation was carried out at home by the dentist on the kitchen table where he was held down by members of his family. He was given a glass of whisky as an anaesthetic and the upper row was removed one day and the following day the same procedure ensued in removing the bottom row. The only amusing part of this ritual was the family cat chasing the discarded teeth on the kitchen floor.

This was one of the enticements advertised to stimulate recruitment; local dentists took out advertisements offering their services free to potential recruits. Even in time of crisis the army would refuse any man with poor teeth as he would be unable to chew the regulation biscuits. How many men lived because of poor dental hygiene? After recovering from his kitchen table surgery William Nelson was later able to enlist in the 7th (Blythswood) Territorial Battalion of the Highland Light Infantry in Bridgeton, Glasgow, on 18 September 1914. In Scotland, residual loyalty to a clan chieftain was still a major factor in recruiting for Highland regiments. At a recruiting meeting in Inverness on 1 September 1914, Cameron of Lochiel remarked that 'just as in the old days... Highlanders responded to the call of their chiefs.'

> In the early winter of 1914 reservists were joining one of the Highland regiments. The men trickled in at most of the stations in Caithness, and they became more numerous as the train entered Sutherlandshire. As the short winter day closed in, snow began to fall; as the train wound through the valleys, all the houses were lit up and the people stood at the doors waving torches and chanting a high-pitched battle song. Except for the railway, nothing was changed. It was thus all through the ages that the clans had mustered, and it was thus that the women, the grandfathers, and the children had sent their men to war. (D.T. Jones, *Rural Scotland During the War*)

Lochiel, approached by Kitchener to raise new battalions for the Queen's Own Cameron Highlanders, quickly declared 'I want to raise a thousand Highlanders for my own battalion and I have no doubt I shall have little difficulty in doing so'. He quickly initiated a recruiting campaign, placing advertisements in the Scottish press:

> I give my personal guarantee that at the end of the war the battalion will be brought back to Inverness, where it will be disbanded with all convenient dispatch. Companies and platoons will be organised according to local districts, so that men from each district of the highlands will always be kept together in their own section, platoon, or company.

Lochiel was not alone in using the ties of heritage and clan loyalty in an effort to raise recruits. He was joined in this by Lord Lovat, who was requested by the War Office to use his position of influence to raise recruits, especially for the Lovat Scouts. In January 1915 Lord Rosebery headed an appeal to the men of the Lothians on behalf of 'their noble and historic regiment, the Royal Scots'. He pointed out that 'lowlanders should be as proud of their regiments as highlanders'. Many others were in a position to adopt a more direct approach to the provision of recruits. Companies, and in some cases individuals, offered a signing-on bonus to those men prepared to enlist.

Sir Ralph Anstruther arrived at the recruiting office in Cupar with his chauffeur, four of his gardeners and one of his footmen. The six unfortunates were then enlisted in the Black Watch. Sir Ralph was not alone in his desire to encourage recruitment among his domestic employees. The new Earl of Wemyss went so far as to threaten to dismiss any of his estate workers between the ages of eighteen and thirty who failed to take the opportunity to enlist. Lord Rosebery drove round his estates collecting his young employees for recruitment while in Glasgow the owners of motor cars were patrolling the streets advertising for recruits, 'shanghaiing' those that they found lounging around and transporting them to the nearest recruiting office.

Meanwhile, local authorities were willing to use any means to promote enlistment:

> At the sheriff court in Forfar the local Chief Constable suggested that those brought before the court on charges such as drunkenness be 'persuaded' to enlist and it would appear that the option of military service for those appearing before the courts was not isolated to Forfar as the number of convicted persons sent to prison in Scotland's four main cities in late 1914 showed a marked drop over the figures for the previous year.

Similarly, in Glasgow the Night Asylum was reported empty of those young unemployed men who were normally resident there. They 'had all disappeared; they had gone to serve their country'. Alastair Crerar was working as a legal clerk in 1914 and recalled:

> I found life very frustrating. The war was involving everything and many of my friends and nearly all of my male cousins were joining the Army or Navy and I wanted to do the same, but for various reasons mainly the fact that I was deterred by my bosses in the office who needed me, and perhaps also sympathy for my mother who had been left a widow little more than a year ago, I couldn't get away yet.

He eventually managed to join the Officer Training Corps, which allowed him to obtain a commission in the 2nd Battalion Royal Scots Fusiliers. The harsh realities of the manpower needs overruled the residual ties to his family:

> A few days into the New Year, the postman brought me a long official envelope containing a beautifully lithographed document in the name of King George the Fifth 'to our trusty and well beloved Alastair Henry Crerar' appointing me an officer in the land forces in the rank of 2nd Lieutenant.

James Campbell was working as Assistant Inspector of Poor at Cambuslang when hostilities broke out. As a Territorial in the Royal Garrison Artillery, he was mobilised at the outbreak of war but found the dull routine of gunnery practices, route marches and practice with limbers did not live up to his idea of doing his bit. He deserted, changed into his civilian clothes in a nearby wood and sent his uniform back by post. He chose to enlist in the 6th Battalion Cameron Highlanders in Inverness as his brother was already there. After training at Liphook in Hampshire, he got his wish for action and was posted to France on 8 July 1915 with 15th (Scottish) Division, in time for the Battle of Loos. T. Chamberlain was employed as a clerk in a timber merchant's office in Glasgow when he saw Lovat's call for recruits. 'Well I joined the Cameron Highlanders because I knew a number of people who had already joined there.' Others saw enlistment in a different light. W. Sorley Brown, Lieutenant, 4th Battalion King's Own Scottish Borderers, recalled in his diary:

> I came to the conclusion that the sword is mightier than the pen in these eventful times. So I hied me down one morning to the local Recruiting Office and offered to join the Foreign Service Battalion of the 4th King's Own Scottish Borderers.

He enlisted in Galashiels and was medically examined by the local doctor, who knew him well. The doctor wasn't keen to pass him and, although he informed the Recruiting Officer 'well, he's passed the tests, but he's always ailing, and I'm not so sure if he's really fit to go out there', Brown was allowed to enlist, going on to serve with the battalion in Gallipoli, Palestine and Egypt. In George Square, Glasgow, an outdoor cinema was erected and was used to show films of local battalions training in an effort to stimulate recruitment. Friends and relatives would crowd round to see 'weel kent' faces and, it was hoped, feel a duty to enlist. Robert Irvine recalled that at this time he was swept up in the feeling of war enthusiasm, often mistaken for patriotism:

> When Lord Kitchener's pointing finger was on every hoarding throughout the country – 'Your King and Country Needs You' – I was one of the innocents who was enmeshed in the web of patriotism at the First World War. I was only a shop assistant at the time, and on reflection I think it was more that I wanted to escape from the humdrum life behind a grocer's counter and see a bit of the country. (R. Irvine in MacDougall, *Voices from War and some Labour Struggles*, p.28)

Many came forward to enlist and lied about their age and, although they were obviously underage, the recruiting sergeant, or officer, would turn a blind eye. The recruiting sergeant and examining doctor were still, even after the outbreak of war, paid a bounty for each recruit passed as fit and sworn in. Initially it was five shillings per man and, although it was later reduced in the light of the number of men coming forward, there was still an incentive to turn a blind eye. Recruiting vans toured the outlying districts of rural Scotland in an effort to enlist those men who had been unable to walk the long distance to regional recruiting offices. Meanwhile, in the cities tramcars carried advertisements urging the young men to enlist in local regiments. For the first time Glasgow trams carried advertisements, in this case for the Cameron Highlanders and the Highland Light Infantry. 'Illuminated tramcars nightly toured the streets of Glasgow with bands on board in an effort to stir the suburbs into action. Determined not to be outdone, Edinburgh took this concept one stage further by converting one of its tramcars into a mobile recruiting station, complete with recruiting sergeant, doctor, and justice of the peace.'

On 1 October 1914, *The Scotsman* reported:

> A new method of attracting recruits was put into operation yesterday through the Edinburgh and District Tramway Company. A car, decorated by Sir Robert Maule with the flags of the 'Allies' – Great Britain, France, Russia, Belgium and Japan – and pictures of the King and Queen, was run over different routes of the system. In the front of the car were the words conspicuously placed 'To Berlin via France', and at the back 'Take your seats for Berlin'. A piper – one of the company's employees – played music on the top of the car, and inside or on the footboard was the recruiting sergeant who was ready to attend to all who were willing to give their services. A justice of the peace was also in attendance.

This tramcar travelled the various routes of the city and suburbs, stopping at all key points and catching the spontaneous recruits before they had time to reconsider, in many cases before the effects of alcohol wore off. Some were determined to get into uniform and did not require the enticement of a recruitment campaign or the inducement of financial reward. William Cameron was lucky on the fourth attempt:

> The first real attempt I made to get into khaki was after I turned eighteen years of age. This was in the month of October 1915 and I was rejected by the Doctor or I would have been sporting an 'Argyll' kilt. My next attempt was under the Derby Scheme when on the 12th December 1915 I was again considered of no use by a Rutherglen man, Doctor Allison by name. I was beginning to think I would never be taken, but alas on the 12th May I got papers from Bath Street telling me to report there when I turned nineteen. I didn't wait till this event came off but I went on the 18th May (with a recommendation from Mr John my old employer) to try to get away with the Glasgow Highlanders but again my luck was out, they said I was too small. I went up to Bath Street the next day and after passing the medical test I managed to get into the Scottish Horse, a crack regiment.

Serving with the 4th Battalion Black Watch, Private Cuthill voiced his opinion of those who failed to come forward and enlist – as he saw it, to do their duty:

> In the last letter I got you were saying that some of the boys had joined the HLI [Highland Light Infantry] well I think it was about time as I don't see why they should stay at home and all of us here.

There was a bit more anger in his later writing: 'I see by the papers that the scavengers are on strike. Well if I had anything to do with them I would send the lot out here and make them do their bit.' Crowds gathered at street corners and at recruiting rallies, listening to speakers calling on the young men to step forward and do their duty. Even the sight of young women giving out white feathers to those men not in uniform, a predominantly English practice, was not unknown in Scotland. Large-scale public gatherings such as football matches were seen as prime opportunities to drum up trade for the recruiters. Local battalions would march round the pitch at half-time, while local dignitaries gave speeches and tried to encourage or perhaps entice members of the crowd to come forward and enlist. At some events there were such histrionic scenes as the burning of a 'fiery cross', a blatant attempt to arouse Celtic nationalism. There was a call for professional footballers to enlist and show an example to the community:

> Let Rangers and Celtic directors forget all about their dividends at present, stop their football playing, and encourage their players to enlist, thus ensuring a spontaneous rush of football enthusiasts to join the colours.

On 26 November 1914, after a home match at Tynecastle, the entire Heart of Midlothian football team enlisted at the Haymarket recruitment office, prompting large numbers of shareholders and supporters to join up. With the majority of the players enlisting in the 16th Battalion Royal Scots, they and a number of their followers formed 'C' Company. The presence of these players, their supporters and a contingent from Watsonians Rugby Club gained for the battalion, in some quarters, the title Edinburgh Sportsmen's Battalion. Interestingly, despite severe criticism of the Football League and its tardy record of recruitment, the Heart of Midlothian team was the only football team in Britain to enlist *en masse*. If Britain was to compete with the large conscript armies on the continent, there would have to be a significant increase in recruitment. The early manpower demand was for infantry and recruits were encouraged to join this branch. Thomas

Williamson was confronted with this fact when enlisting in Dundee:

> The first man to greet us when we went further into the recruiting office was a burly sergeant. 'Well,' he said, in a deep bass voice, 'Are you two chaps going to join up?' We replied, 'Yes' I began to ply him with questions such as, could we join the Army Service Corps, or the Royal Field Artillery, or the Royal Engineers? The sergeant said with a smile, 'no lads, what we are requiring urgently is infantrymen.'

Not all who came forward were successful in enlisting. Twenty-one-year-old Mitchell Lawson was one of seven young men, work colleagues, who went to enlist in August 1914. He was rejected as his chest was too small and he continued to work in the Ice and Cold Storage Company until drafted in 1918 to the Duke of Cornwall's Light Infantry. Lawson served as a non-combatant but was sent to France after the war ended. Of the other six who successfully enlisted four were killed.

One aspect of the recruiting drive was to distribute postcards depicting the history of a particular regiment and a picture of soldiers in regimental dress. Space was left for the name of an individual to be inserted when he offered to enlist – this served to reinforce ties to a particular regiment. W. Nelson received one such card from the HLI. Although Territorial battalions were receiving recruits in large numbers, not all were opting for foreign service. The bearer was able to carry such a card – suitably filled in – until he went into uniform. The card prevented pressure from other parties to enlist. Recruitment marches were used to promote the local battalions, which would spend several days criss-crossing the county, staying each night in the local drill hall and collecting new recruits on the way. When marching through towns and villages these battalions would often send a youth on ahead carrying a placard showing the number of men the battalion still required to come up to full strength.

Men came forward in large numbers for Lord Kitchener's New Armies and the Territorial Force. In August 1914 some 40,138 men enlisted for both services, while in September 58,255 men came forward, the highest monthly figure for Scottish recruitment. The 16th Battalion Royal Scots, which received the majority of Hearts players and their supporters, was one of only a handful of 'Pal's Battalions' raised in Scotland. These 'Locally Raised' battalions were primarily a phenomenon of English recruitment and only seven were raised in Scotland with varying degrees of success. In Glasgow four such battalions were formed. As a result of a council meeting on 3 September, the Corporation of Glasgow raised two battalions, the 15th and 16th Highland Light Infantry. The 15th (City of Glasgow) Battalion became known as the Tramways Battalion, as the majority of original members were employees of Glasgow Corporation Tramways Department. The 16th Battalion was made up predominantly of past and serving members of the Boys' Brigade. A third battalion, 17th Highland Light Infantry, was raised at the same time by Glasgow Chamber of Commerce. The fourth such battalion raised in Glasgow, the 18th Battalion Highland Light Infantry, was raised in 1915 as a 'Bantam' battalion for those under 5ft 3in in height. The other three battalions were raised in Edinburgh. The 15th Battalion Royal Scots was raised by the City Council and created controversy when its ranks were filled by recruits from Manchester. The 16th Battalion Royal Scots was raised by Sir George McCray. The third battalion, 17th Battalion Royal Scots, was raised by the Rosebery Royal Scots Recruitment Committee and was also a Bantam battalion.

3

Training

The urgent manpower needs of the army dictated that the training period be as short and as practical as possible. Recruits were taught the basic rudimentary skills necessary for them to be absorbed into the army. They were taught to march and drill and were introduced to the intricacies of rifle drill, bayonet drill, etc. Initial training was limited, as those left behind on mobilisation to train the new cadres often managed to find their way to the front. Many, fearful of missing out on what was supposed to be a short war – perhaps the only one of their generation – simply ignored orders and went along with their battalions to France. Others were quickly posted overseas when the BEF began to suffer high casualty rates in the early months of fighting. Retired soldiers were called back to the colours to train the new citizen armies. Although these 'dugouts' were usually the product of the Boer War, and some even saw service in the Sudan campaign, they were generally competent enough to supervise the basic training requirements of the army and many saw active service. The number of recruits outstripped the resources available, and they frequently spent their first months in the army wearing their civilian clothes and drilling with broom handles. For many the only uniforms available were made from surplus blue cloth intended for the Post Office, while others were clad in a mixture of dress uniforms and leftovers from the wars in South Africa. New battalions out on route marches made a motley sight and did little to instil confidence. Instruction took place at camps throughout the British Isles, camps which were initially tents but quickly became semi-permanent, with the construction of accommodation huts. By their very nature these camps were established in isolated and often barren localities, where a harsh environment was seen as a positive aspect. In the early months of the war, conditions in training camps situated in Scotland were primitive, with most of the men accommodated throughout the winter of 1914 in tents and temporary huts. Jim Braid ran away from home in Kirkcaldy, Fife, and joined the regular army on 3 February 1914. At the outbreak of war, after six months' training at Aldershot, Private Braid was posted to Nigg Bay in Ross-shire with the 3rd Battalion Black Watch:

> It is like mid-winter up here shivering every night. It is all right through the day trench digging and route marching. Our company were away on a route march yesterday and what a march it was. The Captain would hardly give us a rest. After the last halt we walked for two hours right into camp. They don't march up here, they gallop, nearly everybody was dropping out.

Braid frequently wrote home to his parents in Kirkcaldy, describing conditions in the camp:

> The grub is very poor up here. Nearly all tinned meat and stinking. We have sometimes an apology for ham. What a disgrace. It is enough to sicken a dead dog.

The subject of food was dear to Braid's heart and permeated his letters to his parents. He also asked them 'When do you think the war will finish now. Are we to be home by summer?' In a letter to his parents on 3 October 1914 Braid wrote excitedly:

> We received a wire this afternoon to the effect that 30,000 Germans are killed and 20,000 are prisoners. The war is about

finished now the enemy are being scattered right and left and are starving.

In a later letter he again asked:

> When do you think the war will finish now, are we to be home by summer. The Austrians are about finished now they are unable to stand up against the advance of the Russians. The Russians will no doubt finish the war and the quicker the better.

As we have seen, the Cameron Highlanders had taken the unusual step of opening their own recruiting office in Glasgow and setting their own criteria for recruits. This 'elitism' was passed on to those enlisting in the regiment. When T. Chamberlain enlisted in the Cameron Highlanders in January 1915 he was sent to Invergordon for training:

> We were there for about 3 months but as a draft was urgently required in France we were sent out there. We didn't need the same amount of training as Kitchener's Army.

He seems to be able to ignore the fact that he himself, irrespective of the regiment or battalion he was serving in, was a 'temporary' soldier, as much a part of Kitchener's army as any other. Later in the war, when Second Lieutenant C.N. Barclay of the Cameronians was sent to the same camp to recover from his wounds, he discovered that there had been no appreciable change in conditions. He quickly discovered that:

> Nigg in the winter, living in a hut camp, was a grim place. I was on light duty for the first few weeks of my stay there, and was excused the before-breakfast run, in the dark and often in the snow, which was part of the hardening process which all newly joined personnel – officers and men – were subjected to.

When Barclay had come forward to enlist in August 1914, his training had been minimal to say the least:

> A few weeks training, based at Buckingham Gate, we had learnt to march fairly long distances, had fired some twenty rounds from our rifles – carried out on a couple of visits to the ranges at Bisley – and done a little tactical training on Wimbledon Common.

After just two months' training he was sent to France in late October or early November to replace the heavy losses suffered by the 1st London Scottish at the First Battle of Ypres in October 1914. Barclay was later given a commission as Second Lieutenant in the Cameronians and posted to Fort Matilda, Greenock, for officer training with the 4th Reserve Battalion:

> This unit consisted of about 1,200 men under training and some 40 young officers – of whom I was one – also under training. It must be admitted that the training was not of a very high order… there were just not enough first class instructors available.

There was a lighter side to training, as Ian Maclaren discovered when the 6th Battalion Black Watch was stationed in Edinburgh for home defence in November 1914:

> Today we had a long route march in the morning. While we were halted and had fallen out a bakers van appeared – general rush and scramble – everyone got something, a cookie, bun or bap. The officers themselves took up their position behind and got a muffin each. When on route march we never halt near shops, which is rather exasperating after 10 miles march.

His training continued, although it was constantly disrupted by invasion scares and false alarms:

We should be going soon but great invasion scare here last week. Preparations made so that we could move to any part of coast in quickest possible time. Slept in our kilts etc. have fine dinners here. Today's was soup, stew (very good) and one apple – other meals much the same, but quite nice on the whole.

Thomas Williamson spent his first day in the army at the Royal Scots Fusiliers Depot in Ayr and certainly managed to fit in seamlessly with the requirements of army life:

At six a.m. I heard the bugler sounding the reveille. I tumbled out of bed and, as the place was like an iceberg, I got into my clothes with all haste. Then the cry rang out 'Come along you recruits.' We were paraded on the square (a large part of the barracks) wearing only boots, shirts and trousers. The physical instructor began bawling 'come along now, don't stand there looking as if you were lost.' We were lined up in twos then something began that made us warm. 'By the right, quick march. Don't shuffle; lift up your feet; double up.' Then we had to run round the square half a dozen times. I was on the verge of collapse when the halt was called. Then we had: 'Arms upward stretch, arms downward stretch, outward stretch, knees bend,' etc. etc. For one hour this went on. I soon regained my wind. After this treatment I felt the glow of health flowing through me. I was beginning to think that this outdoor life and the physical jerks would be the finest thing for me.

We had a ten minute smoke, then the clarion call of the bugle 'come to the cookhouse door boys' sounded. There was a rush to the dining room where we all sat down to breakfast served by the orderlies. The breakfast consisted of porridge and milk, then bacon, bread and margarine and a mug of tea. I certainly enjoyed my first meal as a recruit and could find no fault with anything I had eaten.

There were others who were not able to adjust to the demands of army life as quickly as Williamson. Joining his training battalion on 23 December 1916, David Ferguson spent Christmas Eve in the army and was singularly unimpressed:

> Up at a soldiers rising time and a soldiers breakfast. Taking rather bad with both life and food as expected. Received inoculation and blanket-full of kit. The latter I got into some kind of order after a struggle. Donned the kilt as a soldier and otherwise for the first time in my life and did not go into ecstatic's over the privilege.

Private Victor Silvester, Argyll & Sutherland Highlanders, was training in Sutton Veny, Wiltshire. 'I am very unhappy down here and the only thing that keeps my spirits up is the thought of the two months leave before long'. J. Wallace, 5th Battalion King's Own Scottish Borderers, did his training at Hipswell Camp near Richmond, Yorkshire, and witnessed this humorous but harsh lesson to those who would not, or could not, accept military strictures:

> Reveille sounded at 6 a.m. This was not sounded on a bugle but was played by the orderly piper who marched up and down between the huts playing 'Hey Johnnie Cope are ye waulkin yet'. I remember the occasion when all the men in a hut were late for the 'jerks' parade at 6 o' clock in the morning. The men's excuse was that they had not heard the orderly piper playing 'Hey Johnnie Cope'. Our Colonel, who must have had a sense of humour, ordered that the whole pipe band, the next morning, would march single file through this particular hut playing 'Reveille'. I don't know whether the men in the hut enjoyed it but I don't imagine the men in the pipe band would be pleased about it.
>
> The majority of the men in my hut were put into the 40 draft, we did most of our training together, our training consisted mostly of route marches, drill, musketry and bayonet fighting. Certain men received instruction in machine guns. So far as I remember we did not receive any instruction in bombs.

Sergeant H.E. May, the London policeman who had travelled the length of the country to enlist, recalled on his arrival at the Cameron Highlanders Regimental Depot that at meal times the recruits were required to wait outside the dining hall until the Depot Staff, time-serving soldiers and men returned unfit from the BEF were seated. Then the orderly sergeant gave the command and the recruits were able to enter and take seats 'below the salt' – literally the lower half of the table beyond the salt cellar. He remembered:

> There was the good corporal who trained them. He had Gaelic and would cast a disapproving eye over his squad. 'Holy -- --!' And an acid stream, descriptive of their shortcomings, would flow. One of the missing words was perhaps the most obscene that can be uttered.

Thomas Williamson's training with the Royal Scots Fusiliers continued when he was posted to Fort Matilda – between Gourock and Greenock:

> We were marched down to Battery Park which was right against the esplanade wall. We were told to remove our caps and tunics, and then began my first experience of physical training, knee bending, rising on toes, arm stretching, trotting, running, jumping and walking. After half an hour of this strenuous training we got a ten minute breather. We sat on the sea wall, and how I enjoyed the sea breeze... We were soon at it again, another session of physical jerks, jumping over hurdles, etc., but no accidents or incidents; everything going according to the sergeant's planning.

However, experiences of training camps varied. We have already heard how Private Braid found conditions and food at Nigg to be lacking. Albert Hay echoed these points when he was training with the Scottish Horse in Lincolnshire. Hay, 1st Battalion Black Watch, discovered that while undergoing training at Theddlethorpe in Lincolnshire he was 'never very well fed, nor very comfortable in the huts' and that he looked forward to guard duty:

> Our nights on patrol duty were pleasant by comparison, because we could keep warm walking outside, and the four hours 'off' were spent in a dug-out where we were smoked and heated by a small stove.

However when the battalion moved to Alford, Lincolnshire, they were quartered under canvas – twelve men to a bell tent. His diary recalls the daily routine of the training camp:

> Reveille was sounded at 6 o'clock while we were at Theddlethorpe but it was now put forward to 5.30, and we had to be on parade for roll-call and reading of the days order at 5.45, then we washed and shaved and were on parade again for Physical Training from 6.30 to 7.45. Breakfast at 8 o' clock, and various training exercises from 9 until 12.30. Dinner at one o' clock, and more parades from 2 to 4.30 with tea at 5pm completed our day, but we had a half-holiday on Saturday and sometimes one on Wednesday as well.

Conditions greatly improved for the better when they were moved to Skegness, where they were billeted in the Seaview Hotel, three or four to a room, and the promenade was commandeered as the parade ground. Hay was quick to acknowledge that not all aspects of training were resented, and the men quite clearly looked forward to some of the more physical aspects of military training:

> We all liked the physical training and the hours of bayonet fighting, but the latter was much more interesting at the dummies than simply going through the motions of long point, short point, and jab, with various Butt Strokes at times, and we all suffered from skinned hands caused by too heavy charges at the dummies. We

learnt how to make Jam-tin bombs; [an operation afterwards unnecessary owing to the plentiful supply in France of Mills No. 5's], how to dig trenches; about the 'parts of the rifle', and we spent many hours in cleaning the 'brasses' of our equipment, and in other irksome jobs which had to be done, but to us, perhaps the worst ordeal of all was 'kit inspection' until we became 'old soldiers' and learnt the art of camouflage and substitution.

The battalion was later stationed in Cupar, Fife, and practised 'street fighting' in the village of Ceres:

> This was much more fun than the parade ground type of training, but we realised that France was looming nearer on our horizons when we had to cycle to Cupar and test our Gas Masks in a chamber filled with Phosgene gas.

David Ferguson also saw the gas training as a turning-point in his awareness of the war:

> Up to this date we hardly ever knew a war was raging until we passed a gas test with our GH helmets i.e. a rag saturated with chemicals with eye pieces and a clip to grip your nose. A most uncomfortable instrument to wear I can assure you but evidently it was to be a grateful friend to us according to the bleak cold narratives our instructor was blessed to unfold to us.

Throughout Scotland public buildings of any size were being utilised to house the growing numbers of new recruits and the rapidly expanding Territorial Force. Town halls and schools were echoing to the sound of newly mobilised men. Not only public buildings but those industrial buildings which had closed on the outbreak of war were commandeered. When Captain Patrick Duncan was training in Hawick with the 4th Battalion Black Watch he recorded that 'half the Battalion are at Wilton Mills and half at Riverside Mills; all the men get their meals at Wilton Mills.' Those officers with a temporary commission were given a 'crash course' on the finer points of being an officer and gentleman. After his commission Second Lieutenant Crerar recorded:

> After some weeks at North Queensferry, I was sent to Glasgow on a PT Course which was at Maryhill Barracks. This was a very strenuous fortnight where we drilled as a squad of 15 or 20 officers and NCOs under a Corporal who kept us at it, Physical drill and bayonet fighting, and if we slacked off a bit in the August heat it was double round the square half a dozen turns.

Gunner David Bell, Machine Gun Company, later Lieutenant Tank Corps, trained at Elveden Camp, Thetford, Norfolk, and wrote to his Aunt Bell, describing some of the camp amenities:

> Many thanks for your welcome letter which I duly received. The weather here is extremely hot and the only really comfortable place in the 'Shower bath' which I visit at every opportunity. The apparatus may not be designed as well as those at Kingsgate but are a great convenience and have the advantage of being in the open air. Each shower bath is accompanied by a 'Sun Bath' in accordance with the rules laid down by 'Socrates'. It is rumoured that during the early ages Julius Caesar availed himself of the luxury of this same bath.
>
> We have had two great boxing competitions this week but I have not entered for them as I have a horror of being the cause of the premature decease of any of my co-gunners.
>
> Much as I enjoy writing to my beloved Aunt I feel the wants of the inner man so strongly that I must forego the pleasure of any further correspondence at present as I wish to procure some 'Supper' from the YMC A.

Not all military training was undertaken in the United Kingdom – training camps were established in France to 'harden' the recruits just prior to them going to the front or to ensure that those returning from hospital or convalescence were fit enough for the job. The most notorious of these camps was Etaples – legendary for the ferocity of the training staff, many of whom had never been to the front as they were older reservists recalled for the purposes of training. This was one of the primary causes of resentment among the troops. Arriving in France Second Lieutenant Crerar journeyed to Etaples:

> We took a train to Etaples an enormous Base Camp on the coast near Le Touquet, with its legendary training ground the 'Bullring' which could accommodate 10,000 troops. Our first job was to draw equipment for the front at the stores iron ration, gas helmet, steel helmet, first aid dressings, trench boots, revolver, and also a rifle and ammunition. We had two days there training in the hot and very dusty Bullring; bayonet fighting, going through the Gas Chamber with masks on and throwing live Mills Bombs, a grand little weapon where you pulled the pin out and had about 5-10 seconds before it exploded.

Private James Jack, 3rd Battalion Black Watch, provided a sparse description of his time at Etaples:

> Sun Aug 5th – First day in bull ring. Gas and bombing.
> Sun Aug 6th – Bull ring musketry and skirmishing.
> Mon Aug 7th – Idle day washing and payout.
> Wed Aug 8th – Bull ring. Bayonet fighting and exhibition charge before Japanese Generals.
> Thu Aug 9th – Bull ring. Bombing and musketry.
> Fri Aug 10th – Bull ring. Day relief in trenches.
> Sat Aug 11th – Bull ring. Wiring lessons and distance judging.

After recovering from his wounds, and as part of the recuperation process, Corporal Ian Maclaren, 6th Battalion Black Watch, went through the hardening process at Etaples. This was not his first exposure to the harsh regime in the Bull Ring:

> In the 'Bull Ring' I was there a year ago – but present knowledge is second hand, is a scene of terrible everyday fighting every day with bayonet, bomb, rifle, grenade and gas. The bayonet fighting is the most energetic and takes first place – charging of dummies in most realistic fashion, but won't give you any more harrowing details. Parades take place there morning, afternoon and evening, so you can see it bulks largely in the life of most.

There were no allowances made for rank, as Lieutenant J.B. MacLean, 1st Battalion Cameronians, found out when he went through the base at Etaples in May 1917:

> At the QM stores I get my steel helmet, gas helmet, box respirator, first field dressing, iodine tube and iron rations. The latter looks like a horse's feed bag but contains bully and biscuit, tea and sugar, and is only for use in emergency. This afternoon I had nothing to do but in the evening I got my respirator tested in lachrymatory gas. On Monday we shall probably be in the 'Bull Ring' (i.e. training camp) all day and from all accounts it is a H of a place especially the bayonet assault course, which is gone over under adverse conditions, to say the least of it.

On 30 May he recorded:

> Today we had a bad time in the bull ring. In the morning we were twice over their famous 'final assault course' in full equipment. It is a series of rushes from trench to trench, the intervening space being strewn with barbed wire, trip wires, shell holes, etc., and they have fellows throwing huge fir-cones at you all the time to represent bombs. It is somewhat exciting.
>
> One of the jokes made by the bombing officer yesterday was:- When you see a man sprinting round the trench towards you don't stop him and ask 'what is it bill?' beat him by ten yards round

the traverse and say 'what is it bill?' Another: (in a strong Aberdonian accent, he being an officer in the Black Watch) 'If this hits ye, ye'll have an awfu' bother picking yourself together at the resurrection.'

When Thomas Williamson arrived at the camp at Le Havre he was impressed by its 'military appearance', although he never said what he made of the training regime:

Upon entering the camp, what amazed me most was how everything was laid out: row after row of army bell tents, huts, cookhouses, etc. Everything was here in plenty: a huge Army camp, wonderfully equipped, and all that was essential for the welfare of the British Tommy.

In his diary of 27 February 1915, Lance Corporal Alex Thompson, 4th Battalion Black Watch, decribes the BEF rest camp at St Martins, on the heights above the Channel port of Boulogne:

It was a very cold morning and we felt glad we had the sheepskin coats. It was very funny to see us all running about in the dark with the white jackets on, everyone shouting 'Baa Baa'.

When Corporal Robert Caldwell returned to France after recovering from wounds caused by shell splinters, he was sent to the Royal Engineers Base Depot at Rouen, which was similar in many ways to the camp at Etaples:

This was our home for the present. I know because I've been here before. While here we have to go through a little more training which seems silly as we done all this training before in Scotland and England.

On Wednesday we proceeded to the well known Bull Ring. This is a place that every Tommy knows and dread[s]. To put it in the

Tommies language you go through it. The NCOs who take charge here I think are all picked not so much for their ability as for their appearance, a fog horn voice, being a qualification, and when they started on you, they pretty near put the fear of death on you. Our first stunt here was Gas Drill, and Gas Demonstration, this consisted of learning to put on your Gas Mask in a few seconds, then you walked slowly through a trench, charged with Gas.

Thursday our duties were Infantry Drill and a Medical lecture. (I may here state that medical Lectures were frequent occurrences in the army)

Friday our day was spent on Fire Control (Musketry) and Bomb Throwing.

Saturday Bayonet Fighting, Lecture on Military Law, and practice in giving Commands.

Monday Bombing, and lecture by Adjutant on things military. I well remember part of his lecture was that you should always have your Jack Knife open, and slipped down your Puttee, and if you got too close to a German to use your Bayonet effectively, you just pulled out your Jack Knife, and slit him up the stomach, Bloodthirsty. What?

Tuesday Infantry Drill and Lecture on Rifle.

Wednesday done our Musketry at No 2 Sandpit Range. 5 rounds application and 10 rounds rapid. Afternoon off duty.

Thursday started Field Works, Knots and Lashings, Erecting Sheets, Gins, and swinging Derrick.

Friday Trestle bridge, Pontoon Bridging, Forming Raft, etc.

Saturday Gins, Sheets, Derrick and Trestle Bridging.

Sunday Pontoon Bridging and Earthworks.

Monday finishing Strong Point.

Tuesday Lecture on Map Reading and use of Prismatic Compass. Then in afternoon had practical use of Prismatic Compass in finding angles at certain points, from a given Base Line.

Wednesday Road replacing etc.

Thursday placed under orders and consequently had to go through Kit Inspection etc, during day.
Friday day spent at Infantry drill till Dinner Time.
Saturday same.
Sunday and remainder of week spent in camp still awaiting orders.

Training in the Middle East was undertaken to acclimatise troops new to the region. William L. Duncan, Scottish Horse, described route marches in the desert undertaken in temperatures of 120 degrees, with disastrous results:

We've had several route marches into the desert. One way, in the direction of Katana, we covered about twenty miles. Walking in the sand and the heat made it very hard work. Bully beef and hard biscuits are not the best thing to eat to create energy. I believe that hundreds fell out and a few artillery horses died from the result of this march. We got no more route marches after this.

J. Wallace, 5th Battalion King's Own Scottish Borderers, echoed this account:

In the forenoon we went for a route march. We were issued with wire skates. These skates are supposed to make marching on the sand easier, however we found that they often caught together and tripped us.

In the afternoon we went for a march over the desert. Most people imagine a desert to be a flat expanse of sand, but it is very far from that. There are quite a lot of hills here. Out here we are only clad in a shirt and shorts.

Camerons

From Chiseldon to Flanders at last we got the call,
And 'Tipperary' isn't sung as into line we fall;
Whene're we got the news to flit – Glengarry and the kilt –
'Twas 'Break the news to mother' that everybody did lilt.

From hut to hut it rang that night – the setting sun was low,
From throats of boys who never sang before its strains did flow;
All raised their Scottish voices, tho' it was no Highland air,
And that old song of the music halls was lilted everywhere.

How proud that aching heart would be could she but hear the strain'
'And tell her there's no other' came echoing o'er the plain;
Some shouted it unthinkingly, but others I could see,
Thought of that absent mother up in the north countrie.

And O! the vain entreaty in the line that next was sung!
'And tell her not to weep for me', that came from every tongue;
Glengarries darkened all the sky, and eyes were dim as mine,
As the words of that old ballad came swinging down the line.

'Twas thus the gallant Camerons went off from England's shore'
In answer to their comrades' call amid the cannon's roar;
O God of Battles! Listen to our anxious mothers prayer,
And give thy thought and countenance to every Cameron there.

James Campbell, Machine Gun Section, 6th Battalion Cameron Highlanders

4

'Ower the Sea tae...'

After a period of training which varied greatly in length and content, troops were posted overseas to serve in the various theatres of operation. These soldiers were transported by a number of means, such as train, ferry and troopship. Thomas Williamson recalled the send-off for those leaving Fort Matilda for France, including a sermon from the chaplain before leaving:

> We were then given a testament and two packets of Woodbine each. We were then lined up on the road. The regimental band was waiting to play us down to the station, so off we marched, headed by the band playing 'It's a long way to Tipperary'. As we swung along, both sides of the road were thronged with people who had come from Greenock and Gourock to see us off. Just as we were in sight of Fort Matilda Station, people pressed forward to shake our hands. I was marching almost on the pavement. One old woman peered into my face in the darkness. As she did so she exclaimed 'my but yer jist a laddie.' The sight of the old woman and hearing her exclamation made me think of my Granny whom I had left in Dundee. I wondered what she would have said, if she could have seen me now. I was glad she could not see me, it would have grieved her so. As we entered the station, which was closed to the public, the band played popular choruses and kept us cheery. Then I heard the puff, snort, puff of an engine. In a few seconds I saw the huge mighty engine, her tender full to overflowing with coal. The crowds had begun to sing:

'Will ye no come back again?
A' oor hearts will break in twa.
Will ye no come back again?'

When the moment of departure arrived:

We all got aboard the train and we were off on our journey, which would be approximately six hundred miles – Fort Matilda to Southampton. A terrific cheer rent the air from the crowd, cheer after cheer rent the air! We stuck our heads out of the carriages and waved our Glengarries, then our train entered a tunnel and we were on our way down south.

There were similar scenes of public support when the 5th Battalion King's Own Scottish Borderers left Richmond on 10 December 1916 for service overseas:

We marched away headed by the Battalion band and shouts of 'Goodbye' from our pals. The usual tunes played by the bands on these occasions were of course the regimental march-past 'Blue Bonnets over the Border', also our battalion march-past 'Bonnie Galloway and Happy we've been aw the gither'. When we reached Richmond, after midnight, the sound of the band wakened the inhabitants who came to their windows and doors to give us a send off. (J. Wallace, 5th Battalion King's Own Scottish Borderers)

Not everyone posted abroad shared the same enthusiasm. David Ferguson, Machine Gun Corps, had mixed feelings when he sailed for France:

I will say quietly that this was the day when I was sent to France, at least it was called France but I have another name for it. We had, previous to leaving, a whole lot of monotonous tedious and unnecessary inspections by 'brass hats' who had a good job in this country.

Corporal A. Alexander, who had previously worked for the Glasgow and South Western Railway Company, displayed a dry sense of humour when he was notified of his destination:

> Our destination I hear is Egypt then from there work our way up the Dardanelles so at last I will be able to see a bit of life and trust in good luck to get thro' safely... the voyage I understand is about 10 to 12 days so this will make up for the cruises I won't get this year!!

Sailing from Liverpool to the island of Mudros on Friday 21 May on the *Mauritania*, he arrived at Gallipoli on 6 June. Between 6 and 10 June he was wounded in the stomach and sent to Malta to recuperate. The division lost over 4,800 killed or wounded in the attack on the Turkish front between Kereves and Achi Baba Nullah on 12 July 1915. By October of that year Alexander was back once again at Gallipoli.

In May 1915 crowds lined the streets of Edinburgh for over three hours as a procession of hearses wound its way to Rosebank Cemetery, Leith. The 7th Battalion Royal Scots (Leith Battalion) was burying its dead, and scarcely a family in Leith had not been affected in some way. The death toll on that day stood at 215 killed, including three officers, twenty-nine NCOs and 182 men, while another 246 suffered injury. Although large-scale casualties were to become a common factor in the war, those being buried on that day were not killed on some distant battlefield. In the early hours of 22 May 1915 the 7th Battalion Royal Scots left Larbert for Liverpool en route for Gallipoli. Private William Begbie, 'C' Company, 7th Battalion Royal Scots, recorded the event in his diary:

> The 1/7th Battalion Royal Scots left Larbert for Liverpool in two trains – the first contained the CO – Lieutenant Colonel Peebles with the HQ staff and A and B Companies. Near Gretna Green it ran into the rear of some empty carriages of a local train which,

through an oversight, had been left on the main line. The train was overturned and wrecked. Horror was heaped on horror when a few seconds later an express train travelling north ploughed into the troop train, setting it on fire. Three Officers, 29 NCOs and 182 men were killed or burned to death. The survivors, only 7 Officers and 57 other ranks, were taken to Liverpool Hospital. Many of them later died. The total casualties of the Gretna Train Disaster were – 227 killed, 248 injured and only 34 uninjured. The second train carrying 'C' and 'D' companies stopped at a station(?) We were allowed to come off the train but not to leave the station. We all felt that something was terribly wrong but it was not until Captain Dawson told us that we knew the first train had been in an accident, but he did not know the details.

In a letter from France on 30 May, Private William Cuthill, serving with the 4th Battalion Black Watch, touched on the same subject:

> [I] am sorry to hear about that railway smash, it is hard lines on the poor chaps. They never had a chance to save themselves. I think the worst of it is that the troops were coming out here.

During the collision, gas cylinders which were mounted underneath the carriages and contained the fuel for the gas lights exploded. The men, locked into the wooden carriages for their safety and to maintain discipline, were unable to escape the inferno. W. Reid, 4th Battalion Royal Scots, wrote home from Gallipoli:

> I want to state here my thankfulness at having escaped the awful train smash which befell the 1st [means the 1/7th] our train only 30 minutes in advance of the ill fated one. About 200 killed and 300 wounded. Only 52 out of 560 answered the roll call. We knew for certain that some of the Leith boys including the major were shot to save their untold misery.

When Captain Patrick Duncan, 4th Battalion Black Watch, received word that the first battalion was due to pass through Carlisle *en route* to Southampton by train on Tuesday 25 February, he went to see them pass. Travelling from his station in Hawick he waited at Carlisle station in the early hours as three trains carrying the battalion and its equipment passed at 12.30, 1.30 and 3.10 a.m. He observed that 'the men in No 1 were mostly sober, in No 2 mostly drunk, and in No 3 mostly all asleep.' When the 4th Battalion Black Watch was posted abroad, the battalion left its war station at Broughty Ferry and travelled the short distance to Dudhope Castle in Dundee, where it was intended they should spend the day prior to entraining in the evening. Some, including Lance Corporal Alex Thompson, took the opportunity to rush home to Carnoustie as the battalion was not due to leave Dundee until 6.30 that night. They got back late, arriving as the first contingent was marching to the station, and found the event to have a party atmosphere:

> The crowd who were seeing us off had brought a large variety of good things with them for us to eat. We had more fruit than we knew what to do with and chocolates and I think one member of the party had a box of sandwiches.

Thompson considered himself lucky to be in a carriage with only five others – and equipped with a small lavatory. For many soldiers this was the first time they had left home and the journey to France was as much an adventure as the war itself. Corporal Robert Caldwell left Irvine with a draft of men travelling to France:

> What a send off we had, I think all Irvine was turned out. The majority of my lady friends w[e]re very much in evidence, with their parting gifts of cigarettes, etc (that word covers a lot). The most of our draft were drunk in fact, I think out of the 38 men

comprising the draft, I think there were only 2 of us sober. But at last after much hand shaking, gum sucking, and all the rest of it we were off.

Thomas Williamson spent a day confined to an empty cargo shed while waiting to embark at Southampton:

> All day long troops of all kinds had been arriving in the shed until, when the light was fading, it seemed as if a veritable army had sprung up from nowhere. In this huge concourse of men all regiments were represented: Artillery, Royal Army Service, Signal Corps, Black Watch, Seaforth Highlanders, Gordon Highlanders, Royal Scots, Scots Guards, Royal Scots Fusiliers and some of our English regiments. It was an inspiring sight to see so many men who were willing, yes, even to lay down their lives for their country. I couldn't refrain from smiling as the hardy Scot wi' his kilt blowing in the breeze, started chatting away to the English men.

When David Ferguson sailed from Folkestone he was allowed to spend some time in the town before embarking:

> Arrived at Folkestone and was more interested in this beautiful town than where I was destined to go later. Oh yes I was quite keen on getting to France not because I was a hero oh no only because I wanted to get out of it (wounded) or ----- and so as to have a rest one way or another. My appetite for soldiering now had reached a low level.

After arriving at his port of embarkation, Corporal Alex Thompson sailed the short journey to France on board the *Rosetti*:

> Our sleeping quarters below were truly horrible. First of all there were twenty or so occupying a space that might have held half a

> dozen in comfort. Then the floor was very uneven and there were cross beams all over it, which cut into our backs and kept us awake all night. Our equipment was all mixed up and everything was in a muddle. Above all there were about a dozen draughts blowing in a different direction and each colder than it's neighbour.

Due to the adverse weather conditions in the English Channel, the *Rosetti* was unable to dock and Thomson, resigned to spending a second night on board, was determined to improve his sleeping arrangements. 'I unearthed some bundles of straw which the transport people had brought aboard for the mules. Waiting my chance when no one was looking I lifted two and made a splendid bed with them.' His second night on board was therefore more comfortable than his first. R.C. Money received a pleasant surprise when he arrived in France to find that he was not the first member of his family to do so:

> We got down to Southampton I think it must have been pretty early in the morning. I can't remember and we set off from Southampton having embarked in *The Caledonia* I think her name was. Anyway, she had recently been victualled for a passage to Canada. So there was any amount of grub which we were very glad to see and we went off from Southampton at night. Just as the light went. Got into Le Havre in the early morning and it was very early and I saw a familiar figure on the quay and I looked at it twice and yes, it was definitely my father. He had been called up and was a base Commandant. His job was to meet all incoming ships. The French were very kind, very enthusiastic and as soon as we got of the ship we marched about 4 miles up to the camp which was on the top of the hill.

When Captain R.H.W. Rose, 1st Battalion Cameronians, set foot on French soil, his first impression was not favourable. He also appeared to harbour a rather low opinion of the character of the British soldier:

> All the women seem disagreeable, not so the men. I fancy some of the British have behaved badly. It is to be expected coming from a low class. We hear some nasty tales, unfit for publication, of treatment of inhabitants in some places.

Captain A.G. Ritchie, also with the Cameronians, was similarly unimpressed on landing at Le Havre:

> Arrived Havre about 11.30 a.m. and went ashore with Hewitt. No great enthusiasm among the inhabitants, but little children kept running up and shaking hands – lots of drunken French sailors about and heaps of French soldiers of sorts – I suppose they correspond to our New Army. If France has to fall back on such men as these, our new Army need not be ashamed of itself. It was jolly to see our splendid, smart, manly soldiers walking about among this lot.

On landing in France, Lance-Corporal Thompson was detailed to guide his battalion and others through the streets of Le Havre and out to the nearby transit camp. However, he had no knowledge of the town and he soon became detached and had to resort to different means:

> Before long I and all those behind me were lost. I did the only thing I thought suitable. Asking the passers-by if they had seen a Scotch regiment pass, I traced the Battalion and doubled after it.

After arriving in France Alan Macgregor Wilson looked down at Boulogne from St Martins camp and was not impressed. 'A look round at our new surroundings from the heights we are on shows that Bonny Scotland still holds its own.' Corporal Robert Caldwell, Royal Engineers, was a bit more forgiving on returning from service in Egypt:

> I was much impressed by the reception we were given by the French people. The scenery in the South of France was a sight worth seeing, and the hills and landscape, were beautiful and would compare favourably with our finest Highland Scenery. The whole scene, gave one the impression that War, was the last thing to be thought of, although at the self same moment that we were admiring the beauty before us, not so many miles away, shells were flying and lives were being taken, for what purpose, the Creator alone knew.

When troops arrived in France, onward travel was usually by train. While officers travelled in passenger compartments, men travelled in freight cars labelled '40 Hommes – 8 Chevaux'. Men were crowded forty to a car with no space to rest – no heating in winter and no ventilation in the summer heat. As trains travelled so slowly, troops took the opportunity to jump off and walk alongside to stretch their legs and get some warmth into their bodies. If the train stopped they jumped down and brewed up, often with hot water from the engine. On at least one occasion a train was forced to stop when a makeshift fire, lit to provide some heat for the men shivering in the cold of winter, set fire to the floor of the wagon and the occupants had to leap from the train, first throwing their possessions out into the French countryside. It must be said that there was very little risk in leaping from the train, as the average speed of these troop trains was 10mph or less. J.B. Maclean, Second Lieutenant 7th Cameronians, recalled the condition of the French trains:

> We had third class carriages (10th class they would be in England) marked 'Officers'. Our train left at 7.30 p.m. and took just five hours to do the 15 or 20 miles we had to go, but we had a comfortable journey with only three officers to a compartment. As each officer has to keep his kit with him, however, this is not quite so good as it looks. We had a good supply of eatables and a

bottle of port so we were all right. This train was 500 yards long. Three was better than 40 in a cattle truck.

Some of Lieutenant MacLean's later journeys were not so comfortable: 'today we travelled here on a goods train, sitting in an ordinary truck half full of pig iron, but we'll have better accommodation on Tuesday.' Contrary to his expectations, Captain Ritchie found himself pleasantly surprised by the French trains:

> Very comfortable first-class carriages put on for us. Scramble for kit and rations – bully beef, cheese, biscuits, tea, sugar in large quantities. Hewitt and I got a large carriage to ourselves – and I had expected cattle trucks.

Ritchie was not alone in recording his pleasure with the French railways:

> I had a wonderfully comfortable journey, having a 2nd class all to myself, so that I could sleep, eat, read and smoke when I liked. But it was a long and tiresome one, not detraining till about 6 the following day. [left at 2.30 the previous day] the men huddled up in wagons I was sorry for, but they all come up the same way. (Lieutenant M. Thorburn, 2nd Battalion Black Watch)

The French trains were not a fast means of transportation, with some travelling as slowly as 4mph. R.C. Money considered trains 'a very lengthy way of getting there.' He returned from convalescent leave on a French train: 'no one seems to be in charge of the train and the way even officers leave it at every wayside halt or travel on the roof comes as rather a surprise to me.' He continued:

> As there are five in the carriage, sleep has been rather at a discount, and one gets beastly stiff. The men are in some ways

better off in those trucks 'Hommes 35-40, Chevaux 6'! They are 30 or 32 to a truck and so can stretch their legs. Despite the most stringent orders men travelling on the roof of their trucks, fortunately there are few girders! They sit and dangle their legs over the side among other enormities. Apparently none have been killed or injured so far which is as well.

While travelling to join the 2nd Battalion Royal Scots Fusiliers, Lieutenant Crerar also commented on the length and speed of his journey:

That railway journey was a lengthy one taking up most of the day, crawling along and stopping frequently; sometimes we got off at wayside stalls manned by English ladies, and had a cup of tea, and if the train had gone you just caught it up in due course.

As men journeyed ever closer to the sounds of battle, the underlying mood of the journey changed from one of excitement to a feeling of reflection and trepidation. For many it was brought on by a fear of the unknown, while for others it was a reluctance to return to the conditions from which they had temporarily escaped. Alan Macgregor Wilson perhaps gives the best view of such a journey 'up the line' and puts it into clear perspective:

Our train comes in. We find our transport already attached to it, horses etc. Five minutes to entrain and we find ourselves in covered trucks 44 men in each – what sardine would envy us? But there, that's nothing, we are not in the present; we are in the future now, and a train journey on the edge of a knife would be nothing when your thoughts are sixty miles in front of the engine.

However, as well as the serious side of his journey, Wilson does find humour in their situation:

> Various hawkers and curious natives came alongside us: a sight worth seeing a Frenchman and Scotsman conversing – mostly by grimaces, of course I try my hand and fail dismally, but there is yet time to learn.

Not all troops landing in France were destined to stay. A great many travelled across country to Marseille and onward by troopship to Gallipoli, Africa and the Middle East. The conditions on board the troopships were cramped and overcrowded. Troops slept in fetid mess decks or in hammocks, or took the opportunity to sleep on deck – preferring the risk of rain to the smell below deck. During the day every inch of deck space was taken up by troops bored by the length and inactivity of the voyage. Officers and NCOs could only take limited steps to relieve the boredom of the men. Rifle drill and physical exercise could be taken on deck, but time was limited due to the number of men on board. In August 1915 William Duncan from Aberdeen, serving with the Scottish Horse, was sailing to Lemnos *en route* for Gallipoli on board the troopship *Transylvania* and was none too impressed with life on board:

> The first roll call is at quarter past six, the breakfast is sometime between seven and nine. Going down to the mess room was bit of a job. The heat was pretty high and everybody cleared out as soon as possible as everything considered it is not a very inviting spot. Before one gets out one has gone through the first stages of a Turkish bath. I only visit the place once in a day, that is at dinner time, I don't find the other two meals in the slightest tempting. At night one can always get something to keep going by tipping one of the cooks. The next parade is at ten when there is a general parade with lifebelts and ammunition and to get those inspected takes about one hour. We may then get some physical drill and boat crew work. Taking it all over we've a fairly easy time. The usual methods of passing the time away are lying about deck. This is fairly common and many of us are feeling not very fit and we

feel lying down the best position. Those who were lucky enough to bring some readable matter have a read. A good number spend the time gambling with cards and a number of the old soldiers have made quite a pile of money putting the Pugaree on the sun helmets. The Pugaree is a role [*sic*] of white cloth about thirty feet long by one foot broad. It is folded to about two inches broad and then wound round the helmet. The rest of the time is spent trying to get near the wet or dry canteens. There is always cards in these places and it takes a bit of doing to get near the counter. At nine p.m. we are usually in bed and as we now sleep on the deck we are nice and cool.

Posted to Mesopotamia with the 2nd Battalion Black Watch, Private James McGregor Marshall experienced 'strange sounds – strange languages – strange people – the old world – or where civilisation started.' Camped *en route* from Alexandria to Abouker, Private Begbie, 'C' Company, 7th Battalion Royal Scots, received a rude awakening:

During the night we heard shouting and screaming. Scrambling out of the tents to see what was happening, we could see that some men were standing in a circle looking at a dead snake. One of the men had wakened up to find a snake crawling over him. You can imagine what happened in the tent – only one way out and eight or nine men fighting their way out – but luckily an Arab patrol was nearby and the story goes that one of them caught the snake, swung it high in the air and when it struck the sand it was dead.

After leaving Richmond, J. Wallace, 5th Battalion King's Own Scottish Borderers, was posted to Palestine and described his journey on various modes of transport:

Sailed on the 'Duke of Connaught'. I enjoyed the short voyage (Southampton to Le Havre) which I spent mostly on deck. There were 1,500 men on board, and the sight of the men below trying to get a sleep, packed tight like sardines was rather comical.

We disembarked at Le Havre at 9.30 a.m. there the sleet was coming down. We were amused to see a French soldier on guard, walking about, his rifle slung over his shoulder and his hands in his pockets. I'm afraid it didn't give us a good first impression of the French soldier.

The onward journey by rail from Le Havre to Marseille took three days, confined to a small railway carriage. However, Wallace and his travelling companions were in luck and were not subjected to the usual cattle trucks:

The RSM in charge of the draft was a KOSB. When it came to entraining at the station he kept our draft till the last with the result that while the first men were put into large wagons which held 40 Hommes, 8 Chevaux, we were put into 2nd class compartments. There were 8 men in our compartment and we got our kits on the luggage rack.

We are a cheery crowd in the compartment. During the night we sleep as best we can, we can't get stretched out anywhere, it is just a case of trying to sleep where you sit. Our food consists mostly of biscuits, bully beef and McConachies (a stew with vegetables in a tin). When the train stops, which it does frequently, we get out and get some hot water from the engine to make some tea. Occasionally we manage to get a small fire going to boil a mess-tin of water but usually before the water boils the engine whistle sounds and away goes the train and then there's a scramble.

On arrival at Marseille, Wallace and his companions spent a couple of nights in a transit camp before boarding the *Kellyan* bound for Alexandria:

After getting on board we were shown our respective messes. 6 men to each mess. On the roof above the tables were hooks on

> which to sling our sleeping hammocks. I went downstairs and slept on the floor as I thought it safer there than in a hammock.

With the large number of men on board, volunteers were called on to assist the crew in a number of areas. Having worked as a baker prior to enlisting, Wallace volunteered to help the ship's baker during the voyage. 'Working in the bakehouse saves me doing parades and guards. The accommodation for the men is most inadequate, there are 2,000 men on board.' He quite happily spent Christmas night sleeping in the dough trough in the bakehouse. On arrival at Alexandria the battalion was dispatched to Kantara, travelling this last leg of the journey as freight:

> Arriving at Kantara. We had breakfast and entrained for Romani at one o' clock. No passenger train this time, but a goods train going up the line. We climbed on to the trucks and sat on boxes of bully and jam or on bales of tibben (camel's food).

5

In the Beginning

I told the men to keep under cover and detailed one man, Ginger Bain, as 'look out'. After what seemed ages Ginger excitedly asked, 'How strong is the German army?' I replied, 'Seven million.' 'Well,' said Ginger, 'here is the whole bloody lot of them making for us'. (Sergeant I.F. Bell, 2nd Battalion Gordon Highlanders)

Scottish regiments were with the British Expeditionary Force as it landed in France. They took part in the retreat from Mons and the subsequent Battle of the Aisne. On 15 September 1914 the 1st Battalion Cameronians was entrenched in woods near Venizel, on the Aisne. Captain R.H.W. Rose made an entry in his diary which captured the confusion, if not the desperation, of the initial weeks of the war:

Arrive at 12-30 a.m., and cross Aisne at Venizel, move into wood, which we are to hold if 4th Division has to fall back. Very depressed, hear things not going so well. Very cold, very damp, cold feet etc. Have to remain very quiet in wood. Fearful battle going on, infantry and artillery. Some shrapnel burst in our wood, also high explosives, but do no harm, frightfully noisy. See our guns retiring. Don't like our position, as duty not clear. Rest a good deal, but very damp. Battle lulls a bit. Hear things going better. Germans shell part of our wood. Understand situation thus. French pressing up on both flanks, we hold center. Germans' five corps, one crippled. Many French coming up, but not for two days. Our 6th Division up in three days. More rain, very horrid.

Good quantity of rations. Much rain, soaked, a night of absolute misery. Men digging trenches, stand about all night, superintending, men work in reliefs. Withdraw at dawn, CO says trenches are very good work, I think so too. We are now prepared to put up a good fight, if divisions had to retire.

By 4 October Captain Rose was foretelling the way that trench warfare would develop in the ensuing years. In his diary for that day he wrote what he described as 'lessons of the War':

I was quite wrong about rapid fire. It is invaluable. Most of the German attacks have been washed out in 10 minutes, and it would seem that the stereotype form of attack which one has been led to believe would take place will be very rare.

Defence positions are now taken up with very small fields of fire, the enemy can get fairly close, but the last 100 yards or so are impossible against rapid fire. If fire superiority be gained, which necessitates Artillery fire, then attacks may be successful, or a long infantry do (in which case ammunition supply will come in).

The German attacks have been attempted, without fire superiority, which we have always heard are fatal. Troops here face each other at 80 yards, but cannot advance.

Entrenching is most necessary. Deep narrow trenches are best. Head cover is not liked. Without trenches you would stand no chance.

On the Aisne here there are 3 rows of trenches, the 1st if rushed, just lie down and take their chances. No. 2 now opens fire, and if this were rushed, No. 3 ~~would take it up. The 4th~~ platoon is allowed complete rest.

At night men stand up, alternately, all night in the trenches. Communicating trenches to the rear are most valuable, and in our trenches extra rooms etc. have been dug in supporting trenches. During the day more sleep can be obtained.

The 1st Battalion Cameronians were operating as part of an independent brigade under the immediate orders of General French. Captain Ritchie recorded that they spent the time 'driving around in buses – 40 bus[s]es to the battalion'. Captain Ritchie's diary entry for 22 October reads:

> About six we had sudden orders to move – to entrench a position near La Boutillarie – the Middlesex on our right, 6th Division on our left.
> 11 am. It is all a splendidly exhilarating battle. A real battle, not one in which nothing happens. A farm is blazing and sending dense volumes of smoke up and behind us.
> 2.45 pm. The battle seems [to] have slacked off. Wounded are coming past. I hear that Rose and MacAllan are hit.
> Night. A bitter cold night, silence for a long time, but two farms blazing in rear. Several outbursts of firing in the night – beginning with a single shot, then a fusillade, then a mad raging tumult of shot ripping up and down the line. Star shells from the Germans lighting up the line and sky, wild crash of our guns and screams of shells over our heads, streams of light where the shells passed, thud and bright glare as they exploded over the attacking Germans – if they did attack – I think it was only a reconnaissance of our position.

Captain Rose would not have the opportunity to see if his predictions on modern warfare proved true. He was killed in the fighting at La Boutillarie on 22 October. His body was recovered under enemy fire by Privates Barclay and Newbrooks, both of whom were recommended for gallant conduct for retrieving Captain Rose's body during broad daylight and in full view, and rifle range, of the enemy. R.C. Money, 1st Battalion Cameronians, described the action that night after the battalion had been driven forward in their buses:

> Two companies got heavily mauled and Rose was killed. It might have been the village of La Boutillarie. Sent in with two companies

> to defend the village [occupy] as cover for trench digging and protection it was heavily defended and they had to retreat platoon by platoon. The battalion machine guns which were set up on a ridge 1,000 yards away were unable to give supporting fire as they had not been trained in providing indirect fire.

After the action at La Boutillarie Captain Ritchie formed a high opinion of the men under his command:

> I am very badly in want of sleep. Not more than 15 minutes at a time all night. I have to be at them all the time – they are extraordinary men. Far and away more disciplined and quieter and steadier under fire than they are when there is no danger. They are splendid fighting material. While every other regiment in the Brigade is hysterically pumping in lead at an imaginary enemy, my men are perfectly calm and unexcited, thinking only of sleep and food and their rum ration.

That Ritchie and Money were friends is self-evident, but what is also clear is the respect and admiration they held for each other. Ritchie wrote 'Money, O.C. maxim guns, is a very jolly companion. He sniped a German at 700 yards – I saw him pitch over backwards.' He also recorded: 'Money – I put in charge of the farm, and he dug himself in with one machine gun.' After the action at La Boutillarie Money noted 'The General is very pleased with the way Ritchie has run things up here which is excellent.' Money was with Ritchie when he was wounded. A very heavy attack developed against the 19th Infantry Brigade south of Croix Marechal and in his diary Money recorded seven attacks on the night of 28 October: 'They attacked, killed lots of them, Ritchie wounded... left in sole charge of C Coy. plus? Coy. Argylls and MG.' Ritchie had joined the battalion on 11 October, was wounded on 29 October and died from his wounds on 22 November 1914.

Others were more fortunate. The day before he was himself fatally wounded, Ritchie had noted in his diary: 'Hills patrol actually found and brought in, alive and fairly cheery; Pte Berridge, wounded and lying out in the rain without food or water for five days and nights. His brother delighted.' Captain Ritchie's diary ends on 29 October 1914 when he was sent to the field hospital, but there was one final letter sent from hospital in Boulogne on 2 November 1914 which described the attack in which he was wounded. Indeed, he seemed to be rather fatalistic regarding the severity of his own wound, even going so far as to opine that it was inoperable. In this respect he was proven correct and he subsequently died from his wound:

> It was in the early morning of Oct. 30th and they were doing a Night Attack, I had my little post to hold and kept them off alright. But I got hit in the left thigh just below the groin by a bullet which hit the bone. It was splendid the way they brought me down – the stretcher under fire. Motor – Ambulance train – more motor – and then blessed peace in the Allied Forces Base Hospital, Boulogne. Everyone tremendously kind here; a splendid Harley Street surgeon, Heath, and heaps and heaps of nurses and dressers. They are going to chloroform me this afternoon and get on a splint. I don't think they can take out the bullet.

He took great satisfaction in the fulfilment of his duty and the performance of his men:

> I had my little show all to myself. My own company and subalterns and my own arrangements, and they all did so well – the men I mean. I thought I was dying, but when I came to me senses again the fight was still going on and they had put me under shelter and my subaltern [Money] was holding my hand and shouting orders, and it was all very jolly, but only a little bit of a thing.

Although the Cameronians were continually taking casualties, Money's diary reflects his frustration at the battalion's lack of involvement:

> We never really got into action throughout the retreat. We lined up to take action any number of times, even at le Cateau we never really got into action because 19 Infantry Brigade was the reserve brigade and so one spent a very great deal of time moving from the right flank to the left flank and never really coming into action…

Shelter was sought wherever it could be found, and Money also commented on the loss of seventy Cameron Highlanders in their HQ, which had been located in a cave for safety. 'Bad luck, these caves by the Aisne are old quarries, and doubtless in this case the excavation had gone to within a few feet of the upper soil, and no one suspected it.' In this instance, shell fire caused a cave-in and the unfortunate men were buried alive.

Mobilised on 4 August, the 1st Battalion Black Watch had arrived at Le Havre on 14 August and had been a reluctant participant ever since the retreat through the French countryside. When, on 6 September, the Allied retreat turned to attack and the British forces turned to fight, Private A. Mitchell commented, 'This is the first day of our advance after a retiring action that created a World's Record for marching.' H.D. Clark, 2nd Battalion Argyll & Sutherland Highlanders, was also present during the retreat but was a little more content with the continual marching. He attributed this to the wearing of Highland dress:

> The Scottish dress is much better adapted to marching than the English because we don't have army boots. We have shoes, Highland and we have fresh air up the kilt and therefore we can march further and we never had anyone fall out.

Although the BEF had been engaged in fighting a rearguard action during the retreat, the fighting itself was nevertheless bloody and at times desperate. Sergeant I.F. Bell was serving with the 2nd Battalion Gordon Highlanders:

> On rushing the trench, and leaping into it, I found that the dead were lying three deep in it... I slipped over the rear of the trench, to cut across and meet the lads as they emerged from the communication trench, but had only gone about six yards when I received what in the regiment was called the 'dull thud'. I thought I had been violently knocked on the head, but, feeling I was not running properly, I looked down and discovered that my right foot was missing.

Bell was found by the advancing German troops and carried to a forward aid station. Although in great pain from his wound he was still very much aware of his immediate surroundings:

> All the way from the trench to the barn I saw British dead, mostly Highlanders – Black Watch, Camerons, and Gordons – and as they lay there in their uniforms, I thought how young and lonely they looked.

Both sides were exhausted; the Germans were determined to hold on to their territorial gains while the British and French did not have the manpower or material to advance further. The two armies became engaged in what was to become known as the 'race to the sea', in an effort to outflank their opponents. Both sides consolidated temporary positions and the pick and shovel became as important as the rifle and bayonet. By December 1914 the front line had developed into trench warfare. Sergeant S. Saunders, 6th Battalion Gordon Highlanders, described how he sought to minimise the danger of these early days in the trenches. At the same time he highlighted the squalor and discomfort suffered by the ordinary soldier:

As regards being in the trenches – the danger is almost nil... If one keeps one's head up too long one is fired at but one can look up for a few seconds without the least danger. The discomfort however is terrible – the mud awful – it is almost impossible to get it of[f] one's clothes. Shaving and washing are out of the question – water is much too precious.

When the 2nd Battalion Cameronians (Scottish Rifles) took over French trenches in November 1914, M.D. Kennedy was disgusted at the way the French had abandoned their dead and unimpressed with the condition in which he found their trenches:

It was a very deep trench. It was just the single line which was called the frontline but that was not correct because there was only one line and it was really old ditches just deepened and the French had left it in pretty poor condition. No latrines, no firing steps, nothing and they left some of their dead lying about so we had to get to work to try and make things a little better.

By Christmas Day he had concluded that 'the Germans were quite a nice lot – as fed up as we were.' The Christmas truce of 1914 has evoked many memories: carol singing across no-man's-land, gifts being exchanged across the wire, football being played (perhaps the first truly international fixture) and above all else the easy acceptance of the return to killing. The involvement of the Scottish regiments in the Christmas truce of 1914 serves to highlight the changing perception of that period. In some sectors of the front the truce lasted only hours, but in others it lasted for days. Scottish letters show that the truce lasted nine days, from Christmas Day 1914 until 3 January 1915, not just for a couple of days as has been previously thought:

The next morning [Christmas] several of them were standing about in the open and of course some of our men of the 2nd and

6th Gordon's soon followed suit. An order from the commanding officer recalled the 6th Gordon's, but the padre who accompanied him round the trenches suggested the burial of some dead left between the lines` from a scrap on 17th December. This was arranged and the burial service was taken part in by both sides, a German divinity student interpreting the 23rd psalm and the short prayer which followed. Next day and in the days which followed there was no attempt at concealment except when the warning was given that some staff officer was about and then things took on a normal appearance and a few harmless shots were fired. The exchange of food – and drink – was a great game; it was forbidden but went on daily. An arrangement was made from the trenches: a sudden rush by the bargainers and the deed was done.

In a letter dated 28 December Saunders described in detail the impact of the Christmas truce on the Western Front in 1914:

Christmas day in the trenches! And of all extraordinary days, it took the biscuit. An order passed along the line not to shoot. A few minutes after I saw the Germans getting up out of their trenches. I was with the Captain and the Colonel. We rushed along to see that the men didn't shoot and found our men getting out of the trenches as well, and I'm dashed if they didn't walk out, meet the Germans and stand shaking their hands and chatting to them like old friends. On Christmas and Boxing days we wandered about all over in full view of the Germans. It all seemed most peculiar.

The Christmas truce was also witnessed by H.D. Clark, 2nd Battalion Argyll & Sutherland Highlanders:

Came the morning at first light and instead of the artillery hate came a chorus of German carols from their trenches and when the light came up enough we could see them standing up in their trenches singing and the whole atmosphere had changed and our chaps responded and they cheered the Germans singing. Of course, they sang most beautifully and then eventually some impulse brought the 2 sides out of their defences to meet in No Man's Land and there we had a conversation and exchanged, showed each other picture postcards of families and football teams. They were Saxons and very peace loving. They didn't want to be at war at all and the troops didn't penetrate into the trenches. It was only in no mans land. We took the opportunity to clean up no mans land. To remove corpses which had been lying there and give them a decent burial.

You see, usually in Scottish troops it is New Year that matters but on this occasion it was the Germans who started it because they observe Christmas.

Sergeant Saunders later gave an account of New Year in the front line:

> We came in last night fairly easily. Of[f] all extraordinary warfare this takes the biscuit. There was no firing until midnight or thereabouts when a few volleys were fired into the air to welcome in the New Year. We got a crowd together and sang Auld Lang Syne and God Save the King. The Germans sang some songs and played God Save the King on the mouth organ and everyone shouted 'Happy New Year'. Then the Pipe Major came along and played; he had come down especially. We fortunately were able to give him a drop of rum. This morning the men are wandering about all over getting brown bread and other things from the Germans. It doesn't look as if they are short of food.

Although the truce had halted the killing over the festive period, it could not be allowed to continue and had to come to an end some time:

> And so the days went on till the afternoon of 3rd January, when a German Officer and an orderly approached our lines and inquired

> for an officer. I heard the request and scrambling out of the trench, I went out to meet them. We saluted and the orderly acting as interpreter informed me that higher command had given orders for the normal conditions of war to be resumed. I asked for time to enable me to warn those behind the lines and after comparing our watches which showed about two [h]ours of difference in time, we agreed on one hour's respite. A parting salute having been given, I returned to the trench and, after warning those in the line, I sent intimation of the new situation to those in the rear. Only a few stray shots were fired that day, but orders for volley fire were received next day and along the line from the 2nd Gordons, through the 6th Gordons a ripple of fire spread like a 'feu-de-joie', the muzzles of the rifles in approved text book fashion being held well in the air.

In one instance, it was rumoured that during the festive celebrations one German had been 'caught short' in no-man's-land when fraternising with British troops and reportedly urinated on the British wire. He was promptly shot dead, as the insult was too great. In other areas no truce was observed; it very much depended on the troops in the front line.

6

Trench Warfare

During my patrol I heard a very vigorous cannonade on the left. Walking towards a sentry – a firm stolid, rock-bound Scotsman – I said 'What's happening on the left there, sentry'? He mused for a minute and then as the inspiration flashed through his brain, he drawled 'It must be some firing going on, sir'. How beautifully Scotch!! (Lieutenant W.S. Dane, 4th Battalion Seaforth Highlanders)

By 1914, trench warfare was not a new phenomenon. Trenches had been used extensively in the American Civil War, the Crimean War and, to a lesser degree, the Boer War. Practicality dictated events as, in an effort to avoid the intense firepower of modern weapons, the opposing infantry took to the ditches and field drains. Trenches originated out of necessity. Troops could no longer be expected to needlessly expose themselves to the level of fire which could be generated by modern small arms and artillery. Providing the minimum of shelter to troops desperate to get out of the withering fire, the first diggings were nothing more than shallow infantry scrapes in the ground – individual scrapes which were excavated behind walls and under hedgerows. It quickly became the established norm that whenever the infantry stopped for any period of time they went to ground and, as a consequence, if there were no readily available ditches they began to dig. Individual scrapes were soon enlarged to contain groups of men who would share the duties of keeping watch while others slept.

These early trenches were constructed in a haphazard fashion as some battalions dug trenches by company, some by platoon and some by section. This resulted in a dilution of direct command, with the ensuing difficulty in maintaining differing levels of control. The excavations were not directly connected to each other, and while they gave some degree of protection to the troops, there was an increased degree of danger for orderlies, runners and – most importantly in terms of preserving unit cohesion – for the officers who had to cross open ground in order to visit the various small groups of men under their command.

As these shelters became larger they began to connect and become a single entity. It quickly became obvious that it was too costly to attempt frontal attacks, even against the early primitive trenches. As each army tried in turn to encircle its opponent, the line of hastily dug shelters rapidly extended towards the Channel ports. From the English Channel to the Swiss border, Europe was rapidly divided by a man-made barrier on a scale never before imagined. When the 2nd Battalion Cameronians (Scottish Rifles) took over French trenches in November 1914, M.D. Kennedy was appalled, not only at the conditions that the trenches had been left in by the departing French troops but also at the lack of equipment and the restrictions placed on those British soldiers in the trenches:

> The main trouble was the water in the trenches. Up to then we hadn't got trench boots or anything else. It was our first time in the trenches. We weren't allowed to smoke, we weren't allowed to light braziers or anything. Subsequently we were allowed to do all these things.

Trench warfare, as with all other aspects of the Great War, did not remain static in its concept. Instead, it evolved and adapted to the needs of the fighting forces. What began as shallow scrapes, created in a desperate attempt to avoid the withering firepower displayed by both sides in the initial advance through Belgium and France, expanded by 1918 into a sophisticated system of defence in depth. Trenches changed over time. The rough and ready early trenches of 1914 and 1915 evolved into the designed and engineered constructions of 1916–18.

The opposing sides on the Western Front took differing attitudes to trench warfare. Germany had occupied French and Belgian territory and was looking to consolidate and defend her territorial gains. In this context the trench was viewed as primarily defensive. The onus was on the Allies to expel them from French and Belgian soil. Conversely, for the Allies trenches were a part of the offensive. Constructed to hold troops only until the next offensive, they were a temporary necessity of modern warfare. For William Linton Andrews 'our trenches were only for temporary shelter. We never meant to settle in them.' As long as the concept of a short war or the ideology of movement and mobility held sway, the British trenches were viewed as temporary constructions at best. Trenches were considered by high command – some of whom never visited them – as merely a holding area to build up their forces. Since both sides had differing requirements for trenches, both sides took a different approach to trench construction.

In 1914 trenches remained a primitive extension of the original infantry scrapes. With the primary functions of sheltering the infantry and denying any further ground to the enemy, the original trenches were unlined and varied greatly in depth depending on the intensity of enemy fire and the depth of the local water table. In some areas, such as the Flanders Marshlands, it was impossible to dig more than a foot or two before striking water. In these areas palisades were constructed for protection. At Neuve Chapelle in November 1915 it was noted that it was impossible to construct communication trenches and therefore 'communication breastworks were made for communication trenches would quickly have filled with water.'

Life in the early trenches of 1914 and 1915 can best be described as one of squalor with, at worst, a complete disregard for the welfare of the soldier. In a period when trenches were viewed only as temporary shelters from enemy firepower, little thought was given to the welfare of the men. Hardly more than ditches dug out of the soil with the earth thrown up to form a parapet – later reinforced with sandbags as they became available, these early trenches were narrow, unlined and therefore prone to sudden collapse and cave-in. Originally they were dug only deep enough to allow the infantry to fire over the parapet, which meant that men had to expose their head and shoulders above the trench or constantly walk in a crouch to avoid being shot by snipers. Some of the early, hastily-constructed trenches were totally inadequate for the job. In October 1914 it was found that some of the trenches in the village of Fromelles had parapets constructed from hay – not very likely to stop a bullet – while the trenches themselves were too shallow to provide effective cover. However, the need to strengthen the defences was often dismissed as the troops were soon to be advancing. Attack was the overriding doctrine behind British trench warfare, especially in the early years. Trenches were temporary. Although in later years there was a gradual acceptance of semi-permanence, they never gained the same level of prominence in British doctrine as they did for the Germans.

As events progressed, trenches were quickly deepened to provide shelter to all, and began to include a fire step – a ledge on the forward face of the trench, between twelve and twenty inches high, on which the men could stand when required to repel the enemy advances and which would bring them to the right height. The fire step also provided a platform on which the men could sit, sleep and cook their food, and it became essential in order to stay out of the way of those moving along the trench, greatly increasing mobility within the trench. Trenches were of necessity kept fairly narrow to afford shelter from shells bursting to front and rear of the trench, but this led, initially at least, to overcrowding. This in turn led to heavy and continual casualties from random shell fire, especially coupled with the early policy of having the majority of front-line troops actually in the front-line trench at all times – rather than the later policy of having the trenches lightly manned while the majority of the troops took shelter in a safer area, a policy of defence in depth. In some instances trenches were formed by interlinking shell craters, the overlapping craters forming 'natural' trenches. At Arras in April 1917, the support trenches were only wide enough to allow one man at a time – three foot wide at the top with no parapet or parados. Communication trenches were so narrow that two-way traffic was all but impossible – inevitably, in order to speed things up, some traffic would walk on top, exposing themselves needlessly to enemy fire. Eventually, a system of one-way traffic was introduced.

As the war progressed, trenches became more defined in their layout. The typical trench would be around six foot in depth with wooden duckboards to keep the occupants above the water, and parapets and parados were constructed to increase still further the effective height of the trenches. If the water level was a constant factor there would be sumps dug at various locations with pumps to drain the trenches. Individual shelters, or 'funk holes' as they became known, were basic excavations in the wall of the trench, usually the rear wall. They were big enough for the individual to lie curled up in a foetal position. Sometimes there would be a longer excavation, perhaps as a result of the trench wall collapsing and being rebuilt, in which there would be subdivisions of sandbags and a roof supported by branches covered with sandbags with the front still open and exposed to the weather. In a sense they resembled a row of pigeonholes in a mail office or writing desk. The soldier lay on the bare earth or, if he was lucky, he might have a piece of sacking or a groundsheet on which he sat with his legs protruding onto the fire step. These holes offered no shelter from artillery fire; they were primarily to afford space to sleep without others walking on the sleeper. These primitive shelters were prone to collapse due to artillery fire or the weather. With the early trenches having unsupported sides, many men were killed when their shelter collapsed due to the concussive power of nearby shell bursts or when the earth slipped or subsided after prolonged rainfall. A near-miss by an artillery shell would bring about the collapse of the shelter and the soldier's colleagues would have to dig him out, not always in time. Many died from asphyxiation in such situations. Unable to dig out those who were buried alive, or too slow in reaching them, or prevented by continuous shellfire, the soldiers had to leave many bodies buried in the trench walls, which added to the constant smell of decay. In some instances entire trench systems collapsed due to rainfall and the troops were forced to exist once again in a system of unconnected shell holes. Such shallow shelters did nothing to protect the men from the bitter cold or from trench flooding. Men would sleep where they could during the day and work under cover of darkness.

A straight trench could be neutralised quickly by enemy infiltration because it allowed enfiladed fire – fire along the length of the trench. This risk was reduced by digging trenches in a zigzag or castellated pattern, which provided for fire bays and traverses, with turns every ten or fifteen yards to prevent trenches being rolled up by enfiladed fire. This limited the number of casualties caused by a direct hit from an artillery shell – although it would kill all within the affected section of trench. If the enemy managed to get into the trench, each section could be defended on its flanks. Indeed, at varying times and at varying locations, German and British troops shared the same trenches, separated only by barricades placed at these changes of direction, and they carried on the war by bombarding each other with a variety of grenades and bombs. This occurred at Arras in early 1917, when large sections of the Hindenburg Line were occupied by British troops: 'We were the last battalion on the right (or south) and then a few yards further along was the Bosch – with just our sandbag wall and his, a few yards of no-man's-trench between.'

The everyday battle was for existence, not for ground gained or positions captured. Offensive attacks were few and, although casualties were high at such times, it was the accumulating everyday casualties which caused more damage, both physically and to morale. A company might suffer a dozen or more casualties to snipers and artillery every time they went into the trenches and still consider this a light casualty rate. This was attrition rather than the demoralising casualty rate of organised attack and, as such, appeared to be more acceptable. A great deal of effort was spent reinforcing the front line or no-man's-land. The biggest enemy was boredom or the drudgery of continual manual labour. Carrying, digging, stringing barbed wire, reinforcing trench parapets, carrying timber or ammunition, wire parties, patrols, trench raids, listening posts and bombing raids. It was policy not to make life in the trenches too comfortable and, initially at least, men had to find shelter wherever they could.

Troops were required to stand-to on the fire step for one hour at dawn and dusk in case the enemy chose that particular time to attack – although as both sides were doing the same thing this made such a surprise attack highly improbable. The grey light of dawn and dusk was thought by both sides to be the most opportune time for attack – troops stood-to until full light or full dark. Trench warfare had its own routine which had to be learnt quickly in order to survive. Troops would receive the order to stand-to half an hour before dawn and dusk and the whole front line would remain at a high state of alert for the next hour. Men would wait seated on the fire step while sentries stood looking over the parapet. Occasionally there would be a scattering of nervous shots taken up along the length of the trench as men got the 'wind up' and fired at shadows. Once this morning 'hate' was over, the men would spend the next hour cooking their breakfast and resting in preparation for work. This first hour of the day was the most peaceful period, as both sides gathered themselves together for the day ahead. Although work in no-man's-land was confined to the hours of darkness, there was still work to be done strengthening, deepening or widening the trench. Saps would have to be dug for listening posts and for latrines. These saps were narrow trenches dug at right angles to the front line trench in the direction of the enemy to accommodate a patrol, usually two or three men, which would lie there and listen for enemy activity. Officers would come round after breakfast allocating work. Those without work would rest and sleep as best they could.

The soldier in the front line had no conception of the overall plan, and it is a reasonable assumption that he would have cared little one way or the other. His life revolved around a limited world consisting of his immediate locality, a stretch of trench which might extend as far as 100 yards and was filled by his company or platoon. He saw little or nothing of the enemy, as to expose his head for a look would mean attracting the attention of a sniper. While he might see something of no-man's-land when he took his turn at sentry duty, this would only be a view seen through a periscope or mirror clipped onto his bayonet and held above the parapet. His world was limited to his section of trench until he was relieved. Two walls which looked just like any other section of trench. His interest in no-man's-land lay in studying the topography in preparation for nightly working parties: which shell holes could provide shelter; where the wire was the thickest; where the dead lay in order to avoid stepping on them and disturbing the rats. Memorising the position of deserted buildings, trees, ditches – anything which might help to ensure his safety when working in no-man's-land.

The winter of 1915–16 was the period when trench warfare and trench living began to assume an organised structure. The process of life in the trenches became systematic. After the casualties and destruction of Loos there was a period of stability on the front, in part due to the weather but in the main due to the need for both sides to take stock and reorganise. On both sides fresh troops had to be acclimatised to the conditions of modern war – civilian soldiers had to tempered and annealed to the demands of trench warfare. The professional armies had gone. Both sides were now comprised of new blood. Whether conscript or volunteer, the citizen was now at war and the military command had to tread warily. Routines were established and standardised and as the previous material shortages were now made good the opportunity was taken to recondition and strengthen existing year-old trenches and construct new ones. Trenches were lined with timber to prevent collapse in wet weather, wooden duckboards were fitted to keep the men above the water, sumps were dug and fitted with pumps, sandbags used to strengthen defences. This was not something new; it had been done from the beginning in varying degrees. What was new in the second winter of the war was the scale of the work undertaken, as the equipment and material which had previously been in short supply began to arrive in seemingly limitless quantities. Due to the shortage of material and the lack of time spent on maintenance, the trenches were in many areas in a state of dilapidation. Large amounts of time expended on maintaining the trenches, which were suffering as much damage from age and wear and tear as from the advances of the enemy. It was only as war stretched into 1916 and beyond that conditions in the trenches were addressed in a systematic fashion.

For many, the realisation that death could come at any time without involvement in actual fighting and without the opportunity to defend yourself came as a shock. There was a randomness to death – you didn't have to fight in order to be killed or wounded. Luck was seen as a major factor and in many instances death came unannounced: the stray shot, the random shell. Much has been written about the high casualty figures of major battles such as the Somme but, with over two-and-a-half million British casualties, it can be seen that an equally high number came not from archaic set-piece battles but from everyday attrition. The stray shot and the random shell were constant factors. The stoic acceptance of death dealt in a random fashion was something new, something previously unseen in warfare. Of course these shells and shots were not truly stray; they were fired with the intention to kill – maybe not the final recipient or victim – but they were nevertheless intended to kill someone. The stray factor was that they missed their intended target but found another; this was the perceived randomness. On the other hand, the unexpected killing shot might not be the stray that it appeared. Machine guns or fixed rifles would be pre-set on a low or damaged section of parapet and fired periodically during the night in an attempt to hit those soldiers who would have to repair the damage during the hours of darkness. They would also be set at low points or intersections and fired when battalions were being relieved, in an attempt to kill the newcomers before they wised up. Pre-set machine guns would periodically rake the parapet to catch sentries at their posts. It became policy for British sentries to stand on the fire step at night as it was thought to be better if they were hit in the chest rather than in the head – they would have a greater chance of surviving being wounded, although it would take a tremendous leap of faith on their part. It was dangerous to light a cigarette in the trench unless one used a lighter designed to create a smouldering glow rather than a naked flame which could be easily spotted by the enemy snipers. Many men were killed in such a fashion; a second's lapse could spell death. The front-line soldier could never relax his guard. It was this constant need to stay alert and aware that drained the spirit. The quietness would lull men into peering over the parapet, often with fatal results.

No matter what the overall view was, the men on the ground had only the need to exist. Their world consisted of the immediate area of trench. Their life revolved around performing mundane chores in a dangerous environment and learning to adapt to an ever-changing situation in order to survive. Survival in the trenches required constant vigilance or awareness. A moment's exposure above the parapet and a sniper would increase his tally. A momentary lapse of concentration could mean death.

Above all there was the stench of death and decay – rotting flesh and waste matter. When a soldier was killed his indignity did not end there. Bodies could be blown up more than once, disintegrating into their component parts until they were only pieces of indefinable flesh, unidentifiable as an arm or a leg or a head. In this fashion men disappeared from the face of the earth. Literally not enough left to fill a sandbag. Bodies would be blown up and buried several times by shell fire. A burial party would spend nights burying the fallen in front of their trench only to have them disinterred by the enemy artillery. Men would dig through bodies when constructing new trenches or repairing existing ones – only realising what was happening when the digging became spongy, but having no choice but to continue. Decomposing bodies were sliced through by shovel and pick, with sections of human remains becoming part of the trench wall. It was 'normal' to have arms, legs and heads protruding from the trench walls, gradually rotting away until someone, unable to stand it any longer, hacked off the offending part and threw it out into no-man's-land to begin the cycle again. Bodies in trenches would remain unburied; men had to sleep beside them, eat beside them, had no recourse but to walk on them. In the callous fashion that had to be adopted to retain sanity, corpses would be used as chairs or footrests until they could be safely taken from the trench and buried in a nearby shell hole. Men can live with anything. Men learnt to sleep through the cries of the wounded. Hands protruding from trench walls would be shaken by those passing along the trench as a symbol of good luck; disembodied heads would likewise receive comforting pats from passing soldiers. Protruding arms, legs and even bones would find new use as hangers for equipment, keeping it out of the mud or water. Signallers would use protruding limbs to hang signal wires. The disembodied and the dead became part of the framework – troops would be given directions to 'turn left at half man' or take shelter at the headless corpse. With so much death the system must shut down; men would become immune to scenes of death, and perhaps view them in an abstract fashion – they exist but they are not real.

A soldier's first experience of trench warfare was often the journey 'up the line'. As the men progressed towards the front the scenery changed and the danger increased. Roads and communication trenches were under enemy observation and enemy fire. Movement in the front area was undertaken at night – positions were relieved and re-supplied when the cover of darkness hid all movement from enemy observation. Second Lieutenant Crerar journeyed with his men to the front line near Longueval:

> We marched past Longueval where Blyth had been killed in July, and the only landmark was a wooden notice on a post 'Longueval'. Woods were reduced to some bare trees, and the ground everywhere was pitted with shell holes, debris of posts, barbed wire, entrenching spades, shattered ambulances and gun carriages and dead horses and mules. We set of[f] for the Front Line next day, a Sunday, and had a tiring slow journey in full kilts, rifle, etc. up communication trenches, sometimes under quite heavy shell fire. Then followed before we 'went over the top' what I think were the most miserable four days I have experienced in my long life. Our trench was almost constantly under heavy shell

fire as were the communication trenches which prevented rations getting to us, and it was frequently raining.

Second Lieutenant J.B. Maclean, 1st Battalion Cameronians, wrote to his brother Alex describing his journey to the front line in June 1917. His comments were tempered with sympathy for his enemy:

> Last night it was raining very heavily and no doubt the trenches will be pretty muddy. The ones we are going into have been shelled a lot recently and I understand there are only improvised dug-outs in them. You say that it must be quite different coming out now that we are pretty well top dogs, but there are some considerations which make it worse in other ways. Formerly our troops sat for months in more or less perfect trenches and some of them hardly ever went over the top, but now that we are so much on the offensive there is a lot more of that sort of thing and the trenches we occupy are very often captured Boche ones which have been smashed to blazes. You really can have no conception what it's like without being here.
>
> I don't know how the enemy stands the continual stream of stuff we dump on him but it must be hell for him. Of course we get it too but not as bad as he does.

He returned to the subject again in August of the same year:

> We got short notice to quit last night – upwards – and left this morning at 5 a.m. We had reveille at 2.30 and at such times one wishes with great fervidness that there were no war. We have come half way up to the line and are at the moment occupying French army huts. I hear, however, that we move up to the reserve lines tomorrow night and then carry on progressively and have about six days in the front line. This is a very bad part, water being the predominant element and I believe it is more breastworks than trenches. It is also bad in other ways and the battalion we

took over from had ten officer casualties in one six-day tour. The surroundings of this place remind one that there is a war on. Across the road from us there is one of the frequent British cemeteries and today when I went over to have a look round there were eight corpses lying on stretchers awaiting burial. The top part is covered with sacking or a waterproof sheet but the feet are sticking out, which makes it evident they didn't die in bed, and it is a gruesome sight. There are a great many graves of men of Glasgow battalions, chiefly 15th, 16th, and 17th HLI – in one case a trench with about 20 of the 16th HLI all together.

After things cooled off a bit we got started on our trip up of about 12,000 yards. There are only fragments of trench left here and there and when we got up to about 400 yards the Boche light got a bit dangerous, as we were in the open and every time one went up, i.e., every minute or so, we had to flop down. The journey was a succession of rushes in between the flares and bursts of MG fire, but we arrived all O.K. the line up here is not trenches at all on account of the watery ground, but was all breastworks. These have all been blown to atoms and nothing remains but a series of concrete emplacements in which we crouch during the day and from which we emerge at night to do work and patrols, but anything we do in the way of work is sure to be knocked out next morning.

We used to hold the whole 'trench' but half of it was lost about two months ago. I hope he hasn't any designs on the other half. As a matter of fact the ground in between is a honeycomb of shell holes all filled with water so it would be pretty difficult for either of us to surprise the other, but in my opinion he's a jolly sight too near.

When Maclean eventually arrived in the firing line one officer was just going out on patrol. 'He was armed with his revolver and two Mills Bombs and the NCO had a most villainous looking Knobkerrie.' It was not only the journey up the line that he commented on:

Honestly, it is a rotten war and some of the things one sees here make one want to choke the Kaiser and all the rest of them. They have a new gas on this sector, the result of which is to produce broncho-pneumonia combined with boils and blisters. Pleasant isn't it, especially as the stuff usually lies about for a bit before anyone knows it's there. At times it is necessary to keep respirators on for hours but I believe our experts have got the stuff ticketed now and no doubt protective measures will soon be forthcoming.

The first time under fire was a new experience to men who were unused to the noise and horror of war:

First time under heavy fire. Rifles, machine Guns, Trench Mortars, Aerial Torpedoes, and Shrapnel were all turned on us while lying 20 yards from the enemy as covering party for a platoon digging a new trench. (Corporal James Reekie Muir, 7th Battalion Black Watch)

Had my glimpse of a battlefield. Not a bit appetising. The grimness of war was fully illustrated to me by the large number of graves. Most of them however were French and German. Many cases where as many as 40–50 in one grave. (Private David Ferguson, Machine Gun Corps)

Captain Patrick Duncan, 4th Battalion Black Watch, who had been so keen to get into the action when stationed at Dunfermline, noted when he reached the reserve line:

I have spent my first night in these parts and slept all night. We are 1400 to 1500 yards from the German trenches. It will take some time to get accustomed to the rifle and gun fire.

Four days later he moved up to the front line with his battalion and it is evidence of how quickly men adapt to new situations that the sound of firing failed to keep him awake:

> We came up here last night. A good deal of firing etc goes on as long as it is dark. I slept all night from 2.30 am until 6 o' clock. The others say it is pretty quiet here just now. The German trench is between 200 and 300 yards away here.

Lance-Corporal Alex Thompson was struck by the enthusiasm of men new to the line, who had to be restrained from warlike actions. They had yet to learn the art of front-line survival: Don't annoy your neighbour! When the first draft of replacements from Dundee joined his battalion he noted:

> They were greatly exited and were lying facing the firing line, rifles ready for immediate action, which I verily believe they expected. I had to warn them that the very last thing they were to do was to fire.

On Lieutenant Crerar's first sojourn at the front line he received a warm reception:

> On arrival, one of the older officers, Albert King, a South African mounted policeman I think, who had been fighting in German West Africa, and I were detailed to 'B' Company with a Captain in command. That afternoon we were heavily shelled, and while sheltering in a dug-out with Mackenzie, we heard someone screaming and I went along the trench to investigate, passing an officer who'd just had his brains blown out by the bursting of a shell. The man who had been hit was in a dug-out with two others and we bandaged his leg etc. so here I was only five days after being in peaceful Speyside, right in at the deep end.

Crerar was not the only soldier to experience a warm baptism of fire. The noise of battalions changing over in the front line could not be hidden and the enemy would take the opportunity to welcome the newcomers with artillery. Newcomers to the front were also vulnerable to snipers until they realised that vigilance had to be constant. A moment's inattention could mean death. As a new officer as yet 'unblooded', Lieutenant Lionel Sotheby, attached to 1st Battalion Black Watch, was sent up to the trenches to see how things were doing and in the process to gain valuable experience:

> We at last reached the front line where I saw Captain Forrester... He then pointed out a few things and looked over the parapet, explaining where one of our shells had blown up a German machine gun emplacement on the embankment only 100 yards away. We both looked at the spot for barely 5 seconds and our heads could have barely been 6 inches apart when I was suddenly knocked over from the parapet step by Captain Forrester who fell like a log in to the small 1 foot deep trench below. I had heard a great crack which the German bullet makes at close range, and so knew what had happened. There he lay at my feet, a great hole behind the left eye, his eye shot out and most of his brains hanging out, a great stream of blood rushing out. The bullet had come out the other side of the head and must narrowly have missed me too. Somehow a little episode like that has a great effect on one, and despite how callous one is sometimes these things touch one deeply.

In his diary, Thomas Williamson, Royal Scots Fusiliers, described his first taste of combat in France in the summer of 1915:

> What a shambles it was! Several fellows were making their way down the trench having been wounded in the arms and legs. I went down the trench and was ducking my head every time I heard a shell screaming over.

When the Cameronians 'took over Seaforths trenches which were muddy and none too good', R.C. Money recorded '2 men of "C" sniped, neither very serious, right through parapet

– cheeroh for the Seaforths engineering, about a ton of sandbags have to be added to any of their works.' The members of 'U' Company, 4th Battalion Gordon Highlanders, gave a more sobering account of the work of German snipers:

> The night passed uneventfully except for the energy of a particular sniper who made us careful. Scarcely had the day fully dawned when L C Scott got shot through the head while stretching himself. He expired with a sigh, his equipment dyed with blood. This made us all very quiet and sober.

Of course, while German and Turkish snipers were hated and reviled, the use of snipers was not confined to the enemy, as C.N. Barclay found out:

> In the early spring of 1916 I attended a course for snipers organized by two temporary officers (Major Heskith Pritchard and Captain Gray) the former a famous big-game hunter and the latter a Queen's prize winner at Bisley in peace time. Following this I became the Battalion Sniping Officer with 6 of the best shots in the unit under me. We spent our time in the line in sniping posts waiting to pick off the careless German who exposed himself. We usually claimed 2 or 3 victims every day; but we could never be quite certain whether a man had been hit or just bolted down when he heard the crack of the bullet.

Some parts of the line were well known for attracting the attention of enemy snipers, as James Campbell knew:

> When going from one communication trench to another, I was leading and doubled across as it was a risky spot. Andy walked over saying as he came 'What's up with you?' I said 'That's the place where 3 chaps were piped by the sniper last week'. Andy's face was a study as he said, 'And you've the cheek to tell me after I've walked across.'

The activity of snipers was not confined to the Western Front. W. Reid served in Gallipoli with the 4th Battalion Royal Scots. Due to the proximity of the Turkish lines and Turkish dominance of the high ground, sniping took a high toll on Allied troops:

> After 11 months in the army I have at last found myself in the trenches, we came up yesterday to the reserve and are stationed in a place known as the Eshi Line. First impressions astound you at the length of the trenches. Coming up I had to traverse 'Princess Street' 'Leith Walk' and several other well known thoroughfares. Our trenches are not so bad the only danger being spent bullets. We have to deepen our trench so that means work. I had a very narrow escape today a bullet struck my hat and very near stunned me... Last night was in front firing line for the first time not only that but I was sapping in front of the trench was on guard at the other end of a sap only 50 yards of the Turks position was such that you were in danger of being hit from three sides, as it was a three hours guard I was not sorry when the time was up. Come to think of it I was very lucky to get of[f] free from that sap last night we had four men killed in the same place...

Place names were common in the trenches; not only did they remind men of home but they allowed for ease of identification:

> The name of our part of the line is Rothsay Bay, and it's the last seaside resort in the world I'd choose for a holiday. Out of my hotel I have a glorious view of a few sandbags and a mildewed piece of trench. The air is so bracing. The paddling is excellent. When it rains, we are up to the ankles in slush – and wherever we go we can pick up no end of shells if we only put our heads over the parapet. It is rather chilly at night, and I often have to roll out of my hotel to hop around the trenches for exercise. Why did I join the Army? (Lieutenant W.S. Dane, 4th Battalion Seaforth Highlanders)

Lieutenant Dane also wrote on the expansion of trenches, or the 'city of Trenchville', as he chose to call it:

> Our trenches have now grown into little cities with main streets side streets, devious alley-ways, open spaces, telephone boxes, and railways. Here and there you will even find a table, a bed, or a chair. We pay visits, have afternoon teas, and occasionally, dinners. Over the way live our cousins, but we are not on speaking terms just at the present. In the city of Trenchville the streets and even the buildings have names. Here is 'Pip-Squeak' Promenade, there is 'Bomb Bay'. That little trench sliding away there is 'Pomme de terre' Alley. That curve in the line is 'Oui Oui' Crescent. That rise over there is 'R.I.P.' Ridge. This row of dwellings or dug-outs is known as Shrapnel Mansions. No. 6 is called 'The Bug Walk'; No. 10 'Hop o' my Thumb House'; No. 15 'The Angels Rest'; No. 19 'The Pig and Whistle'. Over there is a more spacious residence known as 'Hotel de Fleabite'. While there is a common room known as the 'Opium Den'.

Artillery fire was not only hated by those on the receiving end. Any fire directed at the enemy would result in retaliation directed at the British lines. This helped to create resentment between the infantry and the artillery. Captain Money of the Cameronians noted that when the guns had been firing on the Germans the resulting return fire would, 'as usual', be directed at the infantry:

> Allemands [Germans] dropped a lot of percussion shrapnel, looking for the guns. The gunners concerned sat in a trench nearby while in the neighbouring batteries the men played football in front of the guns. The infantry suffered again.

The main factor of trench warfare was that the combatants were always under observation – someone was always watching. A group of officers consulting a map at a crossroads and apparently killed by a stray shell might actually have been under enemy observation and been killed by artillery fire called in for that very purpose – there was not much of the front which was not under artillery range and zeroed in. They might have been observed from the enemy trenches, a rear high point or an observation balloon, and the crossroads might have been zeroed in earlier for that very purpose. The point is that very few shells were stray; they had a purpose which might not be apparent to the men on the ground at the time. The company HQ in the deserted village or farmhouse was not hit by a stray shell; the coming and going of the company runners had been observed and artillery called in. There was always someone observing movement. On 2 January 1916 three men were killed and two wounded as they were sand-bagging the gable of a house used as a brigade HQ. The men were thought to have received no more than they deserved, as the work was carried out in full view of the enemy. In order to have any guarantee of survival, all movement at the front, or within observation range of the enemy, had to be undertaken at night. It was considered very risky to sleep in deserted or derelict buildings within artillery range of the front as continual coming and going would attract enemy attention and half a dozen artillery shells. When tempted to do just this and take up residence in a deserted village, great pains were taken to ensure 'that they don't see us, and get to think we're in this village, or they'll give us a warm time'. Smoke caused by cooking fires was guaranteed to produce a volley of shells from the enemy. Lieutenant Sotheby described the effect of German shrapnel shells:

> Their high explosive shrapnel is beastly as we have always found out... So terrific is the explosion that at 40 feet up, each shrapnel bullet makes a hole as big as a cricket ball in the ground. It contains over 400 bullets usually... One shell fell close to our Sergeant Major who was going to put up a notice for a trench. He

heard the shell coming, crouched up against the trench, but it burst only 10 yards from him, and the poor chap received most of the effect of it. I won't describe his condition. The other shells buried several and a piece of one entered a dug out and tore one man's side clean away. He died without a murmur, I believe... the other two fellows we dug up after 10 minutes from their entombment. They were a ghastly sight from not being able to breath[e]... another man received from one of the shells a large piece right into his stomach, it doubled him up. He too will die, I'm afraid.

The flies here are simply terrible, huge hordes fly before one when one walks about. Quantities of dead lay about unburied and the stench in places is fearful. This part of the ground has been won and lost many times and people cannot be buried for the most part.

Making his way up the line at the Somme, Norman Collins, 6th Battalion Seaforth Highlanders, was subjected to the full horror of war:

I noticed as we went that the communication trenches had bodies, and parts of bodies, sticking out of the wall for quite a long way. The trench, I suppose, had been dug through the bodies where they lay. Occasionally you would see a loose head or two kicking about.

When his battalion moved to Roeux in May 1917, he noticed little change:

When we entered the trench it had been extremely battered. I remember having to climb out of the communication trench to let the troops who had been fighting pass while we lay on top. The weather had been bad, as I remember, and at several places arms and bottoms of corpses were sticking out of the communication trench. In the support trench the men had tried to repair the line too, and, as the mud had began to dry out, so bits and pieces were sticking out of the wall. A feature of Roeux was the chemical works and another was the cemetery. This had been blown to pieces and a lot of graves churned up, which was a terrible sight.

Lieutenant Hakewell-Smith described the experience of being caught up in an enemy artillery barrage:

One afternoon the Bosch blew some mines and tunnels... Two nights later leading a party to a reoccupy a sap we were observed. There was just a faint 'pouff' from the other side [and] a parabola formed by a trail of sparks. A short prayer by me. Then about ? a second (it seemed ages) of appalling suspense a 'swish THUD' another half seconds eternity an appalling roar. Head half jerked off shoulders and face scorched. Hair singed. Steel helmet goodly scored. An appalling 'fright'.

A direct hit from an artillery shell in a confined space could be devastating, as Lieutenant J.B Maclean discovered:

At one of the battalion headquarters I saw a dug-out where 16 men of the battalion we relieved were all killed with one shell last week. Their grave was simply made by closing up the entrance and wiring it round.

He spoke of the casualties incurred when artillery fire was directed at his platoon:

In my platoon one man was killed and three wounded, and there are also some gassed. The one killed was a corporal and the shell which did it landed plumb in the trench, hit him in the back and absolutely cut him in two. His body had to be left there until this morning when we sent a party up for it, and I can tell you one look was enough for me, as it is not pleasant to see a ragged cross section of a man you were working with a day before.

Dugouts in the British sections were rarely built to the level of the German system. They offered very little protection and were built into the trench wall with a groundsheet or piece of sacking hung across the entrance to shield the light from enemy observation. Troops were expected to live in shell holes covered with tarpaulin and corrugated iron. Some dugouts were merely a large square pit dug close to the trench, with a few boards on top to support a tarpaulin sheet with a light covering of earth and turf. Raised platforms of earth were left on either side, and when covered with an oilsheet and blanket these provided sleeping space. However, by February 1915 some level of standardisation had emerged, as wooden frames were delivered to the front in an effort to aid the construction of dugouts. In the second line or reserve trenches they would be elaborate constructions with bunks, tables, stoves and even carpets 'liberated' from nearby abandoned houses.

The Germans took greater pains to construct their dugouts with a view to permanency, using concrete extensively and digging down more than thirty feet when soil conditions allowed. They included triple-tiered bunks and kitchens. In some instances the German dugouts had wallpaper and wooden panelling to add to the creature comforts – they were building for the long haul and for garrisoning semi-permanent troops. The Germans had a greater incentive to build comfortable dugouts as they were retained in the same area for long periods of service, with some regiments occupying the same section of trenches for several years. The troops therefore knew that they would be returning to the same dugouts and trenches after a rest period, removing the natural reluctance to provide creature comforts which would be handed over to others. It was to their benefit that their facilities should provide the maximum of comfort. This does not mean that they lived in luxury, merely that they had a greater incentive to improve their conditions. They were still under fire, still suffered deprivation, still went hungry. As the war progressed the Germans were quicker to use concrete in the front line to construct dugouts and machine-gun nests.

However comfortable these dugouts were, they were still death-traps under certain conditions. During 'trench raids' it was the practice of the raiding force to move through the enemy trench throwing hand grenades down into the enemy dugouts, in the process killing all the occupants trapped therein. A single shell landing in the entrance could cause it to collapse, suffocating the occupants. The men might also be killed either directly by the shrapnel or by the concussive force of the explosion – many were found dead without a single wound or mark on their bodies, victims of concussion. In an attempt to overcome this, dugouts were usually constructed with two entrances – when a grenade was thrown into one the occupants had a chance to escape through the other. In practice, few dugouts afforded more protection than a shell hole. Most of them were just excavations at the bottom of a trench sufficient to crawl into and stretch out for sleep. However badly constructed the dugouts were, they still provided shelter for the men to rest. A tired man could always find a corner.

Artillery and bullets were not the only danger to those in the trenches. The 2nd Battalion Royal Scots suffered heavy casualties in a gas attack near Chocques, and Private Begbie witnessed the consequences when their trenches were heavily bombarded with mustard gas:

> After about fifteen minutes the first casualties came along our trench. When the bombardment stopped some of the men, thinking that the gas had cleared, took off their respirators. Later I found two men of my platoon groaning and rubbing their eyes so I led them down to the medical post. This post, the dug outs and all the trenches leading to it were filled with men lying on stretchers or sitting on the fire steps. The doctor and orderlies were

giving all the men injections of morphia. On my returning to the trench, I found that the 'all clear' had been given so I took of[f] my respirator. I also found that our trench was almost stripped bare of men. The official record of the 2nd Battalion Royal Scots stated that on that day the battalion lost 12 officers and 363 men were blinded by mustard gas.

Begbie was himself gassed by remnants in a dugout and hospitalised as a result. As the combatants turned to static siege warfare, both sides returned to age-old methods to neutralise static defences. Tunnels were dug out under no-man's-land and mines – tons of explosives – were laid under the enemy front line. These mines were detonated to coincide with attacks by the infantry. Scottish miners were much in demand for this subterranean warfare. The men, recruited into specialised tunnelling companies, not only tunnelled but spent a good deal of their time listening for sounds of enemy activity underground. They would break through into enemy underground galleries where vicious hand-to-hand combat was played out in darkness. When mines were laid they were kept dormant until the time of attack, and when sounds of enemy activity stopped, the troops in the front line would have to continue in the knowledge that there was a large quantity of explosives under their feet, not knowing when the enemy would detonate them. Lieutenant Lionel Sotheby witnessed the work underground:

I went down one of these mines the other day. They are very eerie. There is a shaft about 40 feet deep, with a rope ladder attached. Above is a huge pump worked by two men to keep the water down. At the bottom on the right there is a small tunnel 3 feet high and 3½ feet wide supported with rafters and beams. This leads about 150 yards to a rise up, of about 5 feet, where the tunnel branches to the left and right another 100 yards or so. Here the air is very foul and the sides of the tunnel drip with moisture. At each

> end there is a little recess made, and a hole about 6 inches in diameter is bored 12 feet into the solid earth. Here we have to place men to listen for the enemy mining or counter-mining. The men have rifles and bandoliers only, in case the Germans break through. It is very nervy work, especially as we know the Germans are mining all along the front but the men stand it very well.

In a letter home to his parents, Private Braid also mentioned his involvement with mines:

> I shall be classified for a miner when I come home, in the last position we were in it was all mined. We had mines running from our trenches right under the German trench ready to blow up at any time. I was down two of them guarding them in case they happened to cut through. In one there's a spring, you have to keep working a pump all day in reliefs.

Mines were also used in an attempt to end the stalemate at Gallipoli. Private William Begbie, 'C' Company, 7th Battalion Royal Scots, participated in one such attack:

> The 156 Brigade made arrangements for an operation against the enemy trenches. Two companies of the 7th Royal Scots supported by two companies of the 4th Royal Scots were to attack on the West of West Krithea Nullah and two companies of the Cameronians assisted by two companies of the 7th Royal Scots were to attack on the East of East Krithea Nullah. Hoping to take the enemy by surprise, we had not the usual preliminary bombardment… The signal for the attack was to be given by the explosion of a mine under a Turkish bombing post when our bombers were to dash forward and our artillery were to shell the support and rear positions of the enemy. A deafening report and a pillar of smoke and debris was the signal for us to dash into the enemy trench. Most of the Turks were too shaken by the explosion of the mine to be capable of putting up a fight but after they

recovered there was some brisk fighting. The enemy trenches, having been almost obliterated by our mines, had to be reconstructed and more than 24 hours of hard work with pick and shovel were necessary to rebuild the trench and parapet and we had to dig a communication trench to our old line... The enemy made several attempts to regain possession... but every assault was beaten back even although our trenches were heavily bombarded. The composite Royal Scots battalion was relieved on 21 November by troops of the 157th Brigade and returned to a rest camp in divisional reserve.

When on sentry duty, Thomas Williamson fequently reflected on life in the trenches:

Often as I stood gazing over the parapet, my overcoat up over my ears, my rifle clasped firmly in my icy cold hands, I have thought of the people at home, tucked in, under warm blankets, practically safe from all danger and sleeping soundly. The contrast made me feel sick, sick of the whole thing, but I was still optimistic enough to look forward to the day when their happy lot would be mine.

Not all sentries spent their time reflecting:.

One of our officers came across a man in the trenches yesterday, who was firing furiously at apparently no object at all. 'What the devil are you firing at?' asks the officer. '350, sir' answers the private. (Lieutenant W.S. Dane, 4th Battalion Seaforth Highlanders)

Corporal A. Alexander returned to Gallipoli after recovering from wounds received there. He recorded his return in a letter to his parents dated 8 December 1915:

I am in the firing line again. My mate on the sentry post beside me got wounded first night up, the bullet going in at one shoulder

> and out at the other. He was one of my old platoon and there are very few of us left by now. I was just counting. Out of 48 who came with us only 1 Sgt 2 Cpls 4 Lance Cpls and 11 men are left. The rest are either killed, wounded or away sick. It is six months past on Monday since we first landed here (6 June). And the battalion has never had a rest away from here during that time. I was lucky getting my spell off but it will come to a finish sometime sooner or later.

His comment suggests that the only way to get any form of rest would be a wound – a 'Blighty one' – which would get the unfortunate, or fortunate, recipient time in Alexandria. Not really a holiday but a way out nevertheless. Corporal Alexander was killed on 23 April 1916 while leading a counter-attack to regain an outpost at El Dueidar in Egypt. His name is commemorated on a memorial at St Enoch's station in Glasgow along with 301 other employees of the Glasgow and South Western Railway Company who gave their lives. The memorial was unveiled by Earl Haig in 1922. The members of 'U' Company, 4th Battalion Gordon Highlanders, so named because the members came from Aberdeen University, have left behind them an interesting collection of letters and diaries detailing conditions in the trenches. This description is dated 11 March 1915:

> The trench has a fearful smell of refuse, and dead bodies infest the air with poisonous odours. Just three yards from us was a Frenchman's foot sticking out, the rest of him was covered in, to the right was a disused German trench with eighteen bodies fearfully swollen, the less one thinks about these things the better.

In July 1915 James Campbell, Machine Gun Section, 6th Battalion Cameron Highlanders, noticed the difference in behaviour between raw troops and those who had spent some time in the theatre of war:

> It struck me forcibly how contrasted is the behaviour of old and new regiments under fire. Some Territorial cyclists were passing our place when the shells began to fly and they like 'old hands' got down to it next a wall. But every Cameron who could get out was craning his neck to see where the next one was going to land. Coolness under fire was no name for it. If we are half as good later on we will make a name for ourselves.

Even with the continual stream of replacements to the regular battalions, Lieutenant Sotheby claimed 'I think the regiments (Regulars) are as good as ever.' There was talk of his division, the 1st, being withdrawn from the front for refitting and rest and being replaced with a New Army Division, a proposition with which he strongly disagreed:

> Kitchener's army will not be placed in a lump. That notion is absurd. In these trying circumstances and conditions of heavy artillery, brand new battalions might get a sort of stage fright, so that the presence of the war worn soldiers is needed not only as a stimulant, but to remind newcomers that they have thoroughly seasoned troops on either side.

However, life in the trenches was not one of continual excitement.

> Ordinary trench warfare in reasonable conditions was, for the most part, an uneventful life... roughly, long periods of dullness, interspersed with occasional moments of fright. (Lieutenant C.B. Robertson, 1st Battalion Argyll & Sutherland Highlanders)

After the euphoria of his posting to the 1st London Scottish at the end of 1914, C.N. Barclay described the monotony of the early months of 1915 as the battalion recovered from its early losses:

> We were not involved in any major enterprise, only the rather dull routine of trench warfare – a few days in the front line, then a few days in support a few hundred yards behind the front line, followed by perhaps a week in reserve billets 3 or 4 miles back.
>
> The dangers of the front line were not, I found, as frightening as I had anticipated, and I remember how exceptionally well fed we were, even in the front line when only a few yards from the enemy. I suffered much more from the discomforts than the dangers of those days. It was difficult to get a bath or even a good wash; in some trenches there was often a foot or so of water and one had to stand and wade about in this for perhaps 3 or 4 days at a time. Worst of all was the prevalence of lice. I think I was lousy during most of that winter. Within a few hours of putting clean things on one was lousy again. Where they came from I didn't know.

Thomas Williamson did not have long to wait before witnessing the full horror of war:

> My first sight of death shook my whole nervous system: one of our bombers had been in the act of throwing his bomb when, for some unknown reason, it exploded blowing his head off. I had to step over the headless body. I cannot just say how I felt, the horror of it, the terrible sight revealed so suddenly before me. I felt sick.

Neither did he have long to reflect on the surrounding chaos:

> Just then another blinding flash and another had landed in the trench, further up. It was then I started to fight back. I threw my first bomb over the parapet, then again and again I threw them, gaining courage every moment.

Captain Patrick Duncan, 4th Battalion Black Watch, always felt a sense of relief when his battalion came out of the trenches:

> Coming out yesterday we were up to the ankles in sticky mud, which made the marching very slow and tiring. Your clothes also were covered with mud, which is very difficult to brush of[f]. In places the trenches were covered with water which left big holes, after it had dried up. Apart from some bomb throwing the part of the line we were in was pretty quiet.

Like many others, his immediate thoughts turned away from the horrors of war. 'How is the garden looking just now? Has the dog given up his wandering? One of my good khaki shirts has been lost at the washing.' Lieutenant Thorburn, 2nd Battalion Black Watch, commented on the condition of his men coming out of the trenches after the battle of Loos:

> You cannot imagine such a sight as the return from the trenches when relieved! Clogged with mud, some with no hats, some with German helmets, some with their smoke helmets – cheery, but dead-beat. What trophies they got – Iron Crosses, helmets, coats, books – you have no idea what.

7

'Better Slush than Slaughter'

The trenches were like miniature burns and we simply paddled in them. (James Campbell, 6th Battalion Cameron Highlanders)

Mud – not quite land, not quite water.

All trenches suffered at one time or another from water or, to be more accurate, from the lack of adequate drainage. To be fair, this was not a phenomenon restricted to British trenches; the French and German trenches were every bit as susceptible to water. Similarly, flooding was not confined to the Western Front – heavy winter rains brought flash flooding to the gullies and Allied trenches at Gallipoli where the Turks, like the Germans, had occupied the high ground. This signified a lack of preparation, as trenches became drainage ditches taking the run-off from the surrounding surface water in a landscape in which the natural drainage had been destroyed, or at the very least disrupted, by high explosives. Logic dictates that the winter rains would turn earth and clay into mud. However, in some parts of the Western Front, trenches could not be dug more than a few inches deep as the water table was too high. At Plugstreet Wood (Ploegsteert Wood) the ground was far too swampy for trenches and defences had to be erected as breastworks.

In the trenches of Flanders water was the main enemy. The trenches had been dug in fairly decent weather through the marshes, but in the wet of winter they acted as main drainage ditches. With the winter water level only a foot or so below ground level, the trenches disturbed the natural drainage system, and the deep trenches became main water culverts.

The trenches occupied in January 1915 by British forces were next to the River Lys, which rose so fast with the winter rains that flooding ensued and the trenches had to be abandoned. A new line was built consisting of an above-ground breastwork constructed from wooden hurdles, corrugated iron and mud-filled sandbags. The trenches between the village of Houplines and the river Lys had been constructed utilising the existing field drainage ditch, which turned into a stream when the December rains came. The water could not run off the flat terrain and the trenches served as its channels. After every downpour both sides had to empty the water from the trenches. The trench walls repeatedly caved in and it was a continual struggle to clear away the debris and start all over again. It was only by using timber from a local sawmill that the trench remained serviceable – fully lined with timber, with a timber floor above the water level and cross-braces to keep back the weight of mud pressing against the revetted sides of the trench. If it was any consolation to the troops on the ground, the enemy were suffering the same conditions. In December 1914 the ground around Lillers and St Venant was found to be 'so water-logged, where not under water, that a bombing practice-ground was the largest dry area to be found'.

Not all sectors suffered to the same extent from water. The section of front line at Givenchy was not a wet part and although the consistency of the mud varied from that of thick soup to that of dough it was never deeper than six inches. German shells or heavy rain might cause the trench walls to collapse and flood the trench, but such obstructions were soon cleared.

General Gough, Fifth Army Commander, described the conditions at Passchendaele:

> Many pens have tried to depict the ghastly expanse of mud which covered this waterlogged country, but few have been able to paint

> a picture sufficiently intense. Imagine a fertile countryside, dotted every few hundred yards with peasant farms and an occasional hamlet; water everywhere, for only an intricate system of small drainage canals relieved the land from the ever present danger of flooding... Then imagine this same countryside battered, beaten, and torn by a torrent of shell and explosive... such as no land in the world had yet witnessed – the soil shaken and reshaken, fields tossed into new and fantastic shapes, roads blotted out from the landscape, houses and hamlets pounded into dust so thoroughly that no man could point to where they had stood, and the intensive and essential drainage system utterly and irretrievably destroyed. This alone presents a battle-ground of tremendous difficulty. But then came the incessant rain. The broken earth became a fluid clay; the little brooks and tiny canals became formidable obstacles, and every shell-hole a dismal pond; hills and valleys alike were but waves and troughs of a gigantic sea of mud. Still the guns churned this treacherous slime. Every day conditions grew worse. What had once been difficult now became impossible. The surplus water poured into the trenches as its natural outlet, and they became impassable for troops; nor was it possible to walk over the open field – men staggered warily over duckboard tracks. Wounded men falling headlong into the shell-holes were in danger of drowning. Mules slipped from the tracks and were often drowned in the giant shell-holes alongside. Guns sank till they became useless; rifles caked and would not fire; even food was tainted with the inevitable mud. No battle in history was ever fought under such conditions as that of Passchendaele.

Gumboots were issued early on but were found to be ineffective as the troops had no means to dry them out. Very few were issued in the following winters. Troops found it impossible to walk through the slurry and had to resort to using the sides of the trenches to drag themselves through the mud. The sound of progress through mud could be heard by German sentries and would ensure a barrage of grenades or shells. However, the mud that betrayed the presence of troops was also their saviour as it swallowed the shells – the explosions became plops. Although German trenches suffered from mud and rain, the effects were not so great, due to the German occupation of the higher ground. At Biaches the Germans were seen to be pumping all the water from their trenches down into the British lines. It was recorded that, at Bois Grenier in January 1915, 'the Cameronians had just lived in water'. Lieutenant Norman Collins, serving with the 6th Battalion Seaforth Highlanders, commented in October 1916: 'The mud is really awful. Even on the main roads it is up to our boot tops and off the road will drag a man's boots off with puttees on. In the trenches it varies from ankle to almost waist deep and men have to be hauled out sometimes with ropes.' To be fair, the mud on the roads was probably caused by the amount of traffic, both by foot and vehicle. Collins went on to comment on the conditions in the trenches: 'The men have an awful time. They are up to their waists in mud in the trenches and when in billets they sleep on the muddy floors of old barns, stables etc with more hole than roof.' There was no improvement the following month: 'The mud still continues. I never dreamt of such mud. Yesterday I got stuck and couldn't move, I had to be hauled out. My boot came away from the upper and is now being sewn together.'

Men could live in and cope with the water and mud but it was impossible to do this and fight at the same time. Despite the efforts of the Royal Engineers and the Pioneer and Labour battalions, water dispersal was a recurring problem in the British sectors of the line. The saving grace was that the enemy were similarly affected. While mud increased individual hardship and made living conditions miserable, it was nonetheless welcomed by the troops as it signified an end, however temporary, to the slaughter. Everyday life had to continue, even in conditions which turned roads, tracks and trenches to the consistency of treacle and added to the burden of the soldier. The uniform of the Highland regiments was particularly uncomfortable in the wet and mud. Men on fatigues would remove their kilts and work in their shirt tails with their nether regions exposed to the elements – this was preferred to having ten or so pounds of mud clinging to the kilt or the frozen hem cutting the back of the legs. It was easier to scrape mud from bare legs than from the kilt. Men would also remove the kilt on the way to the front line through the flooded communication trenches, for the same reason. Picture if you will the strange sight of a company of Highlanders appearing through the gloom in nothing but their shirt tails and with their wedding tackle exposed. Devils with skirts? Lieutenant Sir Ian Bolton, serving with the 2nd Battalion Argyll & Sutherland Highlanders, recalled 'My kilt floated up round me when I entered my first trench and later froze. Some of the men removed their kilts altogether.' Captain D. Dick, 12th Battalion Argyll & Sutherland Highlanders, was more innovative than most:

> I discovered a bundle of sandbags of which I took possession. I used them to make a kilt – for the cold froze the pleats of our kilts to the back of our legs – I used them for reserve stockings, and even for a shirt. I came out of that spell of trench duty with no kilt and no rifle, but a stock of sandbags which I had been wearing for a kilt and for my stockings; but I was all in.

A. Gilmor, 14th Battalion Argyll & Sutherland Highlanders, pointed out that standing in water wearing kilts, in his case ten yards of cloth in an Argyll & Sutherland Highlanders box-pleat kilt, reduced the morale and the manpower of the battalion. Some 300 members were hospitalised with trench foot or pleurisy after standing for four days knee-deep in water in December 1916. While his battalion was undergoing a period of rest, Lieutenant J.B. MacLean, 7th Battalion Cameronians, took the opportunity to write home explaining the conditions experienced in the Third Battle of Ypres, otherwise known as Passchendaele:

I daresay you have been reading about the recent 'push' here. Our armies have done well and if you could see the kind of ground they have to go over you would appreciate it more. When the weather is bad fighting on a big scale is impossible, which explains the motto one of our company officers has, 'Better slush than slaughter'.

Quartermaster-Sergeant, later Lieutenant, Alan Macgregor Wilson, 8th Battalion Black Watch, displayed a similar sentiment: 'Oh – Yawn – another day again and pouring of rain. Well, it might be worse. Much better that it rains water than shells.' Captain Dick recalls that, when going up to the trenches of the Somme, the mud was so bad that one fellow was left behind, in the hope that someone with more time would get him out:

We started our way up the communication trench, but the watery mud was up to our waist, and it was sticky. Every two or three yards some one in line would get stuck, and we did our best to extricate him. This meant losing track. One fellow in my platoon we left just stuck in the trench and we hoped that some one with more leisure would be able to free him.

In front of me in line was L/Cpl James Allan, and I was glad that he had a parcel wrapped in white cloth attached to his knap-sack – it was a guide in the darkness. The most unfortunate thing was that James was known to be the tidiest of soldiers, with never a spot on his uniform. We slithered along, then James would suddenly slip down the side of a shell hole, and be up to his neck in mud. I would follow suit, but when James took care at the next shell hole to wash the mud of his hands, he would hold the line back. This happened several times, and at last I got so annoyed that when he was trying to get a chance to wash off the mud, I pushed him with my foot so that he fell over the head in the water-filled shell hole. After that there were no delays, though the dirty cloth of his parcel was not so good a guide for me in the darkness.

Lieutenant Maclean also described the struggle and effort involved in making a journey to the front line in wet conditions:

> It was raining and blowing that evening and very cold and the march up to the trenches was the frigid limit. We had to go along miles (literally) of communication trench in the dark, and as every now and then we struck a shell hole of a bit that had been blown in and had to be climbed over and as everywhere except the 'duck-boards' was deep in slime and mud, you can imagine what we were like. The last 300 yards or so had to be done over the open across clayey ground and it was a regular acrobatic performance getting along as it was very slippy and 'holy'. I fell right into the half filled shell holes three or four times and soon exhausted all the swear words I have ever heard and was reduced to vulgar blasphemy.

For Thomas McCall, Cameron Highlanders, the journey up to the line, undertaken in mud and water, was only the introduction to the work involved in consolidating captured trenches:

> Before we got there we had to march up a communication trench half full of water and mud for a couple of miles, and looked like a lot of sewer rats when we reached the front trench, which had belonged to the Germans. Then started the hard work cleaning up the muck and water, filling sand-bags and building up parts that had been blown in, and making snipers' posts, and all the time trench mortars were hurling over their shells, causing more muck and casualties.

After his struggle through the mud and debris of the communication trenches, Lieutenant Maclean was similarly unimpressed by the conditions in the line itself:

> My own residence was a hole cut out of the side of the trench just big enough to take me in the prone position, and with a waterproof sheet hanging in front to keep out the weather, in which duty it failed miserably. The trench itself in which my posts were,

> had an average of 9" to a foot of mud and water owing to the rain, and we were all provided with rubber thigh boots which kept our feet dry, but which accumulated pounds of mud, and my 'cubby hole' received most of that, so it wasn't exactly a comfortable place. The very first night Fritz came over and raided one of my posts. He got round the back of it somehow and took it in the rear, chucked in a bomb, jumped in (six of them), grabbed two men, shot another and bolted back again.

He quickly discovered that junior officers were required to take the necessary steps to look after the feet of the men under their charge, and were compelled to hold regular foot inspections to prevent the onset of trench foot or gangrene. Dozens of men all sitting on the fire step presenting their feet for the officer's perusal must surely have been one of the more unwelcome duties a junior officer had to undertake, and possibly one of the strangest sights:

> Of course we are wading about in mud and water and in fact got issued with our waders back at the billet and marched up in them. We also have to rub our feet daily with whale oil and change socks as a preventive measure against trench feet. It is not common for the officers to get that as they are moving about a good deal, but the men have to stand in water for hours.

Many were unused to such harsh conditions, and James Campbell observed how nights spent in the open trenches, in the wind and the rain, told on the men:

> The exposure is telling on some already who have not lived an open air life. I am glad that I am blessed with a good constitution. I've never had a cold since I came out here and I've almost forgotten how to blow my nose. It rained heavily all day today and our trenches are in a great mess. After doing the first fifty yards you stop being careful and splash through the muck. It is a great

sensation when a big splash of cold mud goes up on your bare legs.

I was carrying rations to the guns and we had a great job. At one bit I had to lay down my bag of rations, get hold of the sides of the trench and pull my left leg out of the mud. It was very hard work, for the trenches were long and without exception knee deep in heavy clinging mud. The wet bits were not so bad but where the mud had begun to dry up the trench was very difficult to negotiate.

Newspapers at home carried quite detailed 'artist's impressions' of dugouts and trenches, depicting in many instances all the comforts of home. While there were instances of relatively 'luxurious' dugouts, primarily in reserve lines, the majority were of poor construction. Sergeant S. Saunders, 6th Battalion Gordon Highlanders, was aware of the sanitised visions of trench life readily absorbed by those at home:

One sees pretty pictures in the papers of dugouts and reads how comfortable the men are but they must be very different from these. It is HELL – that's the only way of putting it. Everyone is coated with mud from head to toe – I've never seen men in such a mess. Lots lost boots and stockings in the mud – it is no uncommon thing to see men with bare legs and feet. Food is none too plentiful and water is scarce. Rum was issued this morning before breakfast – it upset some of the men being taken on an empty stomach... The trenches are not deep enough and as one walks along one has to stoop down – a most tiring way of walking – all of course in thick mud.

Men, horses, mules and guns all disappeared without trace in the mud. Captain Hay-Young, 1st Battalion Argyll & Sutherland Highlanders, witnessed at first hand the trench conditions in the mud of January 1915:

The trenches here are awful. Men have actually died in the mud before getting to them! Nearly all are knee-deep in mud and water. If you leave go of any of your belongings they sink for ever. The whole condition is impossible, but we are waiting and hoping for a chance to be moving before this trench work has demoralised the men.

Dundonian Thomas Williamson experienced for himself the sensation of being trapped in the quagmire:

I went a few steps and suddenly my feet disappeared beneath the mud. I made valiant struggles to get out but the more I struggled, the deeper I sank in the mud. I was now beginning to panic as I realised like a flash of lightning that I was in a bog. The more I struggled the deeper I sank. Beads of perspiration were streaming down my face with my efforts to free myself. A terrible fear gripped my heart. I was now up to the knees and I knew I dare not try to struggle any more. I could feel the terrible suction around my feet. I looked up to the heaven above, dotted now with a very few stars. I lifted my two hands: in one I held my rifle, covered thick with mud and with outstretched arms I cried to God, asked Him to forgive me, a sinner like me. I called on Him to save me from this awful death, this terrible fate of slow suffocation, but no answer came, nothing but the awful darkness and the swirling suction beneath me. The tears were streaming down my cheeks. What a death, what an end, to die and not get a fighting chance. Oh the agony of it; I was nearly mad. I was beginning to sink deeper. I was up to the waist, and I knew that I was now slowly but surely approaching my end. I peered into the blackness, and at last a despairing thought came to me. I began to shout for help. God had given me a powerful pair of lungs, and I made the best possible use of them now. 'Help, Help, Help!' I shouted. No answer came. I cried again to God; 'O God have mercy on me.' I shouted until I felt my lungs would burst. The suddenly I saw a very small light, roughly speaking about two hundred yards away. I renewed my cry for help and I shouted until I was utterly exhausted. The lights then came nearer and I made a supreme effort to shout again. I then heard a faint dry. 'Hullo there, where are you?' they heard me – I was almost fainting. I looked up to where I knew God was in heaven and it was speechless thankfulness, I could not speak. It was then that I saw dimly the figures of two men, with farm lamps. A rope came whizzing through the air; it dropped short but the second time it was just past my head, and I managed to get hold of it and put it round my body. I was dragged through the mud and stinking water with my head and face almost submerged. I was in such a state I could only stutter, 'thank you lads, you saved my life.' I had been rescued by two lads of the King's Liverpool Regiment.

When Williamson reported to his battalion in a state of obvious shock and distress, he was allowed to rest for a couple of days to recover from his ordeal. For Private Begbie, life in the Dardanelles was just as uncomfortable, as the winter floods made the trenches uninhabitable:

The middle of November witnessed the arrival of typical winter conditions. We were issued with warmer garments but it was impossible to erect huts or shelters which alone could give the troops really adequate protection against the elements at night. After two days of torrential rain, blizzards of sleet and snow swept across the peninsula. The nullahs became swollen rivers and the swirling waters flooded the dugouts and shelters which had been scooped out of the banks. The trenches became canals and the men, careless of snipers, balanced precariously on the narrow ledge of the fire step... The power of human endurance def[ies] calculation. Men compelled to live in the open air seem capable of enduring the utmost extremes of climate. The troops, after being grilled for months by a tropical sun, naturally suffered acutely from the wintry conditions but invariably contrived to joke about the weather. The coming of winter marked an abatement of dysentery but many of the men began to suffer from jaundice which, though less deadly, was no less unpleasant. About this time many of our men were suffering from frostbite.

There runs a road in Flanders
Through meadows to the sea,
A long white road, a good straight road,
As all the world may see.

There runs a road in Flanders
Made dusty by men's feet,
And tramp of marching soldiers,
Rings through the noontide heat.

There runs a road in Flanders
A broken thing of mud,
Where holes yawn wide and cannot hide,
The dull red slime of blood.

There runs a road in Flanders
And long and straight it goes,
A great white path of glory –
How great the whole world knows.

Albert A. Hay, 1st Black Watch, originally 2/2 Scottish Horse

8

'Ower the Bags'

Tommy: 'Good morning, Fritz.'
Fritz: 'Goot morning, Tommee.'
Tommy: 'Come over here and I'll give you an Iron Cross.'
Fritz: 'Come over here and I'll give you a wooden one.'

If trench warfare was the art of survival, then the offensive was the time of maximum danger. Tens and sometimes hundreds of thousands of troops would attack across no-man's-land – leaving behind the relative safety of their own lines – to advance slowly across the killing field separating the two lines of trenches. It is one thing to shelter in the safety of the trench, vulnerable only to the chance shot. It is quite another thing to leave the shelter of the trench while the enemy machine guns and artillery make a concentrated effort to mow you down. Many never advanced more than a few feet before they were cut down by enemy machine-gun fire, with the second and third waves advancing over the bodies of those already dead and dying. Those who managed to survive the first few yards were faced with the journey across no-man's-land burdened with the accoutrements of war – rifles, Lewis Gun, Mills Bomb, pick, shovel etc. – all carefully designed to slow down the advancing infantry and extend their time in the danger zone. There was a distinct difference between 'normal' day-to-day trench warfare and the offensives which produced the high casualty rates. Large-scale offensives were intended for a specific purpose, a specific gain. Ower the bags

– over the top – call it what you will, it was the ultimate leap of faith.

The attack on 10 March 1915 at Neuve Chapelle was witnessed by Corporal Alex Thompson, 4th Battalion Black Watch, who was unaware at the time of the significance of the battle unfolding before him:

> There was a silence – a few guns fired – then – with a roar that shook the earth, every gun in the district opened fire. The crash of that awful salvo must have struck terror into the hearts of the enemy even more than to us who were more or less prepared for it. Daylight was beginning to strengthen and we could see the fresh troops that had been brought up, making ready to go forward to the attack. Still the awful roar of countless guns continued and indeed to me it seemed it would never stop, forgotten now were the cold and wet and all other miseries. I was unable to think coherently. Everything seemed dull and unreal. I felt no danger though I could see large pieces of shell dropping around me and every now and then the earth flung high in the air as a large shell buried itself near at hand and exploded with a deafening report. I remember watching where one had landed and waiting to see where the next one would go, wondering if it would land in the same place.
>
> I have only a slight idea of what took place that day, as strange to say I fell asleep in my dug out and it was afternoon when I was awakened by shouts and cheers from our men in the trench. I tumbled out to see what was doing and was just I time to see the Seaforths advancing over the open in front of our post.
>
> The Highlanders went forward in three long, straight lines. There was no sign of haste – it might have been a parade ground instead of the bloodiest battle-field of the war. A whistle blew and down went every man flat on the ground. A few seconds elapsed then another whistle went and as one man the Seaforths rose once more and swept towards the battered and broken German lines, disappearing shortly in the edge of the wood.

> The day began to draw to a close long before I realised that a great battle had been going on before my eyes and that I had failed to gather the slightest impression of what had taken place.

Thompson's main worry was procuring enough straw to line the bottom of the dugout. J.G. Scott, who was later killed in the Black Watch attack on Aubers Ridge on 9 May, recorded at this time: 'We had to advance over heavy plough and, unfortunately, some misguided fire from our men hurried us up from behind.' Lieutenant Sotheby also participated in this attack and was witness to the brutality of the action:

> When the attacks failed the Germans threw petrol bombs at the wounded and then shot them down while trying to rise... one batch of prisioners taken [German] were all slaughtered because one of their number suddenly shot down an officer.

On 15 March further news of the battle filtered down to him:

> News has just come in that the 'Seaforths' did very very well. They waited until the Germans got quite close in their usual mass and then volleyed at them. Only 1 German reached the ramparts, all the rest were mown down. It is said that the Seaforths behaved just as on parades in Scotland and their discipline was excellent.

Aubers Ridge

Some attacks were futile and hopeless from the outset. What is remarkable is the resolve, strength of character and courage that made men advance in the face of certain death. On Sunday 9 May 1915 the 1st Division carried out an attack on the German trenches near Richebourg on the Rue de Bois. The British attack was in support of a French offensive at Vimy Ridge and Notre Dame de Lorette and was preceded by a forty-minute artillery barrage which was intended to destroy the enemy wire entanglements and front-line trenches. The bombardment was ineffective, with the wire remaining uncut, and German troops were seen to be strengthening the front line even as the bombardment was underway. The attacking infantry went over the top at 5.40 a.m., but by 6 a.m. the attack had ground to a halt, with the surviving infantry pinned down in no-man's-land by the enemy machine-gun fire. The relatively short artillery barrage failed to make any impression on the enemy wire or to make any appreciable dent in the German defences, and the initial British attack in early morning was a disaster. Unbelievably, rather than wait for the cover of darkness, it was decided to attack again in the afternoon. Douglas Haig issued orders for a renewed assault, initially for 2.40 p.m. but revised to 4 p.m. when it was realised that the fresh troops moving up to the front line were being hampered by the number of wounded making their way down the communication trenches. The daylight gave an immediate advantage to the enemy gunners. During the day the Germans were seen to bring up reinforcements and continued to strengthen the line. The British bombardment resumed at 3.20 p.m. and, following the same plan as the earlier unsuccessful attack, the lead companies of the 1st Battalion Black Watch went over the top at 3.57 p.m. and isolated groups of Scottish soldiers reached the German lines as the bombardment ceased at 4 p.m. These isolated groups held on to captured sections of trench and fought a grim life-or-death struggle. Unable to be reinforced and unable to retreat in the face of German machine-gun fire, they fought to the death. The lead companies of the 1st Battalion Cameron Highlanders arrived too late to go over the top with the first rush but advanced without pause into no-man's-land, almost immediately suffering casualties from the German machine guns. As darkness fell, few returned from the enemy line. Although Haig ordered further attacks for the following day, these were abandoned in the face of opposition from divisional commanders, coupled with the lack of fresh resources.

The Battle of Aubers, or Aubers Ridge as it became known, was costly for those Scottish battalions taking part. The British forces suffered over 11,000 casualties in the attack; over 2,000 of those were Scottish. Six Scottish battalions were involved in the attack. The 1st Battalion Seaforth Highlanders suffered 509 casualties, while the 4th Battalion Seaforth Highlanders, a Territorial battalion, suffered 175. The 1st Battalion Cameron Highlanders suffered 249 casualties. The Black Watch had three battalions involved in the assault. The 1st Battalion had 475 casualties, the 2nd Battalion 234 and the 4th Territorial Battalion suffered 174 casualties. Second Lieutenant Lionel Sotheby, Argyll and Sutherland Highlanders, on attachment to the 1st Battalion Black Watch, took part in the attack and was the only officer in the battalion to escape unscathed. He described the action in a letter written on 11 May 1915, two days after the attack at Aubers Ridge:

Perhaps you have heard about it by now. The awful losses on Sunday, which was to have been the great advance. The old fault, wire not cut. The 1st Black Watch, including myself, charged the German trenches 400 yards away. The whole 15 officers were killed, except 4. Of these 4, 3 were wounded and I survived. I tell you it is a miracle, and I felt quite changed as I lay out 15 yards from the German trenches for 4 hours before crawling back.

The attack stalled against the uncut wire. Some men got through but were seen to be disarmed and killed.

Those who penetrated into the rampart on our left held on for about ten minutes and were then stripped of their equipment by the Germans, shot and thrown over the parapet... here one battalion had in part succeeded when a whole lot had failed in the morning. The Colonel has been praised by all the other Colonels and Generals for what the battalion did. Not a man hung back, all charged as far as possible. A finer set of men than these, and most of them Reservists, could not be found anywhere.

> We lost over 500 men. I feel a changed person at present and unable to laugh or smile at anything, feeling almost in a dream. Next time the Germans will get it. Given a chance with wire down and at close quarters, they will be slaughtered, and I feel quite mad at it, and long for a decent smash at them.

The attack by the Scottish battalions was also witnessed by an officer in the 1st Battalion Scots Guards, who describes the second attack in the afternoon as nothing short of murder:

> Although it made one's blood run cold, it was a most heroic sight to see the Black Watch and the Cameron Highlanders filing up to the front trench. They were magnificent; cheerful and quite calm, going in an hour to almost certain death. The Black Watch advanced in line, with their officers five paces in front of their platoons, and their pipers playing in front. The Black Watch got into the German lines, but were unsupported, and our guns had to bombard for an extra half-hour to let them out again. Two companies disappeared and the remainder were sorely shattered. The whole affair was absolute carnage. The second attack was just murder, sending brave men to certain death, and, my God, they met it like men, too.

As the attack was launched it was witnessed by a group of German war correspondents who were visiting the front line. The attack made such an impression on them that the bravery and courage of the Scottish regiments was widely reported in the German press. The correspondent for the *Frankfurter Zeitung* reported:

> Then the British came into action with tremendous fierceness. They would break through, cost what it might. They attacked on three lines. The front regiment was mowed down by our fearful fire, and the following regiment, under a terrible hail from the guns, was unable to advance. Then the British sent one of their

> best Highland regiments to the front, the best they have anywhere. The Black Watch advanced. The gallant Scots came on, but even their really heroic bravery was in vain, for they were not able to turn the fate of the day.

There was also a description of the attack in the *Deutsche Tagezeitung*:

> The British advanced with extra ordinary force. They had in action about a division, and called them to advance in three lines. After the first line had been thrown back with fearful losses, the second line could not advance. The elite regiment, the Scottish Black Watch, was called forward, and bled to death without having obtained anything. Two men actually reached our breastworks, and had to lie in front of them from five in the evening until six the next morning, before we could look at them.

Private Braid also described the action:

> We had a charge the other day and took the German trench which was 300 yards away. You talk about murder, you aught to have been there, they were throwing bombs at us. There were some of our chaps blown to atoms at this juncture, that made the rest of us retire. I made for a shell-hole fifty yards away from their trench and lay there till ten o' clock when I crawled back again in the dark.

Perhaps William Linton Andrews should have the last word on Aubers Ridge. He was with the 4th Battalion Black Watch and witnessed the consequences of the attack:

> When we put up memorial crosses for those who had fallen in the action of the 9th of May, there was a sergeant-major who put a white cross on the grave of his son, and a private who put a cross on the grave of his father.

Gallipoli

In the early months of 1915, with the stalemate of trench warfare in the west, the Allies decided that the opportunity should be taken to prosecute the war on other fronts. The concept was an attempt to return to the fluidity of nineteenth-century warfare. The intention was to use the might of the British and French navies to open up a new front in the Mediterranean by forcing the Dardanelles Narrows, the stretch of water between the Mediterranean and the Black Sea. The intention was to destroy Turkey, Germany's ally in the east, thereby weakening the German ability to project military power and allowing Russia to attack what was thought to be Germany's weakest front. However, when the initial attempts to force the straits using naval power alone failed in the face of the Turkish forts, the Allies proceeded to land troops on the Gallipoli peninsula, with the intention of neutralising the forts and taking control of the straits by advancing overland.

'Y' Beach!
'Y' Beach, the Scottish Borderer cried
While panting up the steep hillside,
'Y' Beach!

To call this thing a beach is stiff,
It's nothing but a bloody cliff.
Why 'beach'?

The initial landings took place on 25 April 1914, with Scottish elements involved from the outset. The 1st Battalion King's Own Scottish Borderers led the landings on 'Y' beach as part of 29th Division. The landings were relatively unopposed, but strong Turkish counter-attacks throughout the night of 25 April and the lack of ammunition resulted in the landing party of King's Own Scottish Borderers and the Plymouth Battalion of the Royal Naval Division evacuating the beachhead on 26 April. The campaign in Gallipoli quickly reached the stalemate of the Western Front and the attrition of trench warfare became the norm. Despite numerous attempts to break out of the beachheads into the hinterland, the campaign was abandoned and the Gallipoli peninsula evacuated in early January 1916. Bandsman G.G. McKay, 5th Battalion Royal Scots, was part of the attacking force:

> We have to be prepared to land waist deep in water. Carry haversack on top of pack, two days rations, bayonet in pack also, spare bandolier of ammunition, 250 rounds issued to all. Emergency ration – biscuits, two oxo cubes, tea, sugar, and bully beef in tins.

McKay participated in the initial landings and his diary records the first two days on the Allied beachhead:

> Sunday 25 April 1915
>
> At 4.15 a.m. we were awakened by the sound of heavy firing and this continued until 9 a.m. when we received a message that our fire was quite successful and a safe landing had been affected by our advance party. Looking through glasses we could see quite well the shells landing and hear the infantry. 10 a.m. we are rapidly drawing near to land; and the noise is deafening. The Turks have been forced back. We are at Gallipoli Peninsular (Cape Helles). Have been watching the fleet shells landing and the havoc 'simply superb'. Rifle fire continuous and much rapid fire. At 1 o' clock some wounded taken on board hospital ship.
>
> Monday 26 April 1915
>
> Battle raged all night and we had to turn out at 3 a.m. and were taken ashore to carry ammunition to firing line. Many dead and wounded lying about. Much Turkish ammunition and rifles

abandoned. Battle still going on. Artillery all landed by 10 a.m. today and apparently successful in keeping the enemy back. We fall with battalion now and seem to be landed for good. Six wounded 'Queen's' so far. Expect to have another night at least. Battle lasts all day and night but Turks retiring. At 6 p.m. our platoon buried thirty dead. Most gruesome. I had the job along with others to empty the pockets and take identity disks. Most fearful and awesome task ever I undertook. This totals 202 dead.

Bandsman McKay was killed two days later on 28 April. On 28 June 1915 the 4th Battalion Royal Scots was once again in action, this time at Gully Ravine, Krithia, on the Gallipoli peninsula. Captain F.B. Mackenzie was wounded in the neck during the attack on the enemy positions and was awarded the Military Cross for his part in the charge on the Turkish trenches. In the recommendation for the decoration, Captain Mackenzie is mentioned as:

…having shown conspicuous bravery and initiative in the handling of one of the battalion machine guns, which kept up a telling fire on groups of Turks gathering for counter-attacks, and when messages sent for re-enforcements failed to have the desired effect, Captain Mackenzie doubled back across the open to where the re-enforcements were lying, and led them up to the weak part of the line where their support was urgently needed.

In a letter home to his sister, Sergeant Grey of the same battalion described the attack and Mackenzie's part in the action:

I landed just beside Mr Mackenzie putting up his machine gun amid a hail of rifle bullets. I know what stuff he is made of. By Heaven! He is a good one! He got it working and mowed down crowds of gathering Turks. I rushed forward to the Turkish trenches with my section and found some of our own men in it. Mr Mackenzie had brought his gun over to our trench, and while

> there was shot in the neck. He came down to our post where we made him comfortable and bandaged him up and I had the pleasure of giving him some tea. He had a narrow shave. The bullet must have missed his jugular vein and spine. He was quite cheery and spoke to me. He is likely away back to Alexandria now.

Another letter on the same subject dated 30 June came from Private Frank Merton, 4th Royal Scots, Machine Gun Team:

> We have come down from the trenches after the most awful experience of my life. The 4th have done gloriously. Never a look back, never a fault, straight on to death and glory they went poor lads. Many will never see Scotland again but they'll never be forgotten. The old 6th battalion's D Company went first and the gun team followed on. All our lads were as steady as veterans. The man who led the gun team was Mr Frank Mackenzie, Greenbank Terrace, and his leading could not be excelled, not by the best officer in the British Army. He was a picture of coolness and leadership and only by his being there did our maxim do such good work.

The remnants of the 7th Battalion Royal Scots arrived in Gallipoli in early June as part of 156 Brigade, 52nd Lowland Division. The battalion left Alexandria for Gallipoli on 8 June on board the *Empress of India*. Private Begbie was one of those who embarked in Alexandria:

> We then sailed to Gallipoli, passing through the 'River Clyde' (a boat that was beached to help in the landing) and waded through the water which, before the landing, had had rows of barbed wire laid by the Turks. After landing we had to dig trenches (reserves and communication). Later we could only dig in the dark because the Turks could see the trenches and at some places see our men walking through them. During daylight all our trenches were shelled at times.

The battalion arrived in time to participate in the assault on 28 June. Private Begbie recalled that the Turks were not unaware of the impending attack:

> The enemy bombarded our trenches from 9 a.m. till 11 a.m. They scored many direct hits on our lines and we suffered many casualties before we even left our trenches. At last the hour came and at the words 'Over you go, lads' the troops gave vent to one resounding cheer and swarmed over the parapets into the perils of the open ground.

As the Royal Scots advanced the Turks withdrew. This created a short pause in the advance, which the attacking forces used to consolidate and to allow the supporting troops to close up. This also inadvertently gave the Turkish defenders time to regroup:

> By this time the Turks, having recovered from their panic, delivered such a terrific fire that our Company fell in bundles and, halfway across, Major Sanderson dropped and Captain Dawson and Lieutenant Thomson were killed as they neared their goal. By now, men were falling on my left and right. I then felt as if a horse had kicked my right thigh. I fell down and later, when I got up again, I had no feeling in my leg and fell again.

Wounded, bleeding and unable to move, not only because of his wound but more importantly because of the threat of Turkish snipers, Private Begbie lay out in no-man's-land waiting for the cover of darkness:

> Trying to move, I heard bullets striking the ground so I lay still. I didn't feel very much pain but the sun, which was by this time high in the sky, threw down intense heat on the sand which was crawling with insects of every shape and size. The worst thing was the craving for water – our mouths were so parched by the heat and sand that our tongues swelled.

Sixteen-year-old Begbie was lucky enough to be evacuated to hospital in Alexandria where sympathetic staff repeatedly raised the question of his age:

> I stayed in this hospital for just six days and was sorry to leave as the food was excellent and the nurses very nice – often coming to my bed for a chat. Sometimes, a doctor or a nurse would ask my age and I had to say 18 or I would have been sent home. I would have liked to go home but not that way.

Even as a scared sixteen-year-old, Begbie had his fair share of pride. To be returned home by the army as a juvenile was a shame he was not prepared to suffer. After recovering from his wounds Private Begbie returned to Gallipoli on 24 July. His diary records the day-to-day struggle:

> Trench work under the prevailing conditions was exacting. Work in the front line was constantly interrupted by enemy bombers and snipers. The higher ground where the enemy trenches were sited gave them the natural advantage.

Shortages of manpower meant soldiers spent extended periods in the firing line. On 3 September Private W. Reid, 4th Battalion Royal Scots, recorded: 'We have been relieved from the firing line and are again in the redoubt line. Have been three weeks in the trenches without getting out this is a record for the division.' After a rest of three days the battalion returned to the trenches:

> We have arrived at the firing line for our third spell and we are in a bombing sap up which we have to go at night looking for the Turks who may be hiding there – this is no picnic. We have spent nights in bomb sap and had to go right up to Turkish and bomb them one time we had to throw note inviting them to surrender it was exciting work going to the trenches.

Above: 1 1st Battalion Cameron Highlanders leaving Edinburgh Castle to join the British Expeditionary Force, August 1914. The photograph shows the rows of onlookers as the battalion crosses the castle esplanade.

Left: 2 King's Own Scottish Borderers embarking at Dublin Quay in August 1914. This scene shows the General Service wagons being loaded on board ship. Although Britain had recently entered into war in Europe, there appears to be no sense of urgency or excitement among those soldiers on the quayside.

Left: 3 Posters depicting Scottish heritage were used to promote recruitment.

Below: 4 Postcards like this were handed out in the streets to promote recruitment. This one was given to William Nelson. (front)

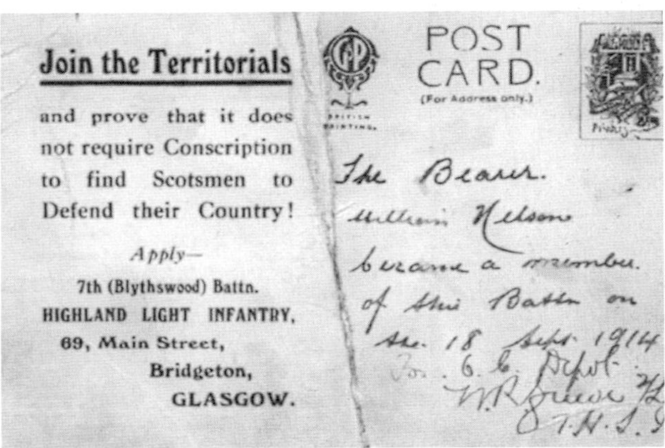

Join the Territorials

and prove that it does not require Conscription to find Scotsmen to Defend their Country!

Apply—

7th (Blythswood) Battn.
HIGHLAND LIGHT INFANTRY,
69, Main Street,
Bridgeton,
GLASGOW.

POST CARD.
(For Address only.)

The Bearer.
William Nelson
became a member
of this Battn on
the 18 Sept 1914
For O.C. Depot

5 Same postcard. (back)

6 The 2/4 Battalion Royal Scots marching up the mound in Edinburgh led by the regimental colours. Large crowds are seen lining the street.

7 Sir George McCrae leading the 16th Battalion Royal Scots, George Street, 15 December 1914.

8 Many of the early camps consisted of tents. This photograph shows the Argyll & Sutherland Highlanders in camp at Aldershot. In the foreground is the cookhouse, itself a lean-to shelter.

9 Route march in the sand dunes to acclimatise troops. Quite a number of the men have their heads down – obviously suffering in the heat. These training marches were in many ways counter-productive – causing unnecessary casualties from heat stroke and exhaustion.

10 The funeral procession for those members of the 7th Battalion Royal Scots killed in the Gretna railway disaster on 22 May 1915, *en route* to Gallipoli. The procession took over three hours to pass.

11 Crash site at Gretna.

Above: 12 Troops parading on Alexandria waterfront before travelling inland.

Right: 13 The funeral procession for those members of the 7th Battalion Royal Scots killed in the Gretna railway disaster.

Above: 14 While some soldiers kill time sitting on the fire step, others sit in 'funk holes', their legs protruding into the trench.

Opposite above: 15 The front-line trench (Contalmaison 1916) – men are clearly seen sleeping in 'funk holes' dug into the side of the trench and reinforced with sandbags. Scattered all around are the accoutrements of life in the trenches, including socks placed on the sandbags to dry.

Opposite below: 16 Men could only walk in the open when in rear areas. Here Seaforths make their way forward. Once within sight and range of the enemy all movement would be done at night.

Above: 17 Part of the trench system in the Somme sector of the British line. The Seaforth Highlanders holding the front-line trench facing Martinpuich in August 1916. This picture demonstrates the barren surroundings. Shellfire and trench construction has reduced the area to a featureless landscape.

Below: 18 Fighting patrol of Seaforths.

Right: 19 5th Battalion Scottish Rifles proudly displaying newspaper headline featuring themselves. The trench appears to be constructed as a breastwork of sandbags – possibly due to the water table preventing deep trenches being dug.

Below: 20 The build-up before the battle at Aubers Ridge. Men of the Black Watch moving forward.

21 The Black Watch attack at Aubers Ridge. The pipers lead the way for the 1st Battalion.

22 The 1st Battalion King's Own Scottish Borderers advancing through the smoke at Gallipoli.

23 The British positions at Krithia Nullah, the scene of heavy fighting.

24 Stocking up on hand grenades before the attack.

Above: 25 Mopping-up party clearing enemy trenches and dugouts.

Below: 26 A caricature of the officers of the 8th Battalion Royal Scots queuing outside their bath house.

Right: 27 Soldiers of the King's Own Scottish Borderers searching for lice on the beach at Gallipoli.

Below: 28 Black Watch on the Western Front searching for lice. Note the bayonet used to keep the shirt in position.

Left: 29 Steam was the most common method of pest control. Here is a mobile clothes steamer, used to fumigate clothes and kill lice.

Below: 30 Work party carrying equipment through the mud at Beaucourt, November 1916.

31 Work carried on even in the trenches. Here we have men from the King's Own Scottish Borderers using a machine to reload machine gun belts in a trench at Gallipoli.

32 A work party clearing debris from the Le Sars–Pys road in France, March 1917.

Above: 33 The Scarpe at Blangy, April 1917. Ammunition being carried forward by pontoon boat while reinforcements march up the narrow-gauge railway line.

Below: 34 Stores being unloaded in Palestine.

Above: 35 Transport took many forms. This photograph shows a transport column in Palestine.

Below: 36 Even at rest the men lived in squalid and primitive conditions. Desolate landscape with trees stripped bare by shellfire – those that are still standing – and a ruined hamlet in the distance. Troops bivouac for a short rest in Fricourt Wood, June 1917.

37 The Black Watch at rest. Men doing their laundry and reading; note the rum jar in the foreground.

38 Men of the Black Watch at rest before the Battle of Loos.

39 Royal Scots church parade in the field.

40 Black Watch hold sports while resting at Bailleul, May 1917.

41 A ration party from the 6th Battalion Cameron Highlanders going up the trenches at Arras, March 1917.

42 Cheese and wine party? Men of the Black Watch relax in the line.

43 Water was scarce and transported large distances by camel in flat-sided containers. Here men of the King's Own Scottish Borderers are filling water bottles from two such containers.

44 Bread being distributed from a field bakehouse.

45 Men of the Royal Scots Fusiliers gather round the field kitchen in Krithia Gully, Gallipoli.

46 A river boat on the Tigris which has been converted for use by the Red Cross.

47 The liner *Mauritania* was used as a Red Cross hospital ship. Hospital ships brought the wounded home – the *Mauritania* was perhaps the most famous.

48 Stretcher bearers struggle to carry injured past waiting Seaforth Highlanders in the narrow front line trench.

Above: 49 Officers' dugouts in Palestine – a hole excavated then covered over to give some protection from the sun.

Left: 50 The Black Watch on the march.

51 Seaforths resting by the side of the road.

52 Rations being distributed to the carrying parties. Black Watch.

53 Watercolour of trench.

54 Route march.

55 Black Watch.

56 Walking the plank.

This time the battalion was relieved after only a short stay, but they returned to the firing line on 14 September and followed this pattern until the evacuation. It was not only in the front line that men continually toiled:

> In support, reserve or in rest, fatigues were the order of the day and most of the night. Since there were no roads, supplies had to be conveyed from the beaches to the front line by pack-mules along the dry water courses – not ideal transport routes and for much of the distance the supplies had to be manhandled by very tired men.

Lieutenant Alexander Nicol was killed at Gallipoli in September 1915 leading a charge at Achi Baba Nullah. In a letter of 12 September sent to his mother, Mrs A.B. Nicol of 85 Brisbane Street, Greenock, by a fellow officer, Lieutenant P.P. Thomson, it is clear that he was trying to sanitise Nicol's death:

> When his platoon was charging, a Turkish machine-gun was causing heavy loss to his men so he rushed at it trying to silence it with his revolver. A burst of fire caught him and he fell killed. I understand that the gun was firing high, so he was shot through the head, and killed instantly. Words of eulogy are superfluous, Alex died a hero, thinking first of his duty and his men.

On 12 November, Lieutenant Thomson once again wrote to Nicol's mother:

> About ten days ago Sgt MacFarlane of C Company and myself placed a cross on Sandy's grave in Achi Baba Nullah. I had it made up by the Royal Engineers.

This time, rather than trying to console Nicol's mother, the letter continued in more bombastic tone:

> Our principal worry is lest the people at home make a premature peace. No matter what happens to us, in view of the Armenian massacres, the Belgian and French losses, Bulgarian treachery, and Greek cowardice, we must carry on until we have smashed for ever Prussian militarism. None realise that more than us out here.

In what was obviously an attempt to bolster support at home he ends by saying:

> Oh how we hope that nothing but complete victory will satisfy our people at home. If any at home think we are pessimistic, tell them we are not: and if we are not, who has a right to be.

In a letter from Gallipoli to his parents, Corporal A. Alexander wrote:

> I can tell you I can't say much but I'll risk a little. We attacked the Turks on Monday 15th and gained our objective where they made a counter attack on us during the following night but they were repulsed after some hard fighting as we knew they would try and recover lost ground we were fully prepared. It was quite an anxious time and to make matters worse it poured all night and thunder and lightening was awful but I came through all right.

The diary of Revd Donald MacDonald, with the Cameronians at Cape Helles, makes brief reading for this period:

> Wednesday 17 November. No water
> Friday 19 November. No water
> Monday 22 November. Nothing landed
> Tuesday 23 November. Nothing landed
> Tuesday 30 November. Half rations. No bread and little water.

There was a distinct improvement to his mood on 4 December when he recorded: 'Stores in. Weather beautiful.' Revd MacDonald also recorded his feelings about the evacuation:

> Monday 13 December. Looking more and more like evacuation.
> Sunday 19 December. When will it be my turn?
> Monday 20 December. My turn must come soon.

W. Reid found that the Christmas celebration of 1914 was not to be repeated in 1915 in the Dardanelles. His diary for Christmas Day records his frustration at fighting a Muslim nation which did not recognise Christmas. 'Christmas day and we would not believe it as there are no signs to show that it has arrived.' The Allied force eventually abandoned the peninsula in early January 1916. The 4th Battalion Royal Scots was one of the last to be withdrawn. On 8 January Reid recorded: 'We have no doubt now as to whether we are going to leave the peninsular or not as we have everything ready to evacuate the place tonight.' The evacuation did take place as his diary shows: 'Have left the peninsular. Was one of the last to get off in a lighter and was transferred to the battleship Prince George, we were torpedoed during the night but luckily the thing failed to explode. Arrived at Lemnos 7.00 am on 10th January.'

Loos

On 21 September 1915 British guns began to bombard German positions at Loos in preparation for a planned offensive on 25 September. Torrential rain and thunderstorms on 23 and 24 September flooded the communication trenches and turned the front line into a morass, while the exploding shells turned no-man's-land into a quagmire which would only serve to slow the advancing troops and make them more vulnerable to enemy fire. Loos was also to see the first use of gas by the British, although the weather was not entirely favourable for its release. In a repeat of Aubers Ridge the German wire remained more or less uncut by the artillery bombardment. The enemy front line was similarly unaffected, with some German units carrying out planned reliefs on the eve of the attack. On the morning of 25 September the wind was not deemed favourable for the gas to be released, as there were pockets of still air, but Douglas Haig gave the order for the release of the gas at 5.50 a.m., forty minutes before the infantry was due to attack. When the gas was released it moved forward slowly in some areas while remaining static in others, forming a thirty-foot-high bank of deadly fog. At 6.30 a.m. the British artillery barrage lifted from the German first line onto the second and the British infantry moved out of their positions and advanced across no-man's-land. The 15th (Scottish) Division made their advance through the clouds of British gas, suffering losses as they did so. As they emerged from the 'relative' safety of the cloud they were met by murderous fire from the German positions. However, disregarding their losses, the Scots cleared the front line and captured the village of Loos by 8 a.m. The 9th (Scottish) Division was detailed to attack the heavily defended Hohenzollern Redoubt and again the leading companies suffered from the effects of their own gas. The advance was slowed because trenches were deliberately flooded by the German defenders as they fell back, but the division pressed on, with the 7th Battalion Seaforth Highlanders reaching the rear of the Redoubt by 7 a.m. While the 5th Battalion Cameron Highlanders, in the face of a murderous crossfire from German positions at Mad Point, reached the front of the redoubt, known as Little Willie Trench, by 7.10 a.m., the 8th Battalion Gordon Highlanders managed to reach the German second line by 8.05 a.m. and were joined by the 12th Battalion Royal Scots. The 6th Battalion King's Own Scottish Borderers were caught in the open, as were the 10th Battalion Highland Light Infantry, and both battalions suffered heavy casualties, as did the 9th

Battalion Cameronians and the 11th Battalion Highland Light Infantry.

The Battle of Loos, 25 September to 19 October 1915, saw high casualty rates among the Scottish divisions, particularly the newly formed Kitchener battalions. The 9th (Scottish) Division suffered 6,058 casualties, including 190 officers, while the 15th (Scottish) Division suffered 6,896 casualties, 228 of which were officers. A total of forty-five Scottish battalions participated in the action at Loos.

Scottish Infantry Battalions at Loos

1st Division	
1 Black Watch	1 Cameron Highlanders
2nd Division	
2 Highland Light Infantry	9 Highland Light Infantry
1 Scottish Rifles (Cameronians)	2 Argyll & Sutherland Highlanders
5 Scottish Rifles (Cameronians)	
7th Division	
2 Gordon Highlanders	6 Gordon Highlanders
4 Cameron Highlanders	
8th Division	
2 Scottish Rifles (Cameronians)	5 Black Watch
9th (Scottish) Division	
8 Black Watch	7 Seaforth Highlanders
8 Gordon Highlanders	5 Cameron Highlanders
11 Royal Scots	12 Royal Scots
6 Royal Scots Fusiliers	10 Argyll & Sutherland Highlanders
6 King's Own Scottish Borderers	9 Scottish Rifles (Cameronians)

10 Highland Light Infantry	11 Highland Light Infantry
9 Seaforth Highlanders	

15th (Scottish) Division

9 Black Watch	8 Seaforth Highlanders
10 Gordon Highlanders	7 Cameron Highlanders
13 Royal Scots	7 Royal Scots Fusiliers
6 Cameron Highlanders	11 Argyll & Sutherland Highlanders
7 King's Own Scottish Borderers	8 King's Own Scottish Borderers
10 Scottish Rifles (Cameronians)	12 Highland Light Infantry
9 Gordon Highlanders	

Guards Division

1 Scots Guards	2 Scots Guards

Lahore Division

1 Highland Light Infantry

Meerut Division

1 Seaforth Highlanders	4 Seaforth Highlanders
2 Black Watch	4 Black Watch

> A thunder-storm to-day. God's guns are rumbling in the heavens. Our little affair down here seems like a puny game between toy soldiers. (Lieutenant W.S. Dane, 4th Battalion Seaforth Highlanders)

On the eve of the attack Captain Patrick Duncan, 4th Battalion Black Watch, recorded in his diary: 'We go up to the trenches tonight, after 6 days out; there was a thunderstorm last night and the weather is unsettled.' James Campbell, 6th Battalion Cameron Highlanders, also prepared for the coming battle: 'Today we handed in our packs containing overcoats. We are going to attack tomorrow and are going light. At 5 p.m. I said goodbye to Peter [brother] in case I didn't see him again.' Thomas McCall, Cameron Highlanders, also took part in the attack:

> The soldier lying next me gave a Shout, saying, 'My God! I'm done for.' His mate next to him asked where he was shot. I did not catch what was said, but he drew himself back and lifted his wounded pal's kilt, then gave a laugh, saying, 'Jock, ye'll no dee. Yer only shot through the fleshy part of the leg.'
>
> The platoon I belonged to arrived at a German trench, where about nineteen to twenty Jerries were shouting for mercy, after pinking some of us as we came forward. Someone shouted 'Remember the Lusitania!' and it was all over with Jerry. We moved on towards the village of Loos, where machine guns were raking the streets and bayonet-fighting was going on in full swing. Prisoners were being marshalled in batches to be sent under guard down the line. The most of the houses were blown in, but their cellars were strongly built and it was in these cellars that many Germans were hiding. I kept well into the side of the street to escape the flying metal, and came to a little estaminet. By the noise going on inside I thought they were killing pigs. I went inside and opened a door where blood was running out from underneath. It was certainly a pig-sticking exhibition. I saw some Highlanders busy having it out with Jerry with the bayonet. My assistance was not required, so I set off for Hill 70, our objective.

Participating in the events of 25 September, Thomas Williamson was spared the full horror of the first wave but as his battalion advanced through the carnage of no-man's-land he found himself affected by the sight of large numbers of wounded making their way back to their own lines:

> The great attack had begun, and our infantry had left the trenches and were at grips with the Bosch. Half an hour after the attack the Royal Scots Fusiliers moved forward in company formation. One fellow, one of our wags shouted 'Noo's the day and noo's the hoor'. I felt a queer sensation inside me, as I kept step with the boys, and then witnessed a magnificent spectacle. Coming across the open towards us were hundreds of our Tommie's, who were all more or less seriously wounded. Men wounded in the face, head and arms were assisting those who were wounded in legs or feet. It was an inspiring sight, comradeship at its very best, all striving to help each other. As they passed us on their way to the first field dressing station, I saw the grim determination on each face. I saw more than that; blood streaming from their wounds, their clothes rent and torn. Others were deathly pale, portraying the awful ordeal they had been through, but in their eyes shone the light of a battle. As they passed us by, those scarred and battered human beings gave us a shout of encouragement 'Up you go Jock, and give them Hell'.

That night as Williamson stood in the trenches the Germans regularly sent up flares to illuminate the battlefield. Perhaps he was of a particularly sensitive nature, but his behaviour that night could be described as unusual. The sight of death affected men in many ways:

> The light revealed to me a few yards in front, two highlanders lying dead. I was so fascinated that I crawled forward and touched the two brawny legs of the dead kilties, legs that had swung along to the tune of the pipes. I could not describe how I felt, those grand heroic lads lying silent in death, far from the land they had died for. Would this awful lust for killing go on much longer? I wondered would I meet a fate such as these lads.

While recovering from wounds suffered in the assault, 'Forrest' Ward, serving in the Cameron Highlanders, wrote to his sister from Birch Hill Hospital near Rochdale, Lancashire, describing the attack and his part in it:

> Many thanks for the parcel received this morning, and I am glad you are all well. My wounds are improving although I am still confined to bed, the swelling in my arm and hand is gradually disappearing, so this is a good sign. I have it dressed every four hours day and night with hot fomentations applied to draw out the septic, and to-day I expect to have the x-rays on it to see what damage is done to the bone, and then we may get started to heal it up.
>
> The wounded here have a good time. Those who are up were away yesterday a motor run to Cheshire and had a nice time, so when I get up I expect to have a few outings. The people about here visit us quite a lot, and we have a fine gramophone to while away the time.
>
> It was Saturday the 25th the advance started. The British started bombarding on the Wednesday and continued till Saturday morning; about 5.30 the bombardment was terrific, night and day hundreds of guns from 4 inch to 17 inch, Naval guns poured shells on to the enemy lines, the first line of trenches was completely obliterated, and the second and third suffered badly. About 5.30 a.m. on the 25th we sent over our gas, but unfortunately previous to this one of the cylinders was burst by a German shell and it caught a few of our men.
>
> However, our boys seemed to be too anxious as they did not give the gas time to travel far enough, and consequently they made up on it before it reached the enemies lines, and again a good number went down with it. However, the Camerons stuck together and made a magnificent charge carrying the first, second, third, fourth and last line of trenches, and then swept through the village behind this. By this time everything was mixed up, but they managed to hold on till night when they were relieved by an English Brigade, and the Highland Brigade returned to our own trenches till daybreak.

Unfortunately, the English lot during the counter attack yielded and gave up a bit of the ground we gained. It is no shame to them, as I believe it was their first time in a trench. However, Sunday passed and on Monday we were more or less in order, but the Germans started shelling our lines and we replied with much gusto until about 3.30 when much to our surprise the shout got up 'Camerons advance'. It was a great surprise as we were told we were being relieved at night, and we were to have a decent rest. However, nothing daunted, the Camerons, or all that remained (about 250) got over the parapet and charged what is known as the Hohenzollern redoubt. Between the two lines the machine gun fire and rifle fire was fierce, and I managed to get into the redoubt and was creeping along to take up my position when a shrapnel burst about 15 yards off and I was one of its victims. I was lucky to be crawling, otherwise I may have been worse off. I immediately got the best cover I could and took of[f] my jacket and equipment, and someone bandaged my arm. At first I thought it was off altogether, but it was only the feeling. My shirt was taken off and I had my back patched. All this was going on amidst a fierce din. At last I managed into a German dug-out with cane bottom chairs no less, and a fine table. I intended lying here till darkness, but the order came to retire and I had to make the best of it. I managed back to our own trench and struggled down the communication trench, but all the trenches were packed with reinforcements and I had a job.

At last I arrived at the first dressing station and was held up as they had again started shelling. About darkness I made another move and arrived in Vermelles about 7.30, then I had my arm dressed again, then something warm to drink, then we got a motor ambulance to Sailly. This is the village we stayed in when not in the trenches; from here we drove to Bethune and slept on the floor of the hospital, then next morning we took the train (about 8.30) for Rouen arriving there after a 28 hours journey, then we slept for a couple of nights in a decent hospital and then crossed to Southampton arriving there about 10 a.m. on Saturday

> and was in Manchester about 8 p.m. arriving here about 9.15 just about all out. I made the journey to Rouen in a kilt and blanket only, from Rouen to here I had a pair of blue trousers, white canvas shoes and blue jacket (some rig out to lie on the deck of a boat with).

James Campbell attended the first roll call held by the 6th Battalion Cameron Highlanders after the battalion was relieved on 27 September:

> Our first roll call numbered 69 all told out of 1,000 on Friday. But all day men straggled in who had been mixed with other regiments and by 6 p.m. we numbered almost 400.

On the following day he recorded: 'Today we had another role call, but failed to number half a battalion. But although dearly paid for, we had won a glorious victory.' He was among those addressed by Sir Henry Rawlinson on 1 October. Rawlinson said the brigade had achieved

> 'the finest and most important victory on the Western Front during the last 8 months' he added 'my opinion now, is that as a fighter, there is none to beat a Scotsman and a Highlander for preference.'

Lieutenant Thorburn, 2nd Battalion Black Watch, agreed with Rawlinson's opinion of the Scottish soldier when describing the assault on the enemy trenches:

> Another warrior was seen to have a Bosch in each hand, gripping them by their chests, dragging them along and butting them in the face with his head, having apparently lost his rifle.

After four days of hard fighting and heavy casualties the attacking force returned to their original start line. Many, like

Lieutenant Thorburn, were despondent at the failure to advance:

> It wasn't till pretty late that we heard (and couldn't believe it) that we were back in the original line. But we did what was required of us – apparently only a demonstration at one part to keep enemy reserves from going down south. All three Generals can't find words good enough for the performance of the Black Watch that day. It must have been wonderful, and could our right and left have done the same, we would be holding the Aubers Ridge now.

Displaying a great deal of luck, J.B. Maclean arrived back after nine days leave and, having missed the initial assault, he was delighted to rejoin his battalion as it came out of the line for a period of rest:

> I got up in the evening and after some trouble located our bivouacs and discovered that I had had the great luck to miss participation in the push. The battalion had been in for about a week and is coming down today so I couldn't have come at a better time. They have been over the top twice and have lost several officers, killed and wounded.

In the aftermath of Loos, James Campbell, who was to win a Military Medal for his part in the action, reflected on the performance of his fellow soldiers and on how the shared experience of combat and the threat of death changes our perception of one another:

> Since the big weekend I respect and like men I previously detested and have lost all respect for other decent chaps. And all because they turned up trumps or didn't when the pinch came. When we were hard pressed I'd have licked the boots of any man who would carry ammunition and keep the gun in action. And, lo, on the Sunday morning, a man I had never drawn well with,

came with a case of ammunition and we worked the gun together all day. It seems funny to think of it, but about 3 p.m. that day we were absolutely encircled with bursting shells for almost ten minutes. When we realized what escapes we had had we solemnly shook hands and defied the Germans to hit us. It was tempting providence but we came through it after all.

He continued his reflection on the aftermath of battle and the normality of life back home:

Some chaps say they would like a 'cushy blighty' which being interpreted, means a wound which will get them home. But I must confess, I prefer a whole skin in France. We got more coal-boxes [large German shells] over this afternoon and when it was all over we were all covered with dust and had it down our necks and into our hosetops and boots. It seems funny to think that at the very same time Rangers were peaceably playing Celtic or some other lot at home.

While recovering in hospital from wounds sustained in the attack, Captain Patrick Duncan's thoughts turned to his fellow officers and friends who had not survived the battle:

Some of our men saw Campbell, lying wounded in a shell hole; although search parties were out for 3 nights after the 25-9-15, no trace of him could be found. The Colonel and poor old Tosh were buried beside each other on the 28-9-15 at a quiet little spot I know well. The poor 4th only got 5 days rest when they had to go a 12 mile march to another part of the line, they have been in the front trenches again for 7 days.

The Battle of Loos has always been seen as a Scottish affair, with battalions from every Scottish regiment present. While this book is not intended as a roll call of casualty figures, it is worth listing a few. The 7th Cameron Highlanders suffered 687 casualties; 9th Black Watch 680; 6th King's Own Scottish Borderers 650; 10th Highland Light Infantry 648; 7th King's Own Scottish Borderers 631; 12th Highland Light Infantry 553; 8th Black Watch 511; 8th Seaforth Highlanders 502; 10th Scottish Rifles 485; 1st Scots Guards 474. Six Scottish battalions lost their commanding officers to enemy fire.

Somme

Originally conceived as part of a joint British and French operation on a sixty-mile front, the initial plan floundered when German forces attacked Verdun in an attempt to defeat the French by attrition. The British offensive on the Somme in July 1916 was carried out to relieve pressure on the beleaguered French forces fighting at Verdun. The bombardment began on 24 June and continued for seven days. There were conflicting reports as to its effectiveness and patrols sent out on the eve of the attack reported that the enemy front line was strongly held. Many of the rounds fired had been duds, while many others had been shrapnel which had little or no damaging effect on the enemy wire or trenches. Servicing the guns of the heavy artillery, Corporal Garside was a member of the 637 Motor Transport Company, Army Service Corps, responsible for transporting ammunition and other stores in the build-up on the Somme in June 1916. In his diary, he described both the bombardment and the attack on 1 July:

> 24 June 1916 [First day of bombardment]
> Loaded with 60 6" shells, cartridges, and fuses. Left Railhead at 10.10 p.m. Went to Mailly. Could see the flashes of the guns all the way up, going directly towards them, held up several times because the Germans were shelling the road. Several lorries stuck in shell holes, had to push them out. Got to Mailly about 3 a.m. Shells falling all around. 5 men killed with shrapnel. One of our men wounded. Unloaded at 72nd Field Battery. Battery in action

all the time and the Germans replying trying to get battery, very unhealthy spot. Can honestly say never felt the least bit nervous. Very hard trying work driving at night without lights and pitch dark. Could not see lorry ahead until within 4 yards of it and then only a black shadow. Shell holes and soft places everywhere, horses and wagons on sides of roads. Could have gone to sleep on lorry if I had dared in spite of shells bursting all round. Got back to [lorry] Park 4.30 a.m. and slept till 9 a.m. Felt alright then. Strange how little sleep suffices 4 hours in 24. Think it is a mistake to go up the line at night, more danger from smashes than shells.

25 June
Bombardment still going on, heard Germans have taken big guns back 8 miles.

26 June
Went in charge of 8 lorries and loaded 335 pit props. Took them to Heavy Artillery Headquarters. Bouzencourt bombardment still going on, started 10.10 p.m. on 24th. Fires all along German line visible from Bouzencourt. Our No. 1 gun blew up German ammunition dump, 4 lorries with fourth shot on Sunday. Complimented on our accuracy. Saw figure of Virgin and Child on top of monument in Albert lying in horizontal position 90 degrees to tower on which it stood.

27 June
Not out. Heard our No. 1 gun.

28 June
Relief lorry on Gun at Bouzencourt for a week. Arrived at 12 midday. Standing within 100 yards of gun. Gun firing every 5 minutes from 2 to 4 o' clock. Shakes the whole village. Air displacement seems to strike with so much force as to make the skin smart. Have to go by Albert and Aveluy with rations from Bouzencourt to No. 2 gun in the Martinsart Wood. Can be seen

from German trenches on part of the road. Under fire all the time for the whole week at Bouzencourt. Passed within 200 yards of German trenches on way to Martinsart.

29 June
Bombardment going on all night. Bouzencourt shelled by Germans. 3 killed. Had a good nights sleep however. Wounded men, chiefly HLI coming down in dozens yesterday. They had been over the parapet the night before and got caught by German fire. Wet yesterday, place simply swimming in mud. Passed through Albert last night. Numerous buildings wrecked by shell fire. All shops closed and civilians cleared out. Seems to be absolutely destroyed. Figure on top of tower is sloping further down than it was – think it must fall soon. 13 men buried in one grave today in a little church yard here just behind our gun. No. 1 gun firing all day. Can see the shell travelling up in the air like a cricket ball. 800lbs weight 12in dia. 3 ft to 3 ft. 6 in long. At Martinsart with rations. No. 2 gun 'Lucky Jim' firing all the time. After hearing about 3 rounds fired – fired in quick succession, don't hear anything else that day. Guns hidden in banks along road the whole way from here to Martinsart and being fired continually the whole time we were passing. Flashes of fire right across our faces. Feel the smart of the hot air and deafened by reports. Some job.

30 June
Germans shelling us here at Bouzencourt. Shells whizzing overhead and exploding while I write this. We may go up any minute – rather unhealthy spot this. Sergeant killed and Pte wounded by shell on football ground. Three men killed and several injured this afternoon. Went to both guns in morning and collected 144 empty cartridge cases, took them to Puchevillers railhead in afternoon. Nearly all ammunition gone from railhead. Hospital train standing there. Motor Machine Gun section passes on way up to the line. Ammunition and food supply dumps shifting towards the

line, pass thousands of Infantry going up the line, cavalry also going up. Expect we shall attack in the morning, bound to be within the next 2 days. Infantry passing up here in steady stream from 2 o' clock, tremendous bombardment commenced from 10 p.m. troops marching past all night long.

1 July
Very little sleep last night, the air fairly hubussed with shells all night till 7 this morning when the Infantry went over. Our 'Lizzie' No. 1 Gun been firing all night and still going. Wounded coming down here in fair numbers now. Say we are well away over the fifth German line. Germans surrendering in hundreds, quite demoralised, no wonder, after the shelling they got. They say 8th Division on right held up. Hope to get forward, heard cavalry are over. Gun teams just gone up to shift Artillery. Wounded say the Germans are on the run, hope the cavalry get in among them. The ground here in Bouzencourt has been quivering all night and is still doing so. They are firing the long range guns only now. Our guns No. 1 'Lizzie' and No. 2 'Lucky Jim' have done remarkably well. Both had a number of direct hits. Constant stream of wounded in ambulance cars, lorries and walking have been coming down all morning. Field Artillery wagons and gun teams galloping up to shift guns forward. Heard from wounded that attack has been a great success. On iron rations now, bull[y] beef, biscuits and tea without sugar and very little milk. Heard from wounded that Germans were in trenches when they advanced and opened machine guns on our men immediately they went over the top.

German trenches had been blown to pieces but Germans were in very deep dugouts while bombardment was on and emerged whenever our men started to advance and opened up on them with their machine guns. Northumberland Fusiliers, Sussex, Lancashire & Yorkshire, HLI Manchesters, all passed up here last night on their way to attack. 3 wounded German prisioners passed here to hospital. Over 600 German prisioners passed through here on their way down. Some fine built men – others just wrecks – all dead beat. Most of them have a look of abject terror.

6 p.m. Great numbers of wounded still coming down, suppose this will be called the battle of the 'Somme'. All wounded who can walk have to. Poor fellows are dog tired and can hardly put one foot before the other and have to keep resting every few yards. Why don't they send motor brakes for them? (Notice there are no charitable institutions for supplying tea or anything to eat within 40 or 50 miles of firing line, also never seen an Army Chaplin or Minister of any description within 10 miles of firing line except French Parish Priests who have stayed in their villages) [lightly scored through]. It is here they are needed especially the charitable people who supply free food and drink more than anywhere else, but I suppose they temper their zeal for charity with a proper regard for their own skins.

Bombardment as lively again tonight as it was last night trying to blow up some German positions that were only disclosed when infantry attacked.

2 July
Wounded still coming down. Pioneers very busy digging large graves close to where we are standing. Heard that some of the infantry who attacked cannot be found. They were fed on bully and biscuits for 4 days before attack, then went forward with one days rations only and have been 2 days and 2 nights without food. Took empty cartridge cases and broken charges to railhead from No. 1 gun.

3 July
More troops went up last night, bombarding all night. Attacked this morning but owing to German defences not been destroyed – failed to get through – machine guns opened up on our men as soon as their heads appeared above sand bags. Great quantities of field gun ammunition going up this morning – streams of wounded still coming down.

Germans are delighted to surrender and go down on their hands and knees and beg for mercy. Whenever they get a chance they run, walk or crawl over to our lines and surrender. The war would be over if it was not for the German officers, the men themselves would give everything they possess to get out of it. Wounded still coming down.

The diary entry for 28 July is short and poignant: 'Graveyards here nearly full now.'

On Thursday 12 October, Lieutenant Crerar was preparing to go over the top in full daylight:

Shortly before 2 we all lined up, the men with fixed bayonets, I with walking stick, revolver and a useful looking heavy knobkerrie with a round metal head with metal studs dangling from my belt. I don't know where I got that; it certainly wasn't a standard issue.

Anyway, at 2.8 I blew my whistle loud and clear and we clambered over the parapet into the open facing the German lines about 3-400 yards in front. Immediately there was an appalling din and we advanced under a hail of thousands of bullets whizzing through the air from rifles and machine guns, and with high explosive shells exploding and throwing up earth and metal, just Hell let loose. After covering about 120 yards with men falling left and right, there seemed to be very few of us still advancing, as the murderous machine gun fire had taken a heavy toll, and a few minutes later, having advanced with a handful of men about another 100 yards, I felt a sledge hammer blow on my left thigh, and fortunately for me tumbled headlong into a shallow shell hole where I lay partially stunned and feeling rather like a shot rabbit in the mouth of its burrow wondering what had happened. I listened to the din of battle overhead and wondered how long it would be before I got picked up by stretcher bearers.

Lieutenant Crerar spent two nights lying exposed to the elements and gunfire before managing to crawl back to the safety of his own lines and have his wound treated. Officer casualties in his battalion were so heavy that one officer who had been injured in a rugby game and unable to proceed to the front was brought up as far as possible by horse to replace the dead and wounded. Norman Collins, 6th Battalion Seaforth Highlanders, recalled the sadness in the aftermath of battle. During the Somme offensive he was appointed battalion burial officer:

> After the attack I was appointed burial officer and was told just to get on with the job of burying the dead. I had a squad of men to help me, carrying the picks and shovels, and also stretchers. Of course some of the men were picking up their brothers and cousins and they of course were very upset, very very upset... In a Highland Regiment, there were many men from the same family, village or town. I mean some of them obviously were just crying, and it was quite natural. If your brother was picked up on a battlefield like that, well, you've only got to imagine what you would feel like, and that's what they felt like... But it was a horrible thing to do, to have to bury your own cousin or brother.

Arras

Private William Cameron, Scottish Horse, had his first taste of action when he went 'over the top' at the Battle of Arras on 9 April 1917. Although it was his first time, he discovered 'it was a most thrilling experience and I am glad to say I had no fear.' James Campbell took part in the fighting at Bullet Trench, as it was known locally:

> Right up and down the trench the German dead are lying thicker than I have ever seen them before. I counted thirty in as many

yards. And there are a good many of our own dead lying around, chiefly Argyles, Camerons, and Gordons. The scrapping about here has been pretty hot.

A description of the involvement of the 9th Battalion Black Watch in the Battle of Arras tells us:

> Early in the month of March our battalion marched to the town of Arras... Our duties now consisted of going up and holding the front line (1 ?miles away) for a few days. But chiefly they were to go on working parties digging extra trenches just behind the front line for the great multitudes of troops that were to attack on the 9th. This work was done at night and was very dangerous owing to our nearness to Jerry's front line. The enemy seemed to spot us occasionally and bombarded us with all sorts of explosive killing stuff. Often we had to hop it, getting one or two wounded in doing so. Well, the night of the 8th April came round and we were told that we were to leave our billets at 2 a.m. the next morning, as we were to attack at dawn (5.30 a.m.). We were also shown photos and maps of our objectives etc. A dozen of us bombers were in a nice billet by ourselves. We started a sing song to keep us from thinking too much of the morrow. 2 a.m. soon arrived and we plodded away up the mud bath of a communication trench, arriving at the front line without Jerry giving us a shell. The officer informed us that at 5.30 a.m. a mine was to go up under Jerry's front line, and in front of the Argyll & Sutherland Highlanders which were a few hundred yards on our left. We waited anxiously in our dismal trench, on as dismal a morning, and at the appointed time up went the mine (previous to this not a shot had been fired) and our artillery opened a barrage fire like a thousand thunderstorms; and at the same time we went over the top, and hurried to the German trenches to get out of the enemy shelling. The Jerry's that were still alive in the 1st and 2nd lines gladly surrendered. Had they not had decent dug outs not one could have survived our artillery. The Camerons who were on our support mopped up

the prisoners, allowing us to go on unhindered. I got my knee badly torn on Jerry barbed wire. We did not go far when the enemy shell fire slackened down. We took it that he was removing his guns to prevent us from capturing them. We reached our first objective with very little fighting and very few casualties. What once had been Foreds Wood was now a few stumps of trees here and there. Here we dug ourselves in for one hour and forty minutes to allow other regiments who had a harder first objective to get up in line with us. All the while the barrage fire was kept up to prevent Jerry from counter attacking. While lying there we looked to the left and on the famous Vimy Ridge saw multitudes of troops running down the ridge towards the British line. We got rather a shock thinking it was our troop in retirement. But our officer after looking through his glasses informed us it was Jerries with their hands above their heads. Believe the Canadians who took part of the ridge had most prisoners that day. The line was by this time straightened. It was time for us to advance again, so we burned red lights on the ground and the Airmen then signalled to the artillery to lift the barrage fire forward and allow us to advance behind it. On starting for the 2nd objective I was with D. Coy. Bombers to assist them to bomb the dug outs. All went well till we got to within a hundred yards of the Triangle Railway, when Jerry opened a proper inferno of bullets among us. We dropped in shell holes, before getting time to do that many, many were killed or wounded. Jerry held us up in our mud holes for four hours and during that time bombarded us with trench mortars, Shrapnel, Lydite, and Rifle grenades. Also a few of his heavies came across. I was lucky to be with D. Coy. As most of the shells fell further behind, some of them falling into A. Coy. It would have been madness to try and advance on that strong point as Jerry had machine guns and snipers into the embankment. After being held up for the four hours the tanks came up (they fairly put the fear into Jerry) other regiments also got round on the flanks, after which we were able to advance and attain our 2nd objective.

Such large-scale action was not confined solely to the Western Front. J. Wallace, 5th Battalion King's Own Scottish Borderers, recalled the eve-of-battle preparations for the upcoming attack on Gaza on 19 April 1917:

> We were attacking Gaza tomorrow. Our objective was Green Hill, and we were not to go beyond it. (For the next six months our theme song was 'There's a green hill far away'). We were to have the support of two tanks and according to our company commander there wouldn't be many Turks left after our artillery barrage had been lifted.

On the day of the attack:

> Reveille at 2.30. Breakfast, water bottles inspected and got ready to move. Each man carried 500 rounds of SAA with a few of us carrying sphere drums of ammo for the machine gunners. We marched in column of route for 3 miles led by our CO Col Simpson, an Edinburgh Dr, we then formed into extended order. My platoon was in the front wave led by our platoon commander Captain Dunn. We were now under shell fire. Two tanks accompanied us but one of them became stuck in a deep wadi bed from which it couldn't climb out so that one became a casualty. The other one got up to an enemy redoubt and damaged the barbed wire, it then became stuck and the crew beat a hurried retreat and joined the infantry. We hadn't many casualties till we reached a ridge on the sky line which we had to get over to reach our objective. When we reached this ridge we ran into a perfect hail of enemy machine gun fire. We lost a big number of men on this ridge.

On the following day Wallace recorded: 'Out of 600 men who went into action yesterday only 200 answered roll call this morning. Out of 21 officers 18 were either killed or wounded.' He later took part in the attack on the village of El Mughar on 13 November 1917:

We advanced over very flat country under shell fire from the enemy. Shells were bursting among us but we kept going forward. Our Battalion's objective was the village of El Mughar. At last we got to a wadi about 200 yards from a large cactus hedge outside the village. There appeared to be a large number of machine guns posted behind that cactus hedge. I went over the top of the wadi along with CSM Townsend. We just got on to the flat when the CSM was hit on the forehead with a machine gun bullet. The Turks appeared to be well entrenched with machine guns behind the cactus hedge. Our boys were falling down in big numbers. Archie Loutill was hit in the arm just beside me, then I got a machine gun bullet through the right thigh, just after I fell I saw Sgt Maxwell look around for his men, most of us were down so he ran for some large stones where he was hit in the upper arm by a bullet. I met him later in hospital where he had had his arm amputated. I must admit that while I lay in the sand with the bullets hitting the ground all round me, I had the wind up, wondering when I was going to be hit again. This was about 11.30 and made what cover I could with my haversack... About 9 o'clock I was lucky in being carried back to a first aid station by two stretcher bearers of the 1/4th KOSB, it was a long carry and they were pretty well done up. I lay there till 4.30 when I was taken to an advanced dressing station in a village which the RSF had captured.

Wallace had the last (13th) operation on his leg in 1929; the damage was mostly due to the delay in receiving treatment. Lieutenant Thorburn, with the rest of his battalion, the 2nd Battalion Black Watch, left the trenches of the Western Front on 9 November 1915 to refit and prepare for the journey to the Middle East. It was intended that they would be part of the force sent to relieve the British force besieged at Kut-el Amara in Mesopotamia. They landed on 6 January 1916 and two days later were in action. Coming from France, it was a shock to find that the fighting in the desert was every bit as fierce and deadly as the Western Front:

I don't suppose men ever went in against such fire, but they never wavered and went right in. Difficult you will understand it is to attack an entrenched position over dead flat ground in broad daylight! We did not reach the position, but dug in at night fall. We lost 18 officers and 375 men, fortunately only a small percentage killed.

In the morning transport not yet up, but we drew rations from a boat, which came up, and I had the finest meal of my life – long streaks of bacon, all fat, cut up and fried in a biscuit tin lid, and eaten (in our filthy hands, unwashed for four days) like asparagus, with real hard biscuits, hot tea ? mud.

Ypres

Private Cameron felt a familiar excitement when he went 'over the top' again on 31 July 1917 at St Julien, the first day of the Third Battle of Ypres – Passchendaele:

This was the best engagement I ever was in, our artillery was using all kinds of shells including liquid fire etc. there were also mines put up on the enemy and really it was just like a firework display.'... We were relieved two days later, soaking through and covered with mud, but feeling happy with a fag in your mouth, and hoping a parcel is waiting on you from home until you get a good 'tightener'.

Sergeant H.E. May, Cameron Highlanders, gave a more sobering account of the action:

Two hours' sleep, then the thunders of an intensive artillery barrage. 5.50 a.m. – over! Men falling. Ahead a burn shown on the map as being 30 inches or 3 feet wide, but found to be a morass 50 feet wide. Wading through mud waist deep, with kilts floating on the surface like water-lilies. Midway over, when the searchlights from the pillboxes swept the countryside and the

> vicious spit of the machine guns was heard. Many fell, killed outright or to suffer the horrible torture of suffocation beneath the mud. You cannot help them; you must push on. A stretch of firm ground and signs of daylight coming up. You see a line of stumpy tree-trunks that, dimly, you realize is the objective. You creep up. A wild mêlée; stabbing with a bayonet. A gushing of blood from many wounds (oh! the nauseating smell of freshly spilled human blood in quantity) and then a cry of 'Kamerad!' and a whine for mercy. Unheeded, for all the enemy died.

He recalls the battalion being stuck in the mud for four days. Shelled on and sniped at from the front; sniped at and bombed from the air, and suffering casualties every hour. One night a sergeant took a party out to set fire to some farmhouses in no-man's-land. There were nests of machine guns in the derelict buildings and the party was armed with tins of petrol:

> Under a rising moon petrol was lavishly poured away. Some under a table. Some on the cloth and a sofa, walls quickly splashed. A flight of stairs in a corner quickly doused when a door at the top opened and a stream of light shone down and there was the noise of much guttural speech. The sergeant had a sheet of newspaper folded lengthwise. A match, a touch, and instantly a flame shot upward. A rapid touch to table and sofa and the sergeant dashed through the door with his kilt apron alight at the rear. They set light to each of four houses; fell foul of a German patrol, and surprised them by fighting with their fists, which seemed so to alarm them that they broke and fled.

The diary of David Thomson Ferguson, Machine Gun Corps, gives a vivid account of the last days of the third Ypres offensive, or the Battle of Passchendaele as it became popularly known:

Thursday 8 November 1917
Arrived Irish Farm situated left suburbs of Ypres. This place is a death trap being constantly shelled and bombed. In fact next day a German squadron came over and dropped bombs all over. I ran for a trench and slipped but soon got up when a piece of bomb struck the ground about a yard in front. Two of our chaps were killed not to mention the wounded.

Friday 9 November 4 p.m.
After being fully loaded up like pack mules we started for the line. All went well altho heavy shelling was going on. We got onto a duckboard track and wended our way slowly in the dark knowing only that it was not a picnic we were on. The first 1? hours went along with nothing starting but everyone was silent. There were 4 teams of 7 men each [machine gun teams] and each team was about or should have been about 20 yards behind the other but we usually got crowded. Things were getting very angry like and each one and all expected death every minute but we had just to plod along. Just then I can remember hearing a terrible swishing noise and then screams and I with others were knocked head over heels. We lost a sergeant killed and one man killed and 6 men slightly wounded leaving only 3 teams now. We left our wounded and dead where they were as our orders were to go forward but we reported at the next dressing station up the line and they went down and attended to whoever survived. We got a rest at this dressing station as we were all very badly shaken and fed up but knew there was worse to come. The next lap to the front line, at least what is called the front line, a few shell holes with two or three men in them maybe up to the waist in water.

We started on the last lap about 10-30 p.m. dark and raining and a miserable night. We could see we were now on the worst part as the track was getting broken and spasmodic with men in Argylls lying dead on each side. I may mention the enemy had hundreds of guns trained on this track as he knew all our men used this one and only way and every half hour or so he would shell constantly for about 20 minutes and if you were caught in a shell it was death of the worst kind. If you got wounded you just had to lie and get another as there was no one to think about you.

However everything was quiet so far and we progressed rapidly. All of a sudden he started shelling and we have to thank our stars the shells he sent at that time were 'duds' i.e. failed to explode. We all scurried and fell tripping over dead anywhere where we could find shelter. I got to a brick wall and was to get into a cellar when I realised it was packed full of dead and water. Evidently a party had been in a same flight as ourselves and ran to the cellar but a shell had landed into it and killed them all. Everything got quiet again and we got together again with no more casualties. We wanted to get on where we were supposed to be going and get finished one way or the other. At last we got to our order quarter. This was a nice strong dug out place where Coy officers etc lived in all safety and sent men out with orders to the front line. It was a gruesome place as it was constantly shelled. In fact at the door mouth a young officer lay on a stretcher. He had been brought in wounded but while going there another shell had come and finished him and there he lay, but at the time happy cause he was wounded and getting away from it all but his luck was out. We lay in this hole for about an hour all of us dead beat and shaken up. It started to rain now as also things began to get a bit livelier. Our lance corporal had our team[']s rum and this was the first time I tasted the spirit and my taste was nothing to shout about. It had the effect of warming me but I was not tempted any further. I may add that before we reached this place we passed a miserable object belonging to a Welsh regiment standing up stuck in a shell hole, dead drunk with rum. A mate was trying to get him out but it was hopeless. I question if they ever got out alive.

About 2 a.m. in pitch darkness and heavy rain we got guides to take us to our kicking off point for morning. At this time we had 3 guns and gun teams but very little ammunition as most of it was dumped. We had to cross a strip of ground just a mass of water and mud and I shall never forget that journey. The first two or three in front soon left the remainder of us to struggle in utter blindness. Men stepped into shell holes and were drowned not under water but with mud. I became stuck in this mud and altho only up to the knees I could not free myself altho I used my rifle to such an extent that I had to leave it where it was. It was no use asking anybody for help as no one had any attention to you, being to busy getting along themselves. However one chap did give me a little help and my knowing my fate gave me increased energy and I managed to get a better footing and keep moving. I jogged along just follow shouting and screaming until I met one of our chaps up to the thighs. He implored me to help him but I must admit I did not want to and he could die for as much as I cared but still I'm glad now to write I did on second thought manage to pull him out altho I had to use the sand bag of rations to do it with. The bag gave me a healthy footing but nevertheless I was nearly stuck again myself. By this time I was carrying only my equipment having had to discard rifle, rations, etc. We or rather I got to some place and I crawled in for shelter and fell sprawling over some more chaps, some wounded and some not. About a dozen of us were huddled up in this place pretty confident we were in a de[s]cent shell splinter safe place. Everyone was very down in the mouth and when nearing six a.m. (time to go over) most of us were physical wrecks.

Saturday 10 November
At a certain time, say quarter to six a.m. every British manned weapon down to machine guns commenced a hideous din. Shells of every calibre whistled and yelled in thousands. Of course this was the prelude to our advance which was to follow in about half an hour. I may say it was simply pouring with rain and altho it was just dawn it was darker with the black clouds hovering above. It was at this time I could discern where I was. We were lying behind a German pill-box (a concrete square house) and our only protection over-head were some stretchers. However the row had now

increased as the enemy was now shelling our lines as heavy as he possibly could. Our officer found us out, there were hardly ? a dozen of us in the place, all the rest were scattered somewhere. He asked to get our guns and go up over. I replied that we had only one gun and one box of ammunition left and that our men were nowhere to be seen. He saw things were hopeless, we were absolutely useless now as a unit so we just lay there under the terrific bombardment. Shells were coming very close and he was continually dropping them about 5 yards away. Of course this pill-box was his objective and in fact he put one clean thro the door at the other side and killed two or three Munster chaps with concussion. We sat all bunched up in this place all day where we could see wounded and prisoners being blown sky high as they came down the line. The enemy was shelling the duck board tracks without mercy for prisoners or wounded. About 5 o'clock there were only 7 of us here now as most of the Welsh regiment chaps had taken the chance when it was quiet for a few minutes to get away. I started to make a drop of tea (we had nothing to eat since Friday afternoon at 3 o'clock) and whether he spotted the light of the Tommy Cooker I don't know but he commenced a terrible bombardment on our place. One shell hit the corner and the chap next to me got a nasty piece of concrete on his head but his steel hat saved him injury. We got this tea warmed and drank it thus when a chap comes flying in all excited with the news that Jerry was counter-attacking and that all the Munsters were killed or prisoners thro having gone too far leaving just a few men to clean their rifles while they chased the enemy with bayonets etc. (rifles were useless in this mud) The result was our whole attack was a failure and anybody who was in front of us had run away. So a sergeant major, (goodness knows where he had been hiding) orders us out to shell holes to man the line. There would be about a dozen of us all told. I with others got our bombs ready. I tried a rifle but it was useless, heavy clogged up with mud. Our officer mounted our only gun and ammo but did not fire as we would need our fire when they got closer. Just out in front a form lay with neither head or arms and just a pair of trousers on. I think he must have been buried and then raked up with shell fire as he was quite clean and not unsightly to look at. The rain had washed the flesh clean and it was coloured blue. The shell fire was not worse and they were dropping all around in front. Jerry was firing so quick and feverishly that nearly all his light shells (the ones that came nearer to us than anything else) were duds. A drunken Welsh regiment soldier was speaking to our corporal just behind me when I heard a terrific swish and saw him (the corporal) turned round sharply and fall dead at my feet, on his back. He had got a direct hit with a shell which passed over my head and went through his left side. This shell was a dud or I aught not to be able to write so. This gave me an awful fright as it did the others and we got the order to go back for shelter behind the pill-box again. The drunken soldier took our corporals paybook etc, altho we expected him to be blown to bits any minute. He then said he was going for stretcher bearers and that was the last we saw of him. A pathetic thing about him was he left two pigeons in a basket sitting on the ground where a shell would likely blow them to atoms. (headquarters used pigeons for taking messages back to the lines).

About half past six when things were a wee bit quietened our officer sent a chap down to a place called Crown Prince Farm (a dressing station) to find out what we were to do. We followed him running down until he went out of sight and we now waited impatiently for his return. It was getting dark and we wanted to get down or moving while it was light. It was time now for this chaps return but he did not appear so our officer sent another chap down. He was away for some time when we were happy to see him return. He came with good news that we had to go down to C.P. Farm. We called our chaps together and made our way down and what a mess on this duck board track. Chaps were lying dead in all positions, some recognisable others blown to pieces. Stretcher bearers with wounded men blown to bits leaving just bundles of blood-soaked rags of blood.

We arrived at this dressing station where all sorts of chaps from different regiments. Wounded prisoners lay everywhere as our own chaps were served first. This place was crowded with chaps moaning and yelling. We stayed there about an hour and then we were led down a track, it was pitch dark now, to another pill-box called Albatross farm. This was somebody's headquarters and on the road down to it we passed the spot where one of our gun teams got blown up while we were wending our way up the line. On the other side of this track were masses of what was once men but now just bits of dirty flesh and rags here and there. A part of this track was under water and we had to wade through up to our middles. If he had started shelling now we would have got it in the neck. We got this place presently, we were to stay here until next morning as we were not yet billed to go out. We had to stay 48 hours in this place so our relief wasn't due till Sunday night. We just crowded round this place sitting down anywhere when our major came up and gave our officer instructions to send 3 men up to Crown Prince Farm for rations. I unfortunately clicked for one and we with our major leading (he was a gentleman in the line) made for up that perilous duck board again. Altho they were quiet the walking was dreadful and by the time we reached the washed away part the water had risen like a high tide. We had to make a chain and clasp one another's hands and went right through this small river. We managed it however and reached this place without much happening. We waited in this place where a crowd were gathered, wounded, ration parties, wire parties, etc. He now started to shell the approaching tracks and we were astonished to see a party coming down and seemingly walking into death. It was very dark but you could see the outline of them. They just were about 30 yards when down came a shell and than screaming and a rush. It was pitiful to hear the cries of the wounded. Those who could help were scampering for safety themselves but our CO managed to get two or three and went out and brought what he could in. I found out the unfortunate party was no other than our No 3 section. They lost their officer and one sergeant killed and two or three men wounded. All this took place within five minutes. About half past eleven a carrying party with rations approached and I was detailed off to lead three of them with their rations to the remnant of our section. I was a bit wind up over this as I was not at all sure of the way, however I led on. We got along out so bad of course everyone was as usual cursing at everything in general. I myself was to busy getting down. The track was simply strewn with dead. In fact I took my guidance from a party of three men (two stretcher bearers and a case) who were lying dead by the side of the track. They had evidently been coming down when a shell had caught them and blown them to bits.

I trudged along but alas I came to a point where the duckboard track ended and a good flowing fast stream stared me in the face. I was lost I knew and unluckily my party guessed so I came in for abuse too bad to record. Of course I knew the stream as I crossed it coming up bit it was at a different point. I told the party to stand easy and told them not to get the wind up. (I was more wind up myself but didn't show it) I ran here and there looking for a likely place to cross and to make matters worse Jerry began to shell and we were standing in the open with no cover of any kind so I called that I had found the place but I was just determined to get across somehow. So we took hands and started the crossing. I soon knew I was off the track as we sank up to the armpits whereas before it just came to our middles. However we got across and I had no difficulty in gaining the commencement of the duck-boards again. I got down to our chaps at last and after the three ration carriers dumped their rations they were off down the line by a different and longer route. I hope they got down alright. We just left the rations as they were as most of the chaps were trying to get a sleep. I tried to get a sleep myself but I was so cramped up in the only dry place I could find that I fo[u]nd it impossible.

Sunday 11 November, dawn.
We got together for moving up to a place called Insh Houses but we started to have something to eat. We had bread and cheese and

bully. I scouted about for a drink of water and made my way to a lot of floating petrol tins. The first one was full of soup but the other was actually brimful of rum. I half filled two water bottles with rum and made up the rest with water. Then I took it to the boys who made a rush and filled up all possible bottles. Of course we first had a swig as we were wet and very miserable.

Soon we made for our position from where we were to be relieved the same evening. (Sunday) We made good progress as we could see our way a little. We found the gun we had lost when coming upon Friday as well as the grave of our sergeant. Somebody had buried him. We took the gun which increased our total to 2 guns (one was punctured with shrapnel and useless) and about 12–14 men. We had lost or were missing about half our section. We soon saw Crown Prince Farm and we went up at this time. We saw our position. There was not a house nor even a ruin of one so goodness knows why they called it Inch Houses. We ran across the open as fast as we could and took up different positions in shell holes. This place was simply covered with dead. They appeared to me to have been mown down as they were advancing in line. I was in a hole along with my officer and three others the rest were scattered about. We tried to dig deeper but we came across more dead and gave up. Fortunately they did not smell which was a blessing we sat there and tried to make something to eat but were in a very dangerous place. There was no shelling simply because the enemy knew no one would dare to take up position there so our safety lay in our not giving our presence away. We found the rations we received were for the 216th Coy an extra company of our division and we got good eating from the parcels that were in their mail. Everything was quiet and we just lay and watched the aircraft fighting and manoeuvring overhead. The rum I had found soon told its tale and most of the chaps had fallen asleep drunk and otherwise. My own made a good drink; it took the bad taste from the water. My officer was very grateful for a drink as he had refused the other chaps raw spirit. During the afternoon the officer (Lieutenant Barker) showed me how he could enfilade the enemy from this place (we were 400 yards from him) but as the section were absolutely useless I told him the gun was out of action which was true. I may add that if he had got his wish it would have given our position away the result can be guessed. The day wore on and two runners from HQ brought us some biscuits and chocolate. Our officer later sent a man (Jones) down to Crown Prince Farm to guide the relief up. Night was soon upon us and no news had come from our man re-relief. We had a fairly quiet night and when morning appeared our officer sent another men (Smith) down and he soon came back with Jones and stated no relief had come at least neither had seen any. Our officer then took the only course open to him and that was to go out. We packed up eagerly and made our way down. A pitiful handful we were too. Up to the ears in mud, most of us without rifles (I should say we were about 14 strong) in fact we were a wash out. We passed a first aid post well down and the sight of a mess tin of hot tea nearly sent me crazy, however I was lucky and got a mouthful. I suppose these RAMC chaps did pity us. We soon got on the road after leaving these death trap duckboards and straggled our way in twos and threes to find our coy. We got back to Irish Farm and were welcomed heartily as we had been given up as lost. After a stiff tot of rum and our back mail given to us we felt a lot better.

As the war progressed, greater planning and preparation was devoted to offensives. Private William Cameron, 7th Battalion Black Watch, spent a week practising for the Battle of Cambrai:

We were away from morning till late at night at the village of _______ near DUISSANS, and here we practi[s]ed the attack two or three days in succession with real 'live' tanks.

After training for the coming offensive the battalion was sent to the line at Haverincourt Wood with the orders:

That no kilties had to be seen, in the district in case of it getting to the enemies ears. For two or three nights prior to the battle we couldn't get sleeping for the terrible noise of heavy transport, and on going outside one night the roads were thick with hundreds of 'Tanks' and Heavy Guns etc. etc. going up to take their various positions for the Day of Battle.

Of the battle itself he records that:

It was a fine sight to see the tanks oblivious to danger, ambling along in front of us and attacking anything from a pillbox to a heavy howitzer gun pit.

Albert Hay, 1st Battalion Black Watch, took part in the fighting on the St Quentin–Cambrai road and witnessed at first hand the duplicity of the enemy:

At eleven o' clock exactly the whistles blew, just like the start of a football match, and we walked forward to be immediately met by machine-gun bullets.

We saw a newspaper held up on a bayonet, and this appeared to be a signal of surrender so our officer ordered me to fire if there was any sign of treachery while he and the sergeant went to meet the Germans. About thirty of the enemy appeared and came towards us but our officer and sergeant had gone only a short way when a splatter of machine-gun bullets just missed them, and I immediately pressed the trigger of my gun firing just over the heads of the Germans. Everyone flopped down on the ground but the German machine-gun did not speak again, and it was only a matter of a minute or two before the group of Germans were in our trench.

During close fighting Lieutenant Baxter captured a trench filled with Germans, everyone of whom wore the Red Cross badge. These men had been firing until the moment their trench was captured, when one of them threw something into a dugout.

It proved to be a machine-gun which was still hot when found. Such incidents were, I believe, happily rare, but even so they inevitably added to the mistrust with which our troops viewed the German idea of what is honourable in war.

William L. Duncan from Aberdeen was with the Scottish Horse in 1918 at the capture of Le Cateau:

The first real test for the Scottish Horse in France was our task to capture Le Cateau. This town changed hands several times at the beginning of the war in 1914 in the retreat from Mons. We were living in huts and trenches near Hurlo. The attack commenced on October the first, my birthday and I wandered. When the boys went over the top I had to dispense the rum ration. As the trench was full I had to creep along under cover of the parapet with the rum jar under my arm. Of[f] they went on the first phase of the attack. When darkness fell the whole regiment advanced. This vast area had been flooded by blocking the canals. Coming near a village we saw a large crucifix. The shaft had been broken by shell-fire. The figure had been set up with the arms outstretched as if appealing to stop. This made one think it might be the last thing of this kind that many of the lads were to see. Owing to the flooding the high areas were very evident and made an easy target for artillery range to repel a night attack. We came through a very heavy and concentrated artillery barrage. We advanced from shell hole to shell hole. The headquarters company here suffered the most disastrous losses of the war. Two shells exploded in our midst, killing all the officers with one exception. Many of the other ranks suffered. For a time there was confusion as those who had the exact knowledge of our position and ultimate aim were simply not there. Finally we heard the sound of a hunting horn. This was being blown by an officer of an English regiment as a means of collecting his men. From there the Scottish Horse got their position, advanced and achieved their objective in capturing Le Cateau. But at a big cost. The highest number killed and wounded in one battle. Many of the chaps had been with us the whole time. Some had come from distant lands with the high endeavour of fighting for the right. Next morning the fallen were collected and buried together in one long grave. I got a big beam from the house, had a cross made and erected with all their names, the writing was done by a monumental mason from Aberdeen.

As the German forces fell back in late 1918 the Kaiser's soldiers were short of supplies and were faced with the necessity of finding material where they could. During the German retreat in late 1918 Private Alexander Paterson, Highland Light Infantry, came across the bodies of his dead comrades:

Just in front lay a Highlander with face upturned, red bubbles at mouth and nostrils. Further on a young subaltern, a few weeks from home, had fallen, striking an attitude with walking stick outstretched. Their faces were still quite recognizable, the weather being cool. A couple of hundred yards from our starting-point lay the main body of our comrades who had fallen the previous day. Their bodies were strewn in every direction. Dozens were heaped around a pitiful little 2-foot trench which they had dug. Many of them were without boots, for the Germans in retiring had taken sufficient time to satisfy their crying need for good footwear.

9

Conditions

> One doesn't need to be a socialist to be quick in recognizing the extraordinary freemasonry of property that the troops so readily acquire out here. (Lieutenant Dane, 4th Battalion Seaforth Highlanders)

Lieutenant Dane was not the only one to fall foul of this. After relieving another machine-gun team in the line, James Campbell discovered his pack was missing:

> The gun team we relieve filed out and one of them went of[f] with my pack. It contained a fine lot of kit and I hope the present owner is not a rogue as well as a fool I am hoping to get it when we get out again. The pack he left behind is just a collection of rubbish. And to crown it all he was wearing his overcoat and mine was in my pack. But I bagged the coat of a poor lad whose troubles are over so I'm not so bad. It will match my cap which I got in the big fight of[f] another poor chap.

Campbell was indeed reunited with his pack and possessions: 'I got my pack returned tonight. The only thing I lost was a home made sleeping bag. The fool filled it with chalk and built it into the parapet.' For many, alcohol played an important part in coping with life in the front line. The men were entitled to a daily rum issue, even and especially when in the line, and looked forward to hearing the cry 'Up Spirits'.

> We had a week in the line during which the shelling eased off and the principle sport was trying to avoid being sniped when visiting the outposts between the lines with a sergeant carrying the jar containing the rum ration. It was normally in the dark, and the old army trick was to have a tin mug stained brown for two inches at the foot, so the unsuspecting lads thought they were getting a better ration than was the case. (Second Lieutenant Crerar, 2nd Battalion Royal Scots Fusiliers)

While it was frowned upon to steal the spirit ration of someone in the same unit, the rum ration of other companies was considered to be fair game. The troops kept faithful to the old adage – not in your own nest. In some instances the desire for alcohol had a funnier side:

> One memory is of breakfast in a reserve trench, cooking bacon, when Black Jock MacMillan, our company runner, who was cooking for us, fell senseless over the fire. He had done fine work all through the battle. There were cries from us of 'poor old Black Jock', whom we felt must have got a stray bullet through the head – only to get a strong whiff of rum. He had apparently got hold of the whole rum ration of a company of a battalion new to the trenches. (Lieutenant C.B. Robertson, 1st Battalion Argyll & Sutherland Highlanders)

At times, the rum ration was clearly more trouble than it was worth, although for many a soldier this was the highlight of the day. Hakewell-Smith experienced another aspect of the rum ration:

> There was a group of 6 men who had a jar of rum and between them they polished off their jar of rum and 4 Jocks never got to the frontline. They were under arrest. Summary of evidence and all that and sentenced to be tried by court martial. They weren't in my company and I was detailed to defend them. One of them was a

barrack room lawyer and he and the others following him insisted on pleading guilty and the president of the court martial explained that this was equivalent to desertion and the only sentence that the court could award was shooting and I was to take them out and talk to them and I took them out and talked to them and so on and they came back absolutely adamant they were going to plead guilty. I couldn't persuade them. The president couldn't persuade them and he had no alternative. They had to plead guilty and the president of the court martial had no alternative but to sentence them to be shot. They were good chaps and the Commanding Officer and the Company Commander each got a confidential letter addressed personally asking the opinion of the Commanding Officer and the Company Commander whether the sentence should be carried out. They both replied that in their opinion the sentence should not be carried out. To our horror the sentence was confirmed and was to be carried out at Ploegsteert church on the morning of whatever it was, April 9 at 7 p.m [*sic*]. There were to be 59 men from every unit in the Division present. To be carried out by the military police. I am not sure but I think Winston went off to see the Divisional Commander and try to get this thing altered and the Divisional Commandeer didn't like it either. So, no the sentence was to be carried out and we all formed up at Ploegsteert church in a hollow square with these chaps against the wall... At that moment round the corner of the church came a motorcyclist holding up a white paper. Stop, stop, stop. I think the Provost Marshal had been warned that this was going to happen. That is my guess anyway and he ordered arms and the chap came forward and handed him a piece of paper saying that their sentence had been commuted to prison or something or other but it had the most marvellous effect.

William Duncan, Scottish Horse, was detailed for guard duty at a railway station but when the cellar was found to contain a large store of wine the Scottish troops were removed and replaced with Irish sentries:

We were looking for a place for a safe and quiet sleep, we thought the vault was just the place. It had been reported at divisional headquarters the position of the wine cellars. The DHQ thinking perhaps that the Scottish Horse were not the lads for the job sent up a unit from an Irish regiment to take over guard duty. After we had collected some straw we crawled into the cellar to settle down to a sleep of bliss. Through the night we heard the sound of popping. We found that the guard were shooting through the barrels thus making an air vent and a bung with the result that the wine came pouring out to find that our straw bed was soaking with wine, also our clothes. Thus ended our blissful sleep. Wine may be all right as a sedative but not to be bathed in. Needless to say, the Irish guard was relieved from this duty.

This was not Duncan's only brush with the excesses of alcohol:

The troops in the front positions had been unable to get rations until darkness. They sent in squads to collect. Some of these groups did not return with the rations. Enquires were made in case they had been wounded. I explored around to see if I could find any of the missing. Passing a ruined house I heard a muffled sound and on enquiry found some of the men stretched out on the floor. I thought they had been hit but much better than that they were gloriously drunk. After being for quite a spell without food this was easily caused. Somehow, this was found out at Scottish Horse HQ. I was instructed to find out the cause and source of this and to place in custody anyone the worse for drink. The cause was a very potent case of red wine. A Military Policeman was put on guard with definite instructions. Sometime later I called round and the sight I saw was laughable. Here was Bill the policeman handing out the wine in Dixie tins. I had a hell of a time hiding the boys who had come under the influence. There was enough trouble round here without adding to it.

As well as overseeing the issue of the rum ration, Lieutenant Crerar discovered that the duties of a junior officer were wide and varied:

> One of our duties which I haven't mentioned was the censoring of the men's letters home, a task we didn't like, but you had to delete any reference to locality, units, or anything that might be useful to the Huns, if a letter fell into their hands. Sometimes a chap would write something about what a terrible danger he was in, which wasn't going to re-assure his wife or mother, and we would tactfully suggest that he change it. My prize memory was a quite affectionate letter from a tough old Regular soldier which finished up with 'Your loving husband Joe. P.S. I wunner who yer sleeping with to-night ye auld bitch.'

Captain Patrick Duncan, 4th Battalion Black Watch, found this to be a pleasant diversion:

> It is quite pleasant to censor the men's letters, as you find they are usually letters written home asking how their people have enjoyed the holiday week and pointing out that they are quite well; I have only had to delete a portion of one letter yet. The Roman Catholics seem to be favourably impressed with the churches here – judging from what they write home.

After evacuation from Gallipoli, Corporal A. Alexander was sent to Egypt:

> I have now shifted another 9 miles further into the desert and instead of writing 'somewhere' I use Nowhere for this is NO MAN'S LAND right enough. My company is doing very important Outpost duties. Nothing but the desert sands for company except for the daily visit by the camels with our water and rations but through it all I keep smiling. It will come to an end sometime.

Reading material was in short supply in the trenches. Corporal Ian Maclaren, 6th Battalion Black Watch, corresponded regularly with his mother, keeping her informed about his life in the army:

> Picked up a Blackwoods magazine in these trenches, very interesting too – Ian Hay and other fine chaps. Just at present have heaps of good stuff to read and don't seem to feel like it when I do have the time. Strange life this.

On 11 August 1916 he wrote:

> Feeling fit as a ferret Mother and no need to worry. We expect to be relieved anytime now but everything uncertain here but certainly will be out by Saturday in fact almost certain now. Mol will be alright on Brigade or Headquarters staff and probably will see very little of trenches for a while. Some of Kitchener's army are about here but not going into trenches yet... Mol will be alright once he gets settled down out here. The worst things out here are lack of sleep and feeling very drowsy, but after one nights good sleep and a wash feel just as well again.

This was followed on 12 August by a request:

> Could you get a pair of shorts made for me, not for going under the kilt but for wearing in the trenches instead of a kilt. Khaki colour would do with pockets as usual, just a pair of shorts like a boys but for my size.

Corporal Maclaren was killed the following day and both his Platoon Commander and his Battalion Commander wrote to his mother offering their condolences:

BEF 16/11/16

Dear Mrs Maclaren,

It is with sincere sympathy that I write to tell you that your son Ian was killed when our battalion attacked on the morning of the 13th. A letter from me may break the terrible news a little easier than the bald War Office telegram.

Ian was killed by Machine Gun fire between the German first and second lines. He died a soldiers death at the head of his platoon.

His body will now have been recovered and will be buried behind the lines.

The battalion was completely successful and it may be some slight consolation to know that he died in so glorious an engagement.

His kit has been dispatched home through the usual channels and I shall send you direct and personal belongings which I can recover.

With deepest sympathy for Mr MacLaren and yourself.

Yours sincerely
J.R. Leslie
2 Lieut.
Lewis Gun Officer.

Private 1/6 Black Watch

17 Novr. 1916

Dear Mrs Maclaren, I am extremely sorry to have to send you bad news of your son Ian, who I regret to say was killed in the big advance on Monday of this week.

Our Battalion was the first to advance in the thick mist and half light of the early morning and when all the officers of the company except one had been killed or wounded, Ian was leading the men of his platoon with the utmost gallantry, and by his example gave them such a fine lead that they finally took the whole of their objective, four German lines, and many prisioners. I could scarcely tell you how vexed I am that he has made the supreme sacrifice in doing his duty nobly. He was a most excellent NCO well spoken of both by the Commanding Officer and our Brigadier, who had hopes of his getting his commission.

Assuring you of my deepest personal sympathy with your great loss.

I remain
Yours very sincerely
J. Wylie
Lt. Col.
6th Black Watch

It was not only Corporal Maclaren who was interested in reading material. Lieutenant J.B. Maclean, 7th Battalion Cameronians, wrote to his brother Alex:

I was glad to receive a letter from you and to see that all goes well. I also got a copy of 'Puck'. If you could send some other (better) paper occasionally it would be appreciated as we are very short of reading matter here.

Even in such desperate times he was selective in his choice of newspaper. At other times his correspondence with his brother held a more sombre note:

On the way up that morning two dead soldiers were carried past us; one of them had died en route and was lying on his face on the stretcher in a pool of blood with his back bare and a big wound in his back half filled by the field dressing. It was a horrible sight, and I wish the people responsible for the war could see a few things like that. Another rotten thing up there is the little cemeteries which are still in the shelled area. It is quite a common thing to see such places where a shell has landed right in among a lot of graves and blown the crosses all over the place.

Captain Patrick Duncan, 4th Battalion Black Watch, also showed an interest in reading material. 'My letters from Scotland are taking a week to reach me, although the "Morning Post" arrives at the Mess the day after it is published.'

Arguably the main problem facing the average soldier in the trenches was hygiene:

> We had a great bath today. The pond was a large steam condenser at a pit near by and naturally the water was warm. It was about 20 yards by 10 yards and was pretty deep. In fact it would have made an ideal swimming pond had it not been for the supporting beams which divided it into small 2 yard sections. But we absolutely steeped in it for three quarters of an hour and enjoyed the bath immensely. (James Campbell, Machine Gun Section, 6th Battalion Cameron Highlanders)

Some officers went to great lengths to bathe while at the same time placing the extra burden of duties on their men. Lieutenant G.J. Brown, 1/4th Battalion King's Own Scottish Borderers, appeared to show little regard for his men while serving at Gallipoli. He landed at Cape Helles on 23 October and on 29 October wrote to his mother:

> It was very warm, so we took the chance to get the nearest thing to a bath. The performance being rather a novel one, I shall describe it in detail. The bathroom consisted of a disused dug-out, about 6ft

> square and 6 deep, and screened from the front. We dug a hole about 30 ins square and 9ins deep, and lined it with a waterproof. Our servants brought buckets of water from the nullah or stream, about a quarter of a mile away. The water is rather brackish, but when the insects and weeds are strained out, it is quite passable.

James Campbell, 6th Battalion Cameron Highlanders, was firmly of the opinion that any bath was better than none at all:

> We got a billet in the old village which we were in before. The first move on arrival was a dip in the mill dam, where the water, though far from clean, was cleaner than we were and had the advantage of being deep.

In the Givenchy sector coffins were used as bathtubs after the seams had been caulked to prevent leakage. In the desert, where water was scarce, J. Wallace, 5th Battalion King's Own Scottish Borderers, was also concerned with cleanliness:

> I did some washing. This is done by digging a hole in the sand and lining it with a waterproof sheet. Getting water is the greatest difficulty, but we try to keep ourselves clean with the small issue we get. The water is transported by means of large, flat zinc containers called Fantasies, two of these are carried on a camel. The water here is brackish and is usually treated with chloride. A few weeks in the desert and one appreciates the value of water.

For Private Begbie, serving at Gallipoli with the 7th Battalion Royal Scots, the Mediterranean presented the opportunity to bathe:

> Our only luxury was to have a swim in the sea and sunbathe on the beaches while the weather was warm. All drinking water had to come by boats. We never did have enough to drink and our

> only wash was in the sea. We had to put our clothes back on although they were full of lice.
>
> My ablutions are performed in a canvas bucket with cold water. I haven't had a bath for nearly three weeks now but there is nothing abnormal in that as things go here and I may manage one soon. The men get a bath and change every time they come out of the line and they don't half need it, although in this weather animal life is much less active than usual. (Lieutenant J.B. Maclean, 1st Battalion Cameronians)

This reference to animal life was clearly aimed at the scourge of all troops: lice. The creature was no respecter of rank and was rife throughout the war. In Scottish regiments lice were known as Scots Greys. Lice were a particular problem in the trenches and, to a lesser degree, in the rear area. No one could escape from the horrors of body lice, which bred and lay their eggs in the seams of the soldiers' uniform. Soldiers would hunt for them by running a lighted candle down the seams, causing the lice to explode from the heat, while in the rear rest areas a hot iron was used in a similar fashion. Delousing, by necessity, became the most frequent pastime. Even when clothes were laundered it often failed to kill off the eggs and the soldier would put on his freshly laundered clothes only to find himself lousy within a matter of hours as eggs hatched. James Campbell recalls:

> There was a church parade in the forenoon but I didn't go. Instead I spent the time rubbing the seams of my kilt with creosol to kill any lice that may come about. It is great stuff, but it can't be used next to the skin or it blisters it badly. So we have to use Harrisons' Pomade on our shirts. It's a great life.

It was impossible to escape the attention of vermin. Thomas Williamson fell foul of this scourge on only his first day in the trenches:

> As the day advanced I began to feel horribly itchy. I was scratching myself in an abominable fashion, until exasperated beyond endurance by this fearful itching, I pulled of my shirt. I was horrified to discover I was absolutely verminous and the lice were walking in droves on my shirt. I immediately began a killing parade and when I finished my nails were thick with the blood of my victims. It was a momentary relief, however. I was to discover later how utterly impossible it was to avoid this plague when one was living underground, lying about anywhere and everyone. I thought it would be a relief when winter came because the heat made the vermin exceptionally lively. Sometimes I felt I would go mad and though that if only the winter was here I would get some peace to live.

Lieutenant Dane recalled: 'Last night I indulged in the luxury of a scratch. This morning I had an exciting bug hunt – total bag, nil. The elusive little devils!' He had no greater success the following night:

> Had a veneer of sleep last night – was tortured by invisible insects with innumerable mouths. This morning I am covered with pink spots like a muslin blouse – and as if my troubles hadn't reached a climax already, I hear we go into the trenches to-night.

When in the trenches little could be done – clothes could be checked for lice but there were no facilities for fumigation or chemical baths. Men became lousy again almost as soon as they dressed. They had to wait for a rest period when they could bathe and put their clothes through one of the many fumigation processes. However, as the unfortunate men soon found out, these only killed the lice; the eggs would hatch out again after a few hours. Still, for the men any short respite was welcome. Cumming Morgan, 9th Battalion Cameron Highlanders, was working as assistant to the Company Quartermaster Sergeant when a platoon officer suggested: 'You might give this man a new shirt, Morgan. The one he had has just walked across to the incinerator.' Lieutenant Sotheby was horrified at what he found when he eventually managed to remove his kilt after coming out of the line after an extended period of front-line service:

> I got my kilt off for the first time in 29 days, last night. The result was awful. I had had much itching, but never thought of lice. To my horror, I found parts of the kilt one mass of eggs and large ones too. Here and there were animals as large as a small winged ant. I turned quite cold at seeing all my defences thus broken down. I tell you my kilt was off miles away from me in less than a second, and I bawled for my servant. Luckily he managed to find an iron and got a fire going. We ironed the kilt for two hours. One heard the eggs crack as the iron went over them. Then your powder was put on, but despite all this, I feel the brutes walking about today. You see it is very hard to get into the pleats of a kilt, and indeed some people here say it's hopeless to try and kill them, but we are having a good try... I believe sitting in front of a fire yesterday hatched some out prematurely.

The army devised a whole range of equipment to fumigate clothes and most of it relied on steam. William L. Duncan, Scottish Horse, described how his company was marched down to Kantara station, on the Suez Canal, to be put through the mobile fumigating station:

> This is done in a train equipped for the job, and it moves to the various camps. The procedure is – the company collects at the rail side, take off all their clothes which are put into a steel case. Steam is connected from the engine and the clothes are cooked for a time. The process isn't satisfactory as you were very lucky if you were able to get back your own clothes in the ensuing struggle for possession when the clothes are thrown out. When the clothes are being cooked a wash down has to be taken with a disinfectant fluid and you're left with nothing but your helmet for cover.

While standing thus adorned we heard the whistle of a train, along came a passenger train, it pulled up just where we were. You can imagine our feelings when we observed a number of ladies in the carriages seated at the window seeing the sights of Egypt. It was rather difficult knowing what to do, raise your hat or turn your back on the ladies. I chose the latter course but was my face red – I think the ladies would be the best authority on the matter.

J. Wallace, serving in Egypt with the 5th Battalion King's Own Scottish Borderers, was subjected to a rather more drastic method designed to rid the body of lice:

Had a dip in a creosote bath then plunged into the sea. Handed in our clothes and blankets for fumigation and were issued with a suit of pyjamas which we wore till next morning.

The cleaned and disinfected clothes were reissued the next morning after rifle inspection – it must have been a sight presenting arms in pyjamas. Lieutenant F.S. Sotheby, 2nd Battalion Argyll & Sutherland Highlanders, wrote:

I am unable to use the lice killer in the trenches as our equipment is not allowed to come off. However it is impossible to keep the lice down, as the eggs get everywhere, and new armies constantly step in.

I am afraid there will be a bad disease soon, the men have taken to drinking water from the ditches... this they boil, but it is condemned and we have great trouble in stopping them.

Thomas Williamson discovered that lice were not the only pests in the trenches:

I went to sleep, to be awakened at times by rats running over me. I struck a match but saw nothing; they had scurried off to their

> quarters. I was to learn afterwards they were pests who ate your food, and fed on the dead in no-man's land.

Sergeant S. Saunders detailed a similar experience with rats foraging for food:

> Had a rotten night last night. Like a fool left a box with some biscuits in it within a foot of my head and was wakened by rats moving the biscuits about. I kept knocking the box with my fist but they would not go out – kept quiet for a few seconds but were soon at it again. Must say I do rather object to having rats running about me.

> Curious how we harden. Have now been about seven days without taking boots of[f] for any length of time, and feet not dry for nine days, yet no ill effects, bar slight soreness, and cold discomfort. (Captain R.H.W. Rose, 1st Battalion Cameronians)

When curiosity compelled him to visit a nearby war cemetery, James Campbell was moved to reflect on war:

> There is a soldiers cemetery next to us and after a look round you get an idea of what war really means. And yet we are all quite callous and scarcely even think of these things. Some of the graves are done up very nicely with lead work and amateur sculptures have done their bit in chalk too. [He is referring here to ornamentation with regimental badges]

When detailed to spend a spell as orderly and cook, Campbell reflected: 'It is strange how we get accustomed to do these things which we always at home relied on mothers and sisters to perform.' Hay-Young, 1st Battalion Argyll & Sutherland Highlanders, could never get used to the squalor in the trenches:

The filth and unsanitary conditions prevailing everywhere make one sick. The suffering of all ranks is considerable. A regiment crawling back at night from the trenches is a pitiable sight: there is no order; the men are straggling about; some can scarcely crawl, and all cry for water: it is very scarce all over the country for drinking.

I am wondering what is to happen here when it gets warmer. I am sure cholera or plague will break out. Everything stinks.

Latrines were constructed at intervals and were usually small saps cut in the back of the trench and moved when the smell became too much or when an enemy sniper found its location due to the number of men using the facilities. In most instances men made use of empty tins and threw them out into no-man's-land, adding to the stench, making it more difficult to move around no-man's-land in the dark and adding to the illness and disease which affected three-and-a-half million British casualties during the war. The French troops used the communication trenches as latrines, to the discomfort of those forced to travel in them:

Sanitary arrangements were negligible. You were too close to the front line to be able safely to leave your dugout in daylight. When 'in extremis' you had to use an empty bully beef tin which was passed by the officer next to the entrance of the dugout who tipped out the contents into the mud outside. I well remember my 18th birthday in these conditions. A more fantastic way of 'waging war' can hardly be imagined. (Lieutenant C.B. Robertson, 1st Battalion Argyll & Sutherland Highlanders)

When Lieutenant C.B. Robertson's battalion moved forward and took over sections of French trench at the Somme in September 1915, he recalled that:

We found the sanitary conditions of the French had been rather strange. For in many places, sticking out of the sides of a communication trench could be seen bits of old dead Frenchman's legs protruding.

Everything has its humorous side, as discovered by Captain D. Dick, 12th Battalion Argyll & Sutherland Highlanders, when he made a startling discovery on one trip to the latrines:

> On our second spell of duty on this sector, we were able to use some old German deep dug outs. They were very comfortable, with bunks and latrines about thirty feet down. The latrines consisted of a wooden spar over which you sat and balanced yourself. I was amazed to see a soldier climbing up from down in the muck. 'Hey what are you doing down there?', I asked. 'I'm getting my tunic that fell in'. 'But you would get another tunic', I said. 'Yes, but my moothie is in the pocket'. Some soldier in the ranks of the HLI our crowd were superior.

Various schemes were established to send 'comforts' to the troops. Parcels would be collected for distribution to local battalions serving abroad. Sergeant S. Saunders recalled: 'Had some cigarettes issued yesterday from 'The Huntley Lassies'. Most had slips inside with messages. Mine had 'cheer up, hope to see you soon' and a name and address. Curiously enough she was an old sweetheart of the Colour Sgt. – the Flaggie as we call him.' However Saunders was not always happy to receive parcels. 'Wish to goodness people would not send things I don't want – they don't seem to realize what it means having to carry all one's stuff on one's back.' Some were better accommodated than others. J. Cumming Morgan, 9th Battalion Cameron Highlanders, recorded in his diary:

> The CQMS and myself built a little hut of corrugated iron with a good sound 3-foot-high parapet all round. Our Quarter-bloke at that time was a big, black-moustached, clear-to-hell-out-of-it sort

of chap, just the very man for a company of 500 skrimshankers like ours. While he was a QMS and I only a lance-jack, in civil life I was a schoolmaster and he a school janitor. However, we worked and lived together in great harmony and friendship for a year. I did the work and he took the responsibility. He was a beadle (church officer) in the Auld Kirk, and a teetotaller. I was a deacon in the Free Kirk, and drank his nightly tot of rum at bedtime as well as my own. Our hut was about 8 feet by 6 feet, and just so high that if the QMS wanted to stretch himself he had either to lie down or go outside. He slept under the duckboard table-shelf-desk on which the rations were kept during the day, and I on a stretcher, with a little 'Queen' stove between us. In the morning at Reveille – perhaps – I rose, lit a fire in the stove, on the top of which I put a petrol tin full of water for shaving and washing purposes. If the chimney smoked, as it usually did, I went outside, mounted the parapet and cleaned it out with drain-rods. Then I drew my breakfast at the cookhouse. When the petrol tin began to steam, the Quarter-bloke rose, shaved and washed, and I, having breakfasted, partly on what I got at the cookhouse, which generally consisted of a square inch of ham fat and a mug of ham tea, but chiefly on bread, butter, cheese, and jam (strawberry) that had never seen the cookhouse, proceeded to do the same, washing contentedly in Sandy's second-hand warm water. He then went for breakfast to the Sergeants' Mess, and I sat down by the stove to rest and smoke. In this job there was not much to be done during the day. Perhaps one went for the rations, or to the AOC dump for clothing or shovels or gum-boots, or to Pop for beer for the canteen, but our busy time was at night when the boys returned to camp. There was clothing of all sorts to be issued, allotments of pay had to be adjusted, remittances to be sent home, and all sorts of correspondence to be conducted between the men and the pay office with regard to their domestic relations. The number and nature of the family secrets I got to know would have made my fortune were I a blackmailer.

Leave, the chance for a visit home, was a precious commodity for the front-line soldier, and brought with it a whole range of emotions:

> My leave is off – I really felt almost like crying like a kid last night when I heard. (Sergeant S. Saunders, 6th Battalion Gordon Highlanders)

While training in Dunfermline with the 10th Battalion Seaforth Highlanders, Private David Ferguson was given a few days' leave:

> Arrived home for six days. No man will ever experience in all his life such a joyful sensation as 'leave'. These six days I spent very happily altho – like one I – knew and was perfectly aware that I wasn't a soldier only trying to be one. Swank does not make a man a soldier.

Ferguson is quick to point out that the joy of having leave was rapidly replaced by the despair of returning to war:

> This day was one of the most miserable days since I was born. What a cloud of depression came down on one. To go back to that horrible life – oh – I found now what duty was. It is more than duty, it is self-sacrifice. Arriving in the old quarters put the tin hat on it so to speak.

Others were quick to exploit men made vulnerable by the thought of leave:

> On April 1st four men from the company were told that they had been granted a furlough and were instructed to proceed to Bethune, a large town some six or seven miles away. Naturally they were overjoyed and set out joyfully, only to discover on reaching the platform and preparing to go into the train, that

> either a mistake had been made or a cruel joke, consequent upon the day of the year, had been perpetrated upon them. (Corporal Alex Thompson, 4th Battalion Black Watch)

Men who were refused leave railed at the unfairness of the system. Lieutenant Thorburn, 2nd Battalion Black Watch, was turned down for leave by Lieutenant-Colonel Wauchope, as he felt one of the officers who had been through the initial attack at Loos should get the leave. Thorburn had been left in the rear in charge of the transport at the time:

> I know I have not suffered the brunt of it all these five months, but five months out here is five months out here!! I didn't think that altho' I had not been all my time in the trenches, those who had would go home twice before I had been at all. However, say naught about it or repeat anywhere 'unfairness', I shall get back one day – with a 'cushy' wound if no other way.

He himself acknowledged that he had a relatively easy life in the trenches. He had the *Times* sent out on a regular basis, along with pheasant and grouse. He also carried a travelling bathtub.

Thomas Williamson was in the front line when he was told he was going on leave. He suddenly became ultra-cautious:

> In the early hour of the morning, about 3 a.m. a sergeant major came up to where I was and he said, 'Williamson, you will leave the trenches at six a.m., you're going on leave.' So with another ten lads and one officer we were bound for Blighty. I could never explain how I felt, but believe me I had my head covered in case of an accident.

Men who were notified of upcoming leave went to extraordinary lengths to avoid danger. Lieutenant Dane noted the soldiers' reaction when notified of leave:

If you want to see a man make himself as scarce as a £5 note in a poor-house, tell him he is going on leave. He may be standing head and shoulders above the parapet; he may be sniping from an exposed position, but directly he hears the news he vanishes like 10/- on pay-day. He puts his head in his boots and creeps away into a far corner of his dug-out – until his turn for duty comes round. When he speaks he speaks in whispers. When he stands on the fire step – he looks like a human question mark – with his shoulders peeping over the top and his head away down by his fourth button. If a shell bursts within 10 miles he crawls on his hands and knees into a 'funk hole'. In his spare time he scrapes the mud off his knees, and while he's on duty he prays that we shan't advance and that the Germans won't attempt an attack. At last he is given instructions to depart. He bends nearly double and creeps stealthily along the communication trench with his head about an inch from the ground. Never once does he dare to look back for fear of being sniped. Not until he is a good two miles from the firing line does he dare to lift up his head – and even then he makes use of trees, posts, telephone wires and every other available piece of cover as an extra precaution against a 'stray'.

Sometimes when I see staff-officers wandering about, I wonder what on earth they do for a living. They must spend fully two hours in dressing, every morning – and the rest of the day they work strenuously at eating, riding, and ???? Are they the people who mix the tea in the sugar? Do they write Plum and Apple Labels for anonymous jams? Do they take a fiendish delight in laying telephone wires about the height of ones shins? And barbed wire in innocent hedges? Are they the people who promise us 10 days rest and give us 4? If it isn't the Staff officers who do these things, who is it? (Lieutenant Dane, 4th Battalion Seaforth Highlanders)

In the trenches, drinking-water was often hard to find, and troops would resort to any means to brew a pot of tea:

Drinking-water was sometimes very difficult to get, and we had to bring it up in petrol tins. One day the water did not arrive. An officers servant came to me and asked if he could get some to make the officer's tea. The only water, I told him, was that gathered in a waterproof sheet which was stretched above our heads in the dug-out to keep us dry. It was the colour of stout, and I was not very sure whether there were any dead Germans buried above us or not. 'Never mind; it will do fine. The officers will never know, as I will put plenty of tinned milk and sugar in it,' and off he went with his kettle filled. The following night he brought me a small mug of hot tea which I enjoyed very much, but suddenly I remembered the water had not arrived, and asked where he got it. 'Oh! just out of your sheet.' I flung the mug at his head and chased him along the trench. (Thomas McCall, Cameron Highlanders)

Fighting with the 1st Battalion Black Watch on the St Quentin-Cambrai road, Albert Hay had to take similar actions:

We made tea with rainwater collected in ground sheets. When it rained we collected water in holes dug in the bottom of the trench and drained it from mess-tin to mess-tin until it was clean enough to be used for making tea.

Gunner David J.R. Bell, Machine Gun Company, continued to write to his Aunt Bell detailing conditions at the front:

I am still getting on all right in spite of the excessive frost (about 20 degrees below zero). Absolutely everything is frozen. I never knew before that bread and cheese could freeze but we have had it well demonstrated to us now for a fortnight and it is quite impossible to cut the bread with a knife. There are two ways of preparing it for eating. One is 'thaw it' by sleeping on it or any other means you can find. I am glad I do not have a moustache as it seems to be a source of annoyance to all the men who have as it collects icicles.

10

Work

Inspections and training during the day and work parties at night. It was actually more dangerous at rest than in the front-line trenches. Fatigue parties, wiring parties etc. were targeted by enemy patrols in no-man's-land. Carrying parties would be exposed to artillery fire and, as they neared the front-line trenches, to machine-gun fire. Those troops in the front-line trenches were protected by the trenches, but most of the work undertaken at night by fatigue parties was done without the protection offered by the walls of the trenches: carrying food, carrying other materials such as wood, burying the dead – in no-man's-land or behind the firing line – repairing parapets, saps, wiring etc. For the army, rest meant work. The idea of large bodies of troops with no function was anathema to the military mind – troops were often worked harder at 'rest' than in the trenches. Norman Collins, 6th Battalion Seaforth Highlanders, disputed the fairness of this convention:

> We had been withdrawn to Auchonvilliers for a rest where we soon got back into our officers' togs. However, while we were out of the line, I was detailed, probably because I was the youngest officer, to go back up the line with a working party. I thought this most unfair because we had just come out of action. This working party had to march to a dump and pick up barbed wire and posts and take them up a communication trench. We were to do some re-vetting in a trench and then we were to get out, after dark, in front of the line and mend wire.

The men preferred being in the trenches than being at rest, for when out at rest they had to form work parties. It fell to the support battalion to furnish working parties each night, and it was more dangerous to be in these parties than to be in the trench – there was at least some protection in the trench. In November 1916 on the Somme, Norman Collins was put in charge of a burial party, to bury those men of his battalion who had been killed during the offensive:

> I thought we were finished, but afterwards I was told to go back into what had been no man's land and bury the old dead of the Newfoundland Regiment, killed on 1st July. I was given three platoons which carried picks and shovels and, still under shell fire, we buried them in shell holes. The flesh had gone mainly from the face but the hair had still grown, the beard to some extent. When bodies have lain out for a long time there is a sweet smell, and it is not as repulsive as one might suppose. I thought 'there but for the grace of God go I', but the sight didn't make me any braver when I had to go into my next attack. The dead Newfoundlanders looked very ragged, and the rats were running out of their chests. The rats were getting out of the rain, [what effect would this have on the troops?] of course, because the cloth over the rib cage made quite a nice nest and I should think this was the driest place they could find in no man's land. However, when you touched a body the rats just poured out of the front. A dozen bodies would be touched simultaneously and there were rats tumbling everywhere. To think that a human being provided a nest for a rat was a dreadful feeling. The puttees on the men's legs liked quite round but when the flesh goes from under the puttee, there is just a bone, and if you stand on it, it just squashes... Then we shovelled the dead into shell holes, most half-filled with water, about thirty rotting bodies to a shell hole, and covered them as best we could.

While serving in Gallipoli with the 4th Battalion Royal Scots, W. Reid summed up the army's attitude to 'work':

We are to be relieved at 2.00 today the 10th. This is my birthday and I am having a good time (I don't think) 24 years of age today. Have got to the rest camp today for a few days get no rest as we are to go out and work.

A later entry in his diary addressed the same subject:

> The first of August has now come and I am getting quite used to the fire of heavy guns though you may be sure that I have a sinking feeling in the pit of my stomach when I hear one coming in my direction. My regiment have a turn now at the 'rest camp' as long as you are there you get to go to the beach to build a breakwater.

In June 1915, while out of the line resting, sections of the 4th Battalion Black Watch were detailed as working parties. Lance-Corporal Alex Thompson was one of those detailed to carry building materials to the front line:

> About half the battalion had been sent out to carry corrugated sheets down to the trenches. It was dark and rainy. There had been some talking and shouting going down the communication trench and one of the first men turning to the man behind him said 'There's too much row, stop your gassing'. The message went back the whole line 'About turn, they've turned the gas on' whereupon the whole party laying down their burdens doubled out of the trench and went home.

The result was that they were ordered to deliver the goods during the day and suffered twenty casualties. Albert A. Hay, 1st Battalion Black Watch, gave a soldier's opinion on work details when he declared 'a turn in the front line was a pleasant change from doing duty on working parties.' Lieutenant J.B. MacLean, 7th Battalion Cameronians, was detailed in charge of a working party improving the British front line, a task which he saw as futile. 'Both sides keep an eye on any improvements made in the front line and promptly unimproved it as much as they can.' It wasn't only the labour side of the work detail that was disagreeable. Lieutenant MacLean recorded:

> Last night I was on a working party improving one of the communication trenches. I saw a bit where the revetting material was being forced forward by a pile of earth and told a man to get up and dig it out. He jumped up, stuck in his spade and then said in a husky voice, 'It's a body, sir.' That sort of thing fairly puts the wind up on a pitch dark night when all the illumination is the frequent flash from guns or signal lights and courage at these times gets a bit shaky. However, it's wonderful how you get used to it.

Not everyone had the same enthusiasm for work parties. Lieutenant MacLean's attitude to work parties differed from Albert Hay's:

> Our working parties march up daily by the various 'tracks' to the point where the work is to be done and work with tin hats and box respirators at hand and stretcher bearers in attendance but so far we have only had two casualties. Of course it is a lot better than the line as we got more or less regular meals and a sleep at night, but it is only a temporary respite.

Captain Patrick Duncan, 4th Battalion Black Watch, appeared to equate work with a 'good rest'. He commented on the conduct of his men as they toiled on nightly work parties in the build-up to the Battle of Loos:

> We are still at our billets behind the firing line and enjoying a good rest; the weather is of the best again. Our chief duty here is to go with carrying and working parties. I was out from 8pm until 2.30 am. I can only remark again that the men deserve every praise for the way they plod along on these jobs.

A man noted for his humorous approach, Lieutenant Dane, 4th Battalion Seaforth Highlanders, took great pains to describe one of these night-time work parties:

> Many are the dark deeds we are doing just now by night. Sometimes, armed with picks, shovels and high moral courage, we sally forth to dig trenches. Sometimes we carry the sinews of war and the skeletons of Dug-outs up as far as the first line. Digging has one compensation. It isn't as bad as carrying. If you wish to enlarge your vocabulary of expletives, come with a carrying party at night. It is pitch dark. You can see about as far as the tips of your eye-lashes. You are given, say, a huge frame 3'0" x 4'0" to carry between two of you. The word is passed to 'quick march' – the 'quick' sounds rather unnecessary. You shuffle along over uncertain roads and treacherous fields, exploring your way as you go. The chap behind complains because you are going too fast. You growl because he isn't keeping up. 'Step shorter, damn you' says he 'Why in the… [censored]… cant y...' and somehow there's a drop like this --- you've stepped with your neck in a shell hole. There's a general shuffling and re-arranging of limbs, a number of muffled expletives, and on you go again. The other fellow, seeing you are shaken, offers to go in front. By this time the size of the frame feels 5'0" x 7'0". 'Thwizz – Thwizz – Rut – a – tut – a –tut –a – tut – a – tut – a – Thwizz – Thwizz'. The chap in front suddenly halts. The frame gives you a jab in the ribs. You both drop down – the frame on top of you. It is the machine gun playing unpleasantly close. You wait until the strafe has ceased. You go on again. You don't walk. You emerge, emerge, emerge, emerge, quietly evading telephone wires, tins, beams, and all the other things that are 'sooner felt than seen'. You keep your eyes fixed on the chap in front. When he jumps, you jump. When he becomes a trunk and a head, you know that there's a hole in front. When he trips over – you trip over. When he falls, you fall. When he swears, you swear. The size of the frame feels by now about 8'0" x 11'0", and growing rapidly. You have finished the open country, and now

> comes the time to negotiate the communication trench. This consists of painful pauses, awkward corners and startling balancing feats. The size of the frame feels by now 10'0" x 13'0". You do the mud glide along the trench, tying your feet into reef knots, and your body into figures of eight. You advance five paces, and wait for half-an-hour – and so you continue (the frame growing all the time) shuffling, swearing, and stopping until the welcome word comes to 'halt'. You put down a frame 20'0" x 30'0", heave a sigh of relief, withdraw all your expletives and light a fragrant Woodbine. 'Thank Heaven' you murmur 'the job's done'. It's 1.35, and we'll be back in billets by 2.15 – with luck.

All work was not carried out in the front line. Corporal James Reekie Muir, 7th Battalion Black Watch, recalls his fatigue party 'making a new railway line for carrying the rations'. J. Wallace, 5th Battalion King's Own Scottish Borderers, described work done at the British camp at Mender, on the outskirts of Gaza, and explained the practical approach taken by the British soldiers:

> We are making large concrete tanks for holding water. We do 6 hours work each day. Reveille at 3.30 start work at 4.30 and knock off at 7.30. Our next spell is from 15.00 hrs till 18.00 hrs. we gather the stones and sand from a wadi and mix the materials on a large board. As usual with these jobs we don't work too hard. After all our remuneration isn't very large for doing strenuous work, especially in a warm climate.

Wallace and his colleagues spent the next few days splashing water on the concrete as it dried in an attempt to prevent it cracking in the sun, while due to the climate and the threat of 'digging fatigue' work parties were limited to a quarter of an hour's digging and a quarter of an hour's rest. J. Cumming Morgan, 9th Battalion Cameron Highlanders, objected to the stigma attached to service in a pioneer or labour battalion:

> The word 'labour' also gave people the impression that we were an uneducated, uncivilized, unwashed lot of beings, whereas we were composed of exactly the same sort of men as every other branch of the service, except that most of us were short-sighted, and some of us wanted a finger, or possessed varicose veins, or suffered from some other stroke of luck.

Work was not always of a physical nature, as Wallace discovered when he was ordered to replace the company cook for a couple of weeks:

> I was detailed to take over the cookhouse duties as the usual cook (McGreggor) has gone down to Ismalia to attend a course of cookery. I will likely be on this job for a fortnight, and it is not a pinch of a job. I have to cook for the whole company. Which means early in the morning to have the porridge, bacon and tea ready for the men. Tea is issued at midday then dinner at night. After dinner is finished I have to get the rations ready for the next day and the firewood to break up. Cooking for a company of men (infantry) means that you are at it more or less constantly from 4 a.m. till about 8 p.m. The only compensation is that you can get plenty of milk and sugar in your tea and of course you can get the best of what's going in the food line.

In a parting shot at the desert conditions, Wallace commented: 'Despite the amount of sand we have put into bags there is still plenty left to walk on'. Work parties were vulnerable to enemy fire and Sergeant May, Cameron Highlanders, witnessed at first hand the risks taken by work parties in the front line:

> A working party was required one night to dig a cable trench. It is impossible to do navvies' work in a box respirator and the party mainly worked without. A deluge of gas shells. Eyes swollen and red; throats parched; flesh inflamed and almost raw where the mustard variety of gas had burnt it – a serious disadvantage to a

kilt. In the morning the gas lay across the valley, thick and nauseous as the miasma vapour of an African forest. Large green banks of chlorine gas threw back iridescent colours to the sun, while rising from it came a fetid, urinous stench that came near choking one. In the garden at the billet lying about the grass were close on a hundred men, denuded of their clothing, who lay about and writhed in veriest agony. The worst gas cases. With the passing of a few hours huge blisters were raised by the mustard gas. One man had a blister that reached from his neck to the bottom of his spine and extended the whole width of his back. In their agony they were retching horribly; straining till they sank exhausted, and then suddenly vomiting a long, green, streamer-like substance. And they were nearly all blind. Christ! This happened on the morning of May 25th, 1918, in the village of Chocques, after nearly two thousand years of Christianity. Would you believe it?

11

Rest

After a period of time served in the front line and reserve trenches, battalions would be withdrawn for a period of rest, usually equal to the time spent at the front. The men would be billeted in the rear and given time to recuperate and overhaul before the next period of front-line service. The quality of billets available to battalions at rest varied considerably. While some were billeted in barns and empty buildings, others were billeted with French families, while others still were billeted in tents. Some soldiers took full advantage of these rest periods:

> 'B' Company's best billet was in a farm at Montbernonchon, called the Fusiliers Depot, as the 2nd had been there several times before. It had a plentiful supply of home-brewed beer, served I think from a pump at the side of the midden. The day we left after lunch the men had done pretty well, and on the long march kept falling out to relieve themselves which caused our Colonel at the head of the battalion on his horse to come riding down to me at the rear to expostulate and get an explanation, after which they had to wait for the 40 minute halts. (Lieutenant A.H. Crerar, 2nd Battalion Royal Scots Fusiliers)

Discovering his billet contained some of the luxuries of life, Hakewell-Smith was enthusiastic in its praise:

> In our billets just behind the front line. This seems a stopping place so far. The place is within easy gun range and so far has not

> been hit. I have a bed and there is a piano, stove, kitchen and every luxury... by the way all wear steel helmets now. Beastly ugly they are too. The battalion looks like a troupe of chinamen and they are appallingly heavy and altogether beastly.

Two days later he was declaring: 'I have come into my own and all is well. The place is like the Garden of Eden. I don't think there was a shot fired the whole night.' He continued:

> I'm simply in rapture. The place is like a fairyland. I never dreamt such a place existed on the whole western front. The Hqtrs of my company is like a palace and my room is worthy of Haig himself. I have a pukka bed, a long glass dressing and writing table, a stove, and a washstand. In addition the scenery is magnificent and the weather like early June.

Lieutenant Dane, on the other hand, found some of the sleeping arrangements rather claustrophobic and cramped: 'There are four beds in my bedroom. I sleep in one – three Frenchmen in another – two children in another – and from the last I always hear about ten female snores. I don't like to look.' In July 1917 the 1st Battalion Cameronians were settling down to a well-deserved period of extended rest:

> Our company mess is in a very nice house with fine garden both back and front, and I am sleeping on the drawing room floor tonight, which is easily the best place I've slept in for some time. The men are all in big barns and are pretty well off. They think anything with a roof on it is a fine billet.
>
> We are now settled down for a 'rest' in a fairly good village. It is well back from the line and the billets are consequently better. I have a small room in a cottage which is quite OK and has a bed in it. The window opens on to a very pretty little garden, and altogether the place is quite picturesque. We work from 7 a.m. to noon and have the afternoon free except for swimming parade in the river [Somme].

I took that one yesterday and had a fine swim myself. We have fitted up a springboard and the men have a great time.

We had a pretty stiff march coming here and were on the move about five days. On two of these we started off at 5.30 a.m. (which necessitated reveille at 3.30) so as to escape the heat of the day, and finished up in some small village about 1 or 2 p.m. The billeting party goes on ahead and we simply walk into billets on arrival. (Lieutenant J.B. Maclean, 1st Battalion Cameronians)

Lieutenant Maclean was keenly aware that there was a price to pay for such a long period of rest:

This is a large town and we had an A1 dinner – some feed but probably our last for some time as we fully expect to set off for the big push in a couple of days. We have had fully three weeks out and it is I cinch that we shall get it 'en plein con' for a while now – at least all the old hands take that view so I am looking forward to some of the real thing.

Not all Maclean's experiences of billets were as pleasant. When his battalion once again went into rest in October of the same year life was not so rosy:

It was about midnight when we arrived and as the transport was not there we had no blankets or mess kits and had to sleep on the floors of the huts in our coats and I don't think I was ever so cold in my life before.

Our division was specially mentioned by Sir Douglas Haig for their work three weeks ago and he inspected us himself last week. He is a fine looking chap, and with his escort of men of the 17th Lancers (one carrying the Union Jack) made an impressive appearance.

Two weeks before his death in November 1916, Corporal Ian Maclaren, 6th Battalion Black Watch, wrote to his mother:

> Just a wee note – out of the trenches and in very nice billets – very ashy fire last night. Today first decent day for a while and mud disappearing for a good bit – I hope. Mail's a bit erratic just now. Feeling very fit and got properly cleaned up for the first time for a while. Feeling very fit. P.S. Please send me a tin of Harrison's Pomade.

Some of the billets were of an altogether more basic nature. When Captain Ritchie was in reserve in preparation for moving up the line, he recalled that:

> The order came to billet in a village. A tramp in the dark and mist, a muddle in the narrow road; steaming human beings jammed up close, carts, and an occasional dazzling, beautifully fitted Rolls Royce Car with a General in it. A supply cart nearly upsetting in the ditch. Struggling horses; mud and slosh everywhere. 500 men crammed tight into a few small stinking barns, manure and muck everywhere. Cackling wildly excited fowls, smells, laughter, furiously angry moments when orders are disobeyed. Officers sitting in a small kitchen. Crowds of women and children. A hot stove, coffee, tinned beef, bread and butter. Warmth and dryness and comfort. Two beds for six officers and straw on the floor. Ready dressed and booted to move at a moments notice. So ends my first day of battle and we never came into it at all!!!

Captain R.H.W. Rose made a similar comment on billeting:

> The men were billeted among the beasts last night. There are unrecognized heroes among them, men who are always cheerful and bright, but others are a constant source of irritation, and behave more like monkeys, if you take your eyes of[f] them for one minute.

James Campbell, 6th Battalion Cameron Highlanders, found this experience with the standard of billets was commonplace:

Our billet is a loft (entrance by a shaky ladder) partly above a stable and partly above a pigsty. The 'niff' is great, especially when the pigsty is cleaned out, as it was today. Now we know why we were issued with respirators. In the afternoon our first section played our second section at football.

He recorded that the battalion enjoyed a mixture of football and swimming for the next three days. When the Black Watch reached billets in January 1915, Lieutenant Sotheby described the rather farcical and lighthearted approach taken by the men:

We billet. The men are warned that if they get drunk, worse quarters will be found them. Hay lofts are used and all outbuildings. The houses are mostly one floor, with hay lofts above. The outhouses queer barns with mud walls and floors feet deep in straw. The upper storeys appeared to be in senile decay, 5 or 6 long branches thrown across some beams and straw atop; that is the ceiling for one room and the floor for another. The first accident soon came, as ladders have to be used to ascend. There was only one ladder for 5 lofts, so struggles ensued. One lot captured the ladder, and one man ascended. The top rung broke and down he came, everyone hugely delighted, one loft was so bad that the men used to keep falling through the ceiling, as fast as they reached their upper room however, they are happy.

The billeted troops were not always welcomed by the locals, which often led to a conflict of interest. Captain Mackie, 14th Battalion Argyll & Sutherland Highlanders, recalled one such incident when his battalion was enjoying a period of rest in a French village. The local coal merchant would not give the troops coal to keep warm:

So was our 'rest' a vain battle with the cold, and for C_______ [the woman of the house], that, suffering some inconvenience it is true, yet made an enormous profit from the shivering British soldiers in her midst. I wish that her cold may be eternal upon her, that the Somme may crawl upon her bosom like an icy snake, and the snow descend upon her for a funeral pall. Not because she denied us fuel, – for she had little of that – nor because she robbed us, but because she robbed us without politeness.

But even Delaney couldn't get coal, for coal there was none. He got a hint though, and to an Aberdonianised Irishman, the hint was enough. A coal truck destined probably for the yard of Monsieur X_______ [the coal merchant who had refused them coal] was on the railway line. That night he collected a shovel and a bag, and went of with the CO's servant who used to be a miner. Next morning I had a nice fire. 'We got a little coal, sir' said Delaney in a reverent tone. I opened the bunker. It was full. 'Good heavens, Delaney' I said 'I hope you haven't overdone it.' 'Oh no, sir, it would never be missed' and as I looked a little doubtful he added 'It was all one bit, sir, and it seemed a pity to break it.' Shades of the giant nugget. 'But Delaney, wasn't there a sentry over the coal?' 'Oh yes, sir' he replied scornfully. 'just a Frenchman, sir.'

In rear areas, permanent rest camps were built. Albert A. Hay described the conditions at a permanent rest camp at Poperingle:

We had only a short march from the station to the camps and our party was accommodated in a barn sort of place with netting-wire beds arranged round the walls and in the centre of the floor. These beds were typical of those erected in many of the permanent billets in France. They are generally built in tiers of three beds, and each bed measures about six feet by two feet, six inches. I always tried to get a bed in the top storey because there was barely room to sit upright in the others, and it is wonderful how comfortable stretched netting-wire is to lie on when a kilt is carefully folded and placed near the middle.

Rest periods were not the only way to get a break from the front:

> I have another job just now – escort to our chaplain, who is under arrest. He is an Irish RC and his crime was refusing to attend parade when Gen Plummer inspected us. However, as there is nowhere for him to run away to I don't bother much about him. (Lieutenant J.B. Maclean, 1st Battalion Cameronians)

Corporal Jack Lunn, 5th Battalion Cameronians, also described in a letter to his father the joy of getting out of the trenches for four days as an escort for a prisoner at hospital – clean sheets, good food etc. A. Gilmor, 14th Battalion Argyll & Sutherland Highlanders, could not get to grips with the absurdity of military tradition, which dictated that when men were on rest they must be 'worked':

> Our time here was spent like the traditional Divisional rest – in the most extreme efforts to make the men into wooden soldiers and only a sense of humour pulled the chaps through the ordeals of squad drill in swampy ground, handling of arms and the like in the most uncongenial surroundings.

In February 1917, while billeted in the village of Hoilancourt near Abbeville, Private William Cameron was transferred from the Scottish Horse to the 7th Battalion Black Watch in a rather dramatic fashion:

> We suffered very severe cold here and I will never forget the day when the draft was paraded in a field, three inches deep in snow and we were told to get off our slacks as we were being issued with the kilt. The 1916-17 winter was the worst experienced in France, so we were broken in in style.

When out of the line, men took the opportunity to clean themselves up. When Cameron's battalion was sent to a camp just outside the village of Vlamertinshe, the men made the most of the opportunity to wash and repair their kit:

> In this camp there was a pond owing to the heavy rains, and the boys were all down through the day with their shirt tails and great coats on, washing their kilts, rifles and equipments etc. etc. which were all caked with mud. I will always remember after washing our kilts, tunics, etc. we couldn't get them dried as it rained all the time and we had to put them all on soaking wet as we were shifting back to the line.

Captain Ritchie, similarly, commented on a 'day of complete rest and cleaning up... It is jolly to see the men all cleaning up – shaving and hair cutting. Bought a pair of horse clippers for the men's hair.' Captain Patrick Duncan, 4th Battalion Black Watch, recalled his first experience of French billets:

> We are now billeted in a town about 6 miles from the firing line. We left the trenches at midnight and arrived here between 4 and 5 o' clock in the morning. It was a very wet, dark, night which made the journey rather difficult; our company had one man hit by a stray bullet. This town will be about the size of Arbroath. It is rather dirty and shabby and reminds me very much of one of the smaller Lancashire cotton towns. The sanitary arrangements in most French towns are very primitive and the streets are not clean.

Although many took the opportunity of rest to attend religious services, not all appreciated the efforts of the ministry. James Campbell had other ideas: 'Had a church parade this forenoon. The minister was in a rather pessimistic style this time. I don't like these persons who always remind you of the dangers you are running. They feed me up.'

While at rest, Lieutenant J.B. MacLean commented on one of the methods of entertainment which served to give the Scottish regiments their unique identity:

> Just now our pipe band is playing up and down outside the huts. It is one of the best in France and sounds A1. Last night we had the company pipers with us coming down, but it is a bit ludicrous as the men are all so done up that there is no such thing as keeping step or anything of that sort, although the pipes certainly buck them up considerably.

Captain Thorburn, serving in the Bareilly Brigade with the 2nd Battalion Black Watch, felt that some got more periods of rest than others:

> There is no rest for the Indian Corps anyhow for such regiments as ourselves in it. With the BEF I believe they have four days in and 4 days out as regular as clockwork, and always go back to the same trenches, which must be wonderful comfort. But we never have less than a week in – often a great deal more – and we never go back to the same trenches. All the dirty work falls on us.

12

Play

Every effort was made to involve the men in sport of one form or another, in an attempt to relieve the boredom. Men returning half-dead from a stint in the front line would readily play a game of football as if they had been given a new lease of life.

> We played the Cameron Officers at football two days ago. The game was a draw of one goal each. They are a rotten lot, the Camerons now: not one of the old lot left; they are all outsiders. (Hay-Young, 1st Battalion Argyll & Sutherland Highlanders)

Even in the heat of the desert there was time for football, although when the 4th Battalion played the 5th Battalion there was a bit of cheating, as the 5th had a professional goalkeeper and won by 9-1. Football was not the only sport played. On Saturday 31 July 1915, the 14th Battalion Argyll & Sutherland Highlanders held a Highland Gathering at the United Services Sports Ground, Devonport. The events included '100 yards race, sack race, wrestling, high jump, long jump, relay race, throwing the hammer, putting the shot, 440 yards race, band race, one mile race, veterans race, dancing – "Reel o'Tulloch", sergeants race, tug-of-war, five-a-side football competition.' Other sporting events were often made up on the spur of the moment, as Lance Corporal Alex Thompson, 4th Battalion Black Watch, discovered when he spent an afternoon watching the rather peculiar event of wrestling while riding a donkey:

> One afternoon we had sports behind our billet, the second, fourth, and fifth Black Watch all competing. Some of the events were very funny, the most amusing being the Wrestling on a Donkey. The donkeys were supplied by the Indians and to start with some of them would not let a white man come near them and bolted all over the field while competitors chased after them.

The winner was a man who rode his beast naked, thereby affording his opponents no easy grip to throw him from his mount. Boxing was always a favourite among the troops:

> We had a most interesting boxing contest in which the second battalion took part. This contest was held on the bandstand in the middle of a big square just behind our billet, which was very suitable for such a purpose. Most of the boxers were very keen and one could suspect old scores being wiped off. The spectators also showed their enthusiasm and there was a great deal of good humoured chaff going. It seemed funny to think that the boys were not content with the ordinary dangers in the trenches but must needs set-to to kill each other when out resting. (Corporal Alex Thompson, 4th Battalion Black Watch)

Not all recreational activity was sport-orientated. During a period of rest at Darnevrourt, Corporal James Reekie Muir, 7th Battalion Black Watch, found alternative relaxation, along with some of his comrades. 'We passed the day with a few Frenchmen and held dancing in the middle of the street. Then departed for the trenches at La Boiselle in the evening.' Lieutenant Crerar found that playing sports in a theatre of war could be every bit as dangerous as fighting:

> We spent the night in tents on flat ground, and as we were going into the line the next day, we decided to have a rugger match against the officers of the Manchester Regiment who were the other battalion in our Brigade. First we had to clear a pitch, of

> wire, the odd unexploded Mills Bomb, and a defunct mule which had lost the argument with one that morning. We had no goal-posts, and could only raise 12 a side, one or two of whom had never played rugger. We were, however, determined to thoroughly enjoy what we never thought of as perhaps our last game of rugger.

With the high number of horses in service it is not surprising that they were used for sport: 'On Wednesday we had the Divisional horse show, the chief patron being Gen. Sir Julian Byng. There was a good display of jumping and one of our officers got second prize, although there were Scots Greys officers there.' Although Corporal Thompson thought wrestling on donkeys was a strange sight, William Duncan, serving with the Scottish Horse in Salonica, was party to an equally bizarre event:

> The regimental hunt which perhaps was unique for an army in service. The Scottish Horse Hunt. We had in the regiment several huntsmen connected with established home hunts. They were instructed to go to the villages and collect hounds, well dogs and they acquired the greatest variety of breeds imaginable. However they were whacked into shape. It was quite a sight to see them on the move. Tally ho and of[f] we go. Quite a contrast from the fashionable home meet. One day the officers insisted that all who could get hold of a mule to ride in the meet. There was great fun, to ride a mule with a saddle is difficult but to ride bareback is almost impossible. There are no shoulder withers to grip with the knees. In a few minutes it was pandemonium, just like the charge of the Light Brigade, bodies all over the place. All this too was within artillery range.

The concert party was a popular form of entertainment. Lieutenant Dane, 4th Battalion Seaforth Highlanders, described one such occasion:

Ye Concert. I hied me to ye baths to-night for to enjoy ye merrie concert. Ye preparations were most thorough, again I say, most thorough. For ye stage, ye engineers (or wood and nail artists) had erected some boards. For ye seats, there were chairs for the nobility, and for ye remainder, Nature had, with becoming foresight, provided ye tender portions of ye anatomy. Ye concert was due to begin at 8 p.m. but being organized by ye Army, it started at 8.45 p.m. Together we congregated in ye dark to hear ye artists let off ye surplus of joy which had accumulated during a session in ye abominable burrows called ye trenches. Some sighed ye love songs – others got out of step with their tongues in Ragtime, a modern invention which offendeth ye sense of propriety, yet tickleth ye sense of hearing. Some warbled ye old-world melodies – others set nonsense to musick. Some delivered ye dizzy ditties – others croaked in crazie choruses. 'Tis good for ye minde now and again to mix with fellow feelings, and much did I enjoy it – Yea, I enjoyed it much. Mister Sanford, Lance Corporal of ye 1st Seaforths, and Mister Morrison, 2nd Lieut of ye 4th Seaforths, gave me much pleasure – verily, much pleasure, did he give me. 'Twas curious to watch ye scores of cigarettes, glowing and dying away like little red stars in ye darkness. Ye concert over, we sang 'God Save The King' and parted to rise at 7 a.m. in ye morning.

13

Food

My Bully Beef

The hours I spend with thee, dear friend,
Are like a nightmare without end.
On you alone for life I must depend
My Bully Beef! My Bully Beef!
Each tin a meal, each meal a groan,
There's gristle, fat and ground-up bone,
I finish up each tin and then –
A biscuit comes alone.

O Woeful Fate! That I should eat
This tramway accident for meat,
In you I find odd arms and legs and feet
My Bully Beef! My Bully Beef!
Each meal a pain, each pain a pill,
But, never mind, I'll bear up still.
The biscuit's waiting by my side –
It can't do more than kill.

With you I'm fed, till I'm fed up
You're breakfast, dinner, tea and sup
You're food and drink and clothes to this poor pup
My Bully Beef! My Bully Beef!
Each bite a joy, each joy pure bliss,
Do I want salmon when I've got this?

You rich who banquet at the Ritz –
Poor devils! What you miss!!

When I get killed they'll pack me in
No! Not a coffin, but a tin
And when I'm served you'll murmur 'mid the din
My Bully Beef! My Bully Beef!
Each limb a tin, each tin good fare,
All my equipment will be there
It may be pleasant eating me
But of my pack beware!

Lieutenant W.S. Dane, 4th Battalion Seaforth Highlanders

In the early years of the war there was no provision to provide the men with hot food; they were issued their rations and expected to fend pretty much for themselves. After morning stand-to the men would gather round small burners, primus stoves privately bought, or Tommy Cookers – pocket-sized alcohol stoves – preparing their breakfast, an activity which occupied both sides. There were many variations of home-made cookers or stoves, using charcoal or the limited supply of coal. The men would normally cook their food as a section, pooling their rations and sharing the work. An added bonus was that there was a greater share of rations when casualties occurred until such casualties were reported. It was not unusual for those in the front-line trenches to go without food and water for several days. Shellfire and attacks would prevent supplies reaching them and in this situation they would have to rely on their emergency iron rations, which could not be opened without the permission of an officer. These emergency rations themselves offered little relief as they invariably consisted of a tin of bully beef, biscuits, a small quantity of tea and sugar, mixed together, and occasionally a piece of cheese. The emergency rations of those who were killed would be collected and consumed. It was only as war stretched on into 1915 and 1916 that provision was made to provide hot meals in the front line. Company field cookers were brought up into the support area and the hot food was taken forward at night in 'Dixies' or straw-lined boxes carried by fatigue parties.

The need for water was equally desperate, as in the heat of action or the heat of the French summer, troops were desperate to relieve their thirst. They resorted to drinking the water from shell holes – on some occasions only to find as the water level was lowered that the hole contained several decomposing bodies. With the scattering of body parts or human remains, and the excrement not only of humans but of the numerous rats, any surface water would be contaminated. To the desperate men, need overtook any risk to health. In Gallipoli it was reported that men 'lied and stole' in order to get water, while in Egypt the official allowance was two quarts per man per day, one for drinking and one for cooking. In one instance, troops used ice out of a shell hole to make tea, assuming that any germs would be frozen and therefore harmless. When the ice on the shell hole thawed out, the men saw the rotting body of a French soldier. Their only comment was that the tea had tasted 'quite good'.

If men were lucky they would be fed before going over the top, but all too often they went into battle hungry. Lieutenant Crerar was one of the lucky ones: 'We were told that we would be "going over the top" as the phrase was, in a daylight attack at 2.8 p.m. that afternoon, and fortunately about 1 p.m. some rations, mainly bread, arrived, our first food since breakfast on Sunday.' While most men had to rely on the food supplied by the British army, some were in the fortunate position of being able to write home on a regular basis with requests for food – in some cases extensive and extravagant requests. Lieutenant Hakewell-Smith wrote home describing how he was 'beat to the world after strenuous rugby match and 25 kilometre march in full marching order' but used the opportunity to request

'2 dozen kippers, some Savory & Moore's special sausages, 2 washing gloves, and "bottle of hair juice".' This last was to deal with the problem of lice. The following week Hakewell-Smith sent in a further request for '2 doz kippers, 12 slabs of Savory & Moore's chocolate and 2 sheets of quinine tablets'. These letters home became regular requests for luxury food items.

During the retreat at Pontoise in the early days of the war, Captain R.H.W. Rose, 1st Battalion Cameronians, discovered that it was not necessarily the most luxurious meals that were the best. 'March some distance, and then have a meal, the tea seems excellent. It has been made in a canteen which is dirty with past meals, a scum of grease on the top, and there is no milk, but we find it finer than any tea we have ever drunk.' Rose quickly learnt to appreciate the small luxuries: 'Getting several small luxuries in the feeding lines, piece of butter at breakfast, also an egg, country jam at tea time. People always being accused of eating too much. This is the depth to which the war sinks you.' He quickly learnt the value of food:

> Food is one of the principal pleasures of life during war. We are doing very well now. This is a menu for the day, which does not vary much. To this is sometimes added a luxury, such as an atom of pate de fois gras, or walnuts. Drink at dinner, red wine with water, but this is now finished.
>
> Breakfast
> Bacon, bread, jam. Tea with condensed milk, and sugar. Small piece of butter.
> (All but bread strictly limited).
> Lunch
> Bully beef in some form, potatoes, bread, cheese, tea,
> (as much as you want, some people excepted owing to special capacity).
> Tea

Bread, very small piece of butter, jam, tea.
Dinner
Stew, bully (latterly fresh meat), with vegetables. Stewed apples or pears. Cheese, tea (sometimes rum).

However, like many others Captain Rose was not slow to take advantage of a letter home, although his requests do appear rather eclectic:

> You will remember my sou'wester and drawers for the kilt – to come rather more than halfway down towards the knee; also my Burberry – my mitts are in the pocket of it. Other wants may turn up later as I find that I require them. Little extras, such as sausages, white mealy puddings, ham, oatcakes, cake, sardines, sweets, chocolates, sent at odd times, are terribly appreciated in the trenches. 'Needles Army Fruit Tablets' are very good, and a much-enjoyed sweet. A bottle of Cherry Whisky, sloe gin, or such keeps out the cold when clogged in mud and shivering. Café au lait, too, and cocoa for morning stand-to about 5 a.m. is necessary.

In a letter sent on the 4th or 5th April 1915 Private Braid, now with the BEF in France, once again discussed food:

> I take the opportunity in letting you know how we fare with rations etc. we get one oz bread, equal to a slice per day and the rest biscuits which require a mash hammer to break them and of course the bully beef. If it was not for ourselves we would be starving. We go into the old farms for potatoes and boil them with the bully.

In a letter dated 3 August 1915 Braid again complained about the food, this time making extraordinary claims:

> We are being treated like dogs at present, we complained to the Company Officer about the shortage of bread and he is making

> enquires into it. Our issue of cigarettes are becoming less now, we get so much on Sunday to do us the whole week, 16 cigs last night. Another thing is the currants, raisins and dates are being issued to us instead of jam. What are they doing with the currants etc that people so kindly send us as comforts? They are giving them to us as rations and doing us out of some jam.

Private Cuthill of the 4th Battalion Black Watch agreed with Braid:

> We are getting great feeding just now and I don't think. One slice of b[r]ead for a day's rations and plenty of work, then they have the hard neck to say we are the best fed army in the world. Heaven help the army that gets less than us.

When Bandsman G. McKay, 5th Battalion Royal Scots, sailed from Alexandria to Gallipoli on board the transport ship *Melville* on the eve of the British landings, he was impressed by the standard of fare provided: 'Grub very good on board ship. Breakfast, hash and bread and butter and tea. Dinner, pea soup, pots and beef, and rice and prunes.' However, once ashore, W. Reid, 4th Battalion Royal Scots, quickly found out that the food on the peninsula was of a lower standard: 'When up here the favourite food is what we call peninsular pancakes. They are composed of bully beef and biscuits fried in ham fat, in the absence of anything else they are most enjoyable.' Food was a subject constantly mentioned in the letters sent from J.B. Maclean to his brother Alex:

> I got my rations nightly, usually in a filthy wet sandbag and generally consisting of one extensively filthy loaf, a tin of sausages or bully COLD (business of shuddering), some jam or cheese and a candle. My only implement was a clasp knife. For drink we had the rum issue and we got water once and I also had a flask of whisky. It rained every blessed day and I discovered the acme of all

> human misery – stand to at 4.15 A.M. wet, muddy, dark, cold, hungry, thirsty, and with half a chance of a scrap with the Hun for breakfast. Of course that gentle person no doubt was experiencing much the same sensations.

Maclean understood the practicalities of obtaining hot food in the trenches:

> I think the principal trouble at present is the cold. We can't cook up here as the smoke would be seen, but we manage to make hot tea using a candle as the heating agent; otherwise everything is cold, and a steady diet at all meals of tea, bully or cold roast, bread, butter and jam, with perhaps biscuits or tinned fruit, gets a bit monotonous in winter time, and one's idea of heaven is a warm room with a respectable dinner on a table and no earth mined in the grub or tea.

In the later years of the war hot food was provided in the trenches, brought up at night by carrying parties in hot containers, which were kept warm in boxes packed with straw:

> During the night the men get stew and tea which is brought up in 'hot food containers', and also rum and I take a share of each and the last is not the least. Although the stew is A1 stuff, the men much prefer the tea and rum, as is evident from their remarks when they hear which it is, and that seems rather funny as the stew is the principal meal they get.

However, even on 8 November 1918, three days before the armistice, Maclean could still find something to complain about: 'My food was of the most ragtime description – wet bread and intensely filthy cheese and once or twice a mess tin of tea made over a candle.' In the days leading up to the Somme, Private, later Captain, D. Dick, Argyll & Sutherland

Highlanders, found out that there were times when having a broad Scots accent paid dividends:

> After our long spell in the line we were taken back to rest in a village where there was still a semblance of civilization. We could have decently cooked meals, instead of the tins of beans and bully, and we could go to an estaminet and order eggs and chips, and have a chance to speak French. The Scottish soldiers were a bit confused when they ordered 'twa eggs and chips', and found three eggs on their plate; for 'twa' sounded very like 'trois' in French.

Greed brought its own problems. Sergeant S. Saunders, 6th battalion Gordon Highlanders, found that he was 'having trouble with the men – they say we keep too much jam for the sergeants mess – so we do as well.' When Private Lachlan MacDonald from North Uist was serving in Salonica with the 10th Battalion Cameron Highlanders, the provision of food was so poor that the battalion was compelled to make its own arrangements. Fortunes changed when the men found a large quantity of barley seed in the deserted farms and villages:

> There was a lot of barley seed at the farms and in good conditions and our rations were very poor. But in one village there was a big building and a mill. But it was left with pieces taken out of place. We had an officer who was good at the hunt and it wasn't long until he got the pieces. We found a big German engine in a wood beside the river. They could not get it across and so the officer got horses from the artillery to pull it to the mill. After that he found two boys that were working in a meal mill at home. They started to make Barley Meal. So we soon had porridge and they gave some meal to other Scottish regiments.

During the fighting to capture the village of Loos in September 1915, Thomas McCall came upon a strange sight:

> Two other sergeants and myself ran down into a cellar. To our surprise we found an old fellow in a white jacket, apparently an officers' cook. The table was laid with plenty of eatables and wines. The officers had a pressing engagement elsewhere. As we were feeling rather hungry, and to guard against being poisoned, we forced the cook to eat and drink first, and then we all had a good tuck in and felt the better for it; and took old Jerry upstairs a prisoner.

Sergeant H.E. May, Cameron Highlanders, recalled spending four days in the front line without food:

> On the fourth night came relief. Staggering out to a rest billet and dropping exhausted. A feed of bacon, bread and butter, and tea. Real hot tea, scalding; plenty of it, and you rejoice – until you remember you're eating dead men's rations beside your own, for without the dead men there would be no plenty.

May was quick to point out that there were other times when the men were well catered for:

> In a near-by farmhouse were cows, calves, horses, chickens, rabbits, pigs, and the varied stock one finds about a farm. In a cellar were hundreds of bottles of red and white wine, port, and champagne, to say nothing of a dozen barrels of beer. The troops lived very well in the ensuing days when not engaged with the enemy, on consolidation, or wiring.

Finally, food was a lifesaver in more ways than one. Robert Lothian Ramsey from Crail in Fife was with the Black Watch at the Battle of Loos. His life was saved by a tin of bully beef when he sheltered behind a haystack. He was shot in the neck but the tin of bully – his emergency rations carried on top of his pack – absorbed most of the impact and he survived and was sent home to recuperate at Stobswell Hospital.

14

'Who Pays the Piper'

Provision for the wounded was minimal. When troops were going forward into the attack, wounded would be left where they fell, sometimes for days, until they could be collected by stretcher bearers or more often by their comrades, returning to their own lines after the attack. For many, to suffer a wound meant death as they lay in no-man's-land unable to shelter from artillery and machine-gun fire. The lucky ones might manage to crawl or roll their way into a shell hole, but without water and medical attention they were only prolonging the inevitable. The wounded would spend days sheltering in no-man's-land, crawling toward their own lines at night – many spent days covering 100 yards to safety. Lying wounded on the soil of no-man's-land meant that wounds quickly turned septic, as the very soil itself contained blood and bits of flesh, human and animal waste, all continually churned up by the artillery and all of which would promote gas gangrene. Even when recovered by stretcher bearers, the wounded soldier was not safe – he often had a long and tortuous journey through the front-line trench crammed with the equipment of war, which only became an obstacle to the passage of the wounded. The twists and turns of the front line which were designed to minimise losses from shellfire made the movement of a stretcher and its attendants slow and difficult. The condition of the battlefield meant that journeys to an aid station could take several hours – once out of the front line and in to the communication trench the wounded were going against the flow of men and material, constantly being pushed to one side as the need for replacements and ammunition dictated priorities. Unlike the rear areas where two men could quite easily carry a stretcher along a metalled roadway, at the front it usually required four men to carry one wounded colleague – and often, due to the condition of the ground, it took six or eight. This severely limited the number of wounded that could be brought in before loss of blood or the extremes of weather led to death. It was accepted that wounded would make their own way to the field dressing stations if at all possible; indeed for many that was the only way to ensure survival. This gave new meaning to the term 'walking wounded', as soldiers would often be seen crawling along the roadside towards the aid station. Soldiers would walk minus an arm or, using their rifle as a crutch, minus a foot or part of a leg. Men with the most horrific injuries would be termed 'walking wounded'. It certainly appears harsh that men were 'expected' to do this, but when the alternative was death there was no real choice. Imagine the first day of the Somme with its high casualty rate: how many of those died due to lack of medical provision, and how many survived due to their own resolve?

Captain M. Thorburn witnessed the suffering of the wounded while serving in Mesopotamia with the 2nd Battalion Black Watch:

> The sufferings of the wounded are so awful, poor devils. I suppose it can't be helped, but they go often 3 or 4 days without their wounds being dressed – that is, without their first field dressing being removed, and no food until it is possible to get it for them. As soon as possible, of course, they get them moved off down the river to hospital, but they can't get them all of[f] at once.
>
> On the 8th, after the battle on the 7th, there were our officers walking about waiting to get on a boat to be taken to hospital – one shot in the face and broken arm, two others shattered arms, one both wrists hanging, another with lung pierced, all just band-

aged. I leave out the more sordid parts. It is certainly very difficult to evacuate wounded.

For many men, like Norman Collins, the constant smell of death hung over the battlefield:

> There was an overwhelming stench of death here. I saw many wounded men, and you never got them in, you couldn't get them in, and they might have their intestines blown out. You could lose most of your guts and still live, dying gradually. It was terrible hearing the wounded out in no man's land at night, crying out in pain, and it affected us very much. We did try and go out at night to bring them in, but many were too badly wounded to help, and it was better just to give them a dose of morphine.

Arrival at a field dressing station was no guarantee of survival, as James Campbell discovered. At the Battle of Loos his brother was wounded in the leg but was later killed when the dressing station he was in was shelled with gas shells:

> At first I could scarcely credit it as, when Peter went to hospital there was no sign whatever of him being gassed. But in a moment or two when I considered that I had had no news whatever from him I realized to the full my loss. And when I thought of mother and Jenny it was mental torture. During our lives Peter and I were together and we were not like ordinary brothers. I cared more for him than anyone else on earth and to think of him is agony. And yet I can think of nothing else. He could not have died for a better cause but oh what a poor consolation that is.

When J. Wallace, who served in Egypt and Palestine with the 5th Battalion King's Own Scottish Borderers, went to visit two of his colleagues recovering from minor wounds, he too was faced with the reality of infection and the limited abilities of the dressing stations:

A good breakfast, a swim and roll call were the principal events this forenoon. After dinner Jim Chalmers, Ken Elder, J Seaton, Jack Johnstone and I went to tidy the graves of Wm Miller (Balcarres St) and a chap Huggans. They got slight wounds when we were at the Apex but died down here from aseptic poisoning.

After an extended period in the front line, exposed to the extremes of winter, Private D. Dick, 14th Battalion Argyll & Sutherland Highlanders, collapsed on parade. On waking up in hospital he recalled:

You can have no idea of the surprise I had when I really woke up and found I was lying in a bed, with white sheets. I began to wonder if I had been wounded. I felt really ill all over. The lights were dimmed, so it must have been night. Just then a door opened in the ward and a nurse in white came in. She looked just like an angel. She came straight up my bed, and bending over me she said. 'Can't you sleep? Jock?' It was the first English woman I had seen or heard since we left Britain. So I told her[e] all about it – the mud and the frost and the trench feet and the frost bite, and the dysentery caused by drinking shell hole water, for the only alternative was water in unwashed petrol cans. She understood, for she went away and brought a syringe, which she pushed into my arm. 'This will make you sleep alright, Jock. Good night', with that she was gone again, and so was I.

J.G. Scott passed judgement on the men of the Black Watch: 'They do die game these fellows, and the wounded are very brave: sometimes we can't get them attended to for a long time.' Captain J.D. Mackie, 14th Battalion Argyll & Sutherland Highlanders, recalled the feeling of being wounded:

I always wondered what it was like to be wounded. Now I know. As my knowledge is shared by the greater part of the male population of Great Britain I can claim no monopoly but I may set down what others are to modest to tell.

Private Callaghan was going to bayonet a Boche and I went over to stop him. I don't like the Boches, but I couldn't see the fellow stuck in cold blood. He had a Hebraic nose and a yellowish skin, and he held his arms so high above his head that I thought his tunic must burst at the armpits. His eyes looked as if they would bulge right out of his head and he had an incipient moustache.

We were on our objective and except for a few 'Kamerads' there weren't many Germans to be seen. I halted the line and shouted them to cease firing and dig. Up and down I hurried bellowing to them to stop shooting and use their entrenching tools. I cursed McGregor who should have brought us up the picks and shovels, but I might have saved my breath, for McGregor, though I knew it not, was dead.

Then a horse kicked me, and I felt a sort of double impact as his hind leg straightened – absurd – there was no horse there. One of my men perhaps had lost his temper at my cursings and had given me an 'accidental' bang with the butt of his rifle. I was taking some staggering paces in a little curved run, and I fell to the ground rather heavily. Then I got up again and something warm and comforting, trickled down my cold thighs – it was a sharp morning – and I knew I was wounded.

Lieutenant Henry Bowie, 2nd Battalion Black Watch, was wounded at Shaik el Saad in January 1916:

I was spun right about and dropped. I rose up and saw that a great deal of my left arm had been blown off just below the elbow. The blood was spurting in different jets and I stuck the fingers of my right hand in the hole made holding the blood back in this fashion for nearly an hour.

First aid was not immediately forthcoming and he 'lay out in the sun for two hours and then tried to make for the field ambulance.' It was the lack of transport and medical arrangements that really disgusted Bowie:

> They made arrangements for 250 casualties, they have got nearly 4.000 instead, 14 hours on the P1 with no place to lie on, not a sq foot of deck and nothing to eat. Four of the wounded died on the way down and no wonder. I should say 25% died out here in this country through inattending and proper medical arrangements. The Indian Government is blundering awfully over the whole business.

When Lieutenant Bowie was eventually transferred to P5, a riverboat converted to Red Cross use, he found no change in his situation:

> The rains have commenced and everyone is lying in inches of water. No beds, cabins, or saloons on the craft on this river. Everybody is lying on the deck, the cover overhead fails to keep the rain out, it helps to concentrate in into various streams instead. The conditions of officers and men are ghastly. Things like these occurred in the Crimea. They certainly were not worse of then than what we are now, and this 1916? Some of the wounds are dreadful and have not been dressed for a week. They are dosing the men with brandy, whisky and rum to keep their spirits up.

Alan Macgregor Wilson began the war as a Quartermaster-Sergeant with the 1st Battalion Black Watch and was subsequently commissioned in 1915 as a Lieutenant in the 8th Battalion:

> I do not hear the guns today. Yesterday and today they have been quiet. The lull before the storm. But still the ambulances pass with their freight of sadness. The eternal stream. But how much more sad i[s] the thought of those who have been left. Finding their last resting place in foreign soil. The luxury of a coffin is denied. They are too many these fallen heroes. I wonder sometimes how long

will it take for these sons of Britain to be forgotten. Never, I hope, and least when judgement calls the bestial German to look.

Captain Patrick Duncan also lay in the open until assistance came:

> Both my wounds are healthy and healing fast; I enjoy my food. I am much more worried as to how the present fight is getting on, and grieved over the loss of our Colonel and so many officers, than concerned about my own legs. Tosh and Campbell went immediately before me from the support into the firing line on Saturday morning 25th inst. As they turned to the left and I to the right along behind the parapet I never saw either of them again. I lay for an hour just outside the parapet when I was carried in and put into a dugout where I remained until the evening when I was removed to our dressing station.
>
> I am very thankful that my life has been spared for the present any how; the fact that my wounds were got so early in the morning prevented me from getting over to the German lines, because I just had to lie where I fell.

Walking wounded were expected to make their own way back to the field dressing station and, as Sergeant H.E. May, Cameron Highlanders, describes the scene as the wounded returned from the front line, the term 'walking wounded' should be taken with a pinch of salt:

> Down the track went a constant stream of battered humanity. Men minus an arm; those with huge dark stains on their uniform to show where they had been hit – Highlander and Sassenach. Here a man badly burned by a petrol bomb; there a poor devil with his leg gone at the knee, who dragged a weary way backward, using his rifle as a crutch. On the faces of all a look of hopeless horror as they fled from the terror behind them. One must see something like that to realize the insane folly of war.

Thomas Williamson also described the experience and sensation of being wounded:

> Suddenly a shell came tearing into the trench. I felt myself being lifted to what I thought was a terrific height. I then landed flat in the bottom of the trench. I could not move. I did not know where I had been hit, or what was the extent of my injuries. Then, as my eyes became focused, I saw the officer, his face smashed in. He must have been instantly killed by the same shell that rendered me hors-de-combat. I was feeling very sick as I lay on the ground – sodden earth in the front line trench. I could never describe how I felt. Why were they not coming to help me? Little did I know what had happened further along the trench. Our killed and wounded were lying everywhere. Now that my brain had cleared a bit, I could hear the shouts of help from the wounded. 'O God,' I said 'when, oh when, will this fearful carnage cease? It is more than we humans can bear.' As I lay there moaning with the pain I was trying to endure at last the stretcher-bearers came down the trench. As they lifted me onto their stretcher, I felt as if I had been kicked all over the body. They carried me down the communication trench; turning round the traverses was a difficult problem, the sweat was pouring off their foreheads, and running down their cheeks.

Although he began his military service as a Gunner in a Machine Gun Company, David Bell was later commissioned as a Lieutenant in the Tank Corps. He wrote to his mother on 24 August 1918 describing his wounds:

> Very many thanks indeed for your letter and the white heather from Derry Hill. The wound was really nothing at all and won't injure my beauty. It was caused by bullets hitting my gun and splinters splashing through the mount onto my forehead. They only made little scratches about 1/8" deep which did me absolutely no harm.

Two days later he was writing again, this time with more disturbing news:

> I was wounded yesterday about 11 a.m. but I am quite all right. My right thigh is broken just above the knee by a piece of shrapnel and I have a few other slight wounds in various places. I was operated on last night and I am quite all right and comfortable and expect to come across to Blighty in a few days as soon as they have got my leg properly fixed for transit. Don't worry Mother Dear I am all right and will soon be home.

A third letter illustrates the remarkable stoicism displayed by many:

> I may have to lo[o]se some of my toes o[n] my right foot but on the other hand there is still a hope that I may not. I am feeling remarkably strong and hope soon to get over to Blighty. Now don't worry about me dear dear mumsie for I shall be all right and back with you soon.

Others displayed a more poetic view:

> There will be times when there's a sinking in your stomach and a singing in your head; when men beside you are staring upwards with the stare that does not see; when the sergeant has taken it through the forehead and the nearest officer is choking up his life in the corner of the traverse. But – there's still your rifle; perhaps there's a machine gun standing idle; anyway, remember my words then, and stick it.
>
> Stick it, my lads, as those others have done before you. Stick it, for the credit of the regiment, for the glory of our name. Remember always that that glory lies in your hands, each one of you individually. And just as it is in the power of each one of you to tarnish it irreparably, so is it in the power of each one of you to keep it going undimmed. Each one of us counts, men, each one of

us has to play the game. Not because we're afraid of being punished if we're found out, but because it is the game.

The Regiment, my lads – the Regiment.
It is only the Regiment that counts.

Private Victor Sylvester, Argyll & Sutherland Highlanders

15

Letters from...

War changed men, or more importantly it changed their perspective on life. Letters to and from home played a major part in sustaining individual resolve:

> Looking back on the life of a young officer on the western front, it is strange to realize that for a young man just turned 20 it was a privilege to be given such a considerable responsibility for the care of a large body of men mostly older than himself, and to win their trust. (Lieutenant A.H. Crerar, 2nd Battalion Royal Scots Fusiliers)

In a letter to his parents, Corporal Alexander began by dispensing advice to his brother Jamie, who had just enlisted: 'Tell him to keep his heart up and put all his heart and soul into it, don't trust too much to anyone and mind No 1 and he won't go wrong'. The tone of the letter soon changed into an attack on those who had not volunteered but who had chosen to wait until conscripted:

> This Derby affair [this is in reference to Lord Derby, the Director General of Recruitment when conscription became law in January 1916] will be making some of the slackers hop. I only wish I had some of them out here having a taste of this. They may be sorry they did not take their chance along with the others. Soldiering is bad enough without having to do it against your will, eh, but I suppose they will get the same thanks as the rest of us once it's over.

Private W. Reid was serving in Gallipoli with the 4th Battalion Royal Scots when the battalion returned to the firing line on 29 August 1915: 'Got into the firing line again and are in a quiet corner not much to report. Was on guard in the firing line and was surprised at 2.00 am to hear a dogs mournful cry in the deserted village of Krithia, this incident makes one think of the suffering which war brings in its train.' J.B. MacLean wrote to his brother Alex: 'I received your p.c. from Montreal and I'm glad to hear you were declined for military service, and no doubt you are glad to have it off your conscience.' In a further letter to his brother he touched on the subject of winning medals:

> The battalion has also got two more MCs for the fighting in April. I have practically no chance of ever getting anything like that unless I did something marvellous, as I am not one of the Sandhurst brigade, and hence nothing we do is right to some people.

This was a subject to which he often returned:

> People at home think the MC is easy got but the ordinary infantry officer has to do something thrilling before he gets a recommendation even. I'm not thinking about anything like that and all I want is to get out with a whole skin.

By August 1917, with the onset of the Passchendaele offensive, MacLean's letters were beginning to show a more realistic, if not pessimistic, tone: 'The reserve trenches here are A1 with very fine dug-outs but it is a hot part and I've begun to realize there is a war on.' His letters of October 1917 show no change in this new perception:

> I note you are persistently optimistic as to an early finish of the war, but I'm afraid it will take a bit longer than you appear to think, although I have no doubt we shall down the Hun all right.

> I long for the piping times of peace again and I shall be happy when, if ever, they come again. No one but a lunatic enjoys a life like this, and when I get the chance I intend to make up, and a bit, for some of the present discomforts.

By May 1918, on his return from hospital, he has come to realise that luck plays a major part in survival:

> Since coming up here I have heard that during my absence the battalion has been 'over the top' and has of course had many casualties, including a good many officers, so I have been exceedingly lucky in just being away at the psychological moment and I naturally feel thankful.

Left with his own thoughts on the eve of battle, Lieutenant Thorburn contemplated the day to come:

> With a warning in the morning by the most deafening crash of guns, I assault the enemy's position. Not the cheeriest thing to brood upon all day, especially to-nights work. For the assault we will see red, but to-night we will be in a mortal funk! However, it has got to be done, so I must just go and do it and hope for the best.
>
> One thing! The lucky man who comes through it all should have a good long rest, as the regiment will nearly cease to exist.

Thorburn received six bayonet wounds and head injuries while taking the Turkish positions on the morning of 21 January 1916. Hospitalised at Basra, then taken to Bombay, he was subsequently awarded the Military Cross for his action in leading the attackers into the trenches. Lieutenant W.S. Dane, 4th Battalion Seaforth Highlanders, continually used humour as his defence against the horrors of war:

> Good Heavens! How the time does go! Here is September, and we are still in the same place. Before we know where we are, we

shall be wearing gum boots, overcoats, mufflers and mittens. If we don't do something soon I shall die of stagnation.

Lieutenant Lionel F.S. Sotheby, Argyll and Sutherland Highlanders, was attached to the Black Watch and was always aware that he was an outsider. In a war where shared experiences and comradeship were essential for survival, his isolation added to the strain:

There is only one thing I regret, and that is not being with the Argylls. The Black Watch is a nice regiment and is the premier one of Scotland, but to be 'attached' takes a lot of spirit away. I adored the Argylls ever so much, because the officers were some of the nicest people I have ever met... Here I have been landed in another regiment not knowing customs or a single man, except those I met at Havre. They are a great regiment and have not had any officers attached from other regiments before... I think they resented it, and consequently it was an uphill fight to get them accustomed. You can have no idea how a regiment such as this views the appearance of comparative strangers.

Sotheby's affinity was with the men under his command: 'I have no wish to be anything other than a Second Lieutenant out here – one is part of the men themselves then, and that is what I like.' Similarly, his feelings about war itself were strong:

I have no intention of leaving the line. It amuses me intensely, as one becomes totally callous of the dead, and death that are around you. Horrible to say this is the truth. I don't know what I shall be like after this war. I feel I am passing through a peculiar stage, just as a caterpillar becomes a chrysalis and then a butterfly. I cannot explain. It comes unseen and makes you oblivious of almost everything at times, save one intense desire to kill, kill, kill, the Germans in front. Sometimes I get bored as it seems one has to remain out until you

> get wounded or killed, at other time[s] I live in a perfect heaven fairly revelling in it and enjoying the ramparts immensely.

Others viewed the war in a different light:

> It was all taken you know as part of the game and I don't think any of us realized that there was a very unpleasant side to war until we got into the first trenches ever. We were digging them and then a lot of one's friends got killed. (R.C. Money, 1st Battalion Cameronians)

After a period of absence, R.C. Money returned to his battalion, 1st Cameronians, on Friday 30 June 1916, the eve of the Somme offensive, and felt uneasy among so many new faces, replacements for casualties:

> Must frankly admit that I am a lot softer than I was 14 months ago, or else it is being among comparative strangers, for I am not so keen and eager as I was then – or perhaps I am too newly out from home. I daresay it will be better when one gets settled down to it. A beautiful evening only marred by war.

The original timetable for the Somme had been held up by weather, and when travelling to rejoin his battalion, Money experienced the British bombardment:

> They tell us there was some bombardment, but it didn't disturb our rest, gas is to be sent over tonight if the wind favours us. I am not sure that I care about battle fighting as much as I did.

Many men survived because they were able to detach themselves from the realities of war. War only became personal when friends were killed, as Captain D. Dick discovered:

> It was reported round the trenches that an HLI officer had been killed by a German trench mortar, I wondered if it might be Alex.

It was, and I was saddened by the fact, as well as becoming angry against the unknown Germans who had been responsible for the death of my friend. The war had become personal.

Kenneth Kershaw enlisted in Stirling Castle as a private in the Argyll & Sutherland Highlanders on 6 August 1914. His previous experience in Russell School Officers Training Corps, as well as the fact that he had lived in both France and Germany and could speak the languages fluently, ensured that he was commissioned as a second lieutenant in the 9th Battalion Gordon Highlanders in September of the same year. He was killed at Loos between 25 and 27 September 1915. In a postscript to a letter written on 30 June 1915 he expressed his enthusiasm for the war:

Thank heaven this tedious time is over, Thursday will be the happiest day of my life without exception. I am chosen to fight for my country, my whole and only one ambition in life. Pray nightly that I may catch a column of Germans with one of the machine guns at close quarters, I have no time. Three cheers for all the world bar those __ Germans, devilish glad we are not going to the Dardanelles.

While some, like Lieutenant Dane, could use humour as an escape from the realities of war, not all were so lucky. J.G. Scott, serving with the Black Watch, wrote to his father:

Right in the thick of it now. It is hard to describe the approach to the firing line, or any of the day, without bringing in the grey side of the war. However, all that part is to be buried in oblivion in this country, I hope, and I'll try in all my letters to follow the splendid example of all the cheery officers out here and get along describing the funny bits. At the same time, one thanks God very humbly that the homeland itself is practically intact. Such a scene of death, decay, ruin, and desolation unspeakable I never could have imagined.

Ten days before he was himself killed on the first day of the Battle of Loos, Sergeant Joseph Miller Barber, 9th Battalion Black Watch, wrote to the brother of one of his comrades who had just joined up:

> I hope you will get to like it, if you have not done so already, in that queer monotonous sort of way we all do. Grousing all the time and all the same having a feeling inside that we will be sorry when it's all over, when we will have to look about and see how we are going to get through the rest of our lives.

The idea of dying a hero's death was not appealing to all. The letters of Captain Patrick Duncan of the 4th Battalion Black Watch cover the entire period of the war and give a deep insight into the thinking of one man. He wrote from France to his brother Bob in Dundee on 1 August 1915:

> It is an appalling state of matters that men professing the same Christianity should, after 1900 years of teaching, bring such desolation on a peaceful county town. It is far worse than the middle ages, when those fighting were ignorant religious fanatics but at this time of day both sides have been educated and know better.

He did not view the war as a moral necessity but rather saw it as a form of commercial adventure:

> The fact is that all Christian countries have been really bent on material prosperity to the exclusion of everything else, and this includes Christian governments. The fact is there has been the same ruthless spirit in industry and commerce as is now pervading the combatants in this war.

In October, after the losses sustained at the Battle of Loos, Patrick Duncan wrote to his father while recovering from wounds in the Duchess of Westminster Hospital, Paris: 'I wish someone would take hold of the situation and see the matter through and have fewer "meetings" and conferences.' He continued, with regard to the reported shell shortage: 'I sincerely trust that there are plenty of munitions now in France, because shells are more effective than men against machine guns and defences etc.' The following month he was writing to his brother Bob encouraging him not to join the infantry but to join the Mechanical Transport section or some other skilled unit, claiming he would 'get better food in those branches and probably more comfortable sleeping quarters than with an infantry regiment'. He continued by telling his brother 'you need not risk your health un-necessarily'. In a letter to his father written on 5 November, Duncan touches on the subject of the Derby Scheme, the forerunner to the coming conscription act, and its impact: 'How is recruiting getting on? How many men are the authorities in your district asking? Is it a workable scheme, and can you give me particulars.'

The letters from Captain Duncan changed significantly over time. In August 1915 he was writing: 'I keep very fit and have begun to realise that to be happy out here you must try and forget yourself and live from day to day only. A self-conscious man is unhappy; a cheery man never thinks about himself. I will try and practi[s]e the latter disposition.' A few weeks later, in the build-up to the British offensive at Loos, he wrote: 'Things may be going a little quicker shortly. I often look back to outings we had together, with great pleasure. We came out of the trenches last night and are billeted pretty near the firing line.' He wrote from hospital while recovering from leg wounds suffered at Loos:

> I have everything to be thankful for, and I am very much so, although a little anxious. The anxiety is not about my legs but about the position of affairs in France and in the Balkans. I wish someone would take a very firm hold of the situation and see the matter through, and have fewer 'meetings and conferences' etc etc.

I sincerely trust that there are plenty of munitions now in France, because shells are more effective than men against machine guns and defences etc.

I would watch Greece, carefully, the queen should not be trusted for a moment.

By May 1918, after four years of war, his attitude had changed: 'I wish very much to develop a "love of danger" but it won't come. It is an unpleasant mixture, the feeling of peace and contentment, engendered by this country side, compared with the anticipation of frightfulness that may come.' Perhaps his most poignant comment came in September 1918, two months before the armistice: 'Men are really fiends when they throw all moral law aside.' Captain D. Dick had also adopted a more pragmatic approach. After recovering in hospital he was sent to Dreghorn camp, Edinburgh:

> By that time the glamour of war was over – I had enlisted in the spirit of the knights of old, fired on with ambition to get the chance of being a hero – and gaining a medal. War, I now knew was a matter of doing one's duty, of standing by your comrades and not letting them down under any circumstances, and of keeping your fears to yourself.

Writing to his parents, Private Cuthill of the 4th Battalion Black Watch was determined to prevent his brother enlisting:

> You were saying that James was home with you and I hope that he will soon be all right again but tell him never to come out here. I may tell you that I have seen some strange sights since I came out here. Some of them I don't wish to see again. I wish I was back in Bonnie Dundee again.

He also expressed firm views on trench warfare: 'I tell you that I am sorry that I ever seen it [France]. It is not war here it is pure murder. You don't get a fighting chance, you have simply got to wait and chance your luck.' In a later letter to his parents, Private Cuthill continued in a similar vein, in a further attempt to persuade his brother to stay at home:

> I hope he never sees France. I tell you that I am sorry that I ever seen it. It is not war here it is pure murder. You don't stand a fighting chance. You have simply got to wait and chance your luck.

It is clear here that Private Cuthill's concern is about the randomness of trench warfare, the impersonal mechanics of the war. In the expectation of impending death, many men took the opportunity to leave 'last letters' in safe keeping to be sent on to their loved ones in the event of the writer's death. When, on the last day of February 1918, his battalion was detailed to stop the German offensive, Hakewell-Smith wrote a dramatic letter in the expectation of being killed:

> If you ever get this letter you'll know that my battalion has attempted to stop the great Boche offensive, and that one of these things will have happened. Killed, missing, or wounded and missing. If I am posted missing you must allow 3 clear months to elapse before assuming the first case. Buck up old girl, don't worry. I am perfectly happy and confident. Give them all my love at home and tell them I hope in the eventuality would be able to repay in some small measure the great kindness you and they have all done to me. The warning has been very short and you must excuse a scribble but I want you to know how much I appreciate everything you have done for me and I shall always pray for you. Ones thoughts at times like these are necessarily very near to god and all the people one loves. My only sorrow is that I can not now repay in the earthly world anything to aunt May and Granny and the others… the very best of love dear D [Miss Dorothy Currey, London] and may God keep and help you for all your kindness to me.
> P.S. I am quite happy and confident.

There was a follow-up to this in a letter dated 11 March 1918:

> What a deuce of a fright you must have had. I am most awfully sorry, but it was due to an over-zealous post corporal. Things were looking very black when we went into the line and I handed that letter into the orderly room to be sent off if the worst came to the worst. Unfortunately the aforementioned post corporal saw it on the adjutants table and thought it was a late letter and popped it into the mail bag.

Unfortunately, such mistakes were not unusual. Walter Morrison was serving in the Hood Battalion, Royal Naval Brigade, when he was wounded at Gallipoli. After recovering in hospital on the island of Gozo he came home to Dundee to recuperate and was present when the telegram arrived telling his mother that he was dead, killed in action.

A letter sent by Lieutenant Hakewell-Smith clearly shows the strain of life in the trenches:

> Have had an absolutely hellish time in the trenches. The battalion is still in. Three of us have been sent out for a rest. One night I was nearly a raving lunatic and if we had not come out I would have most assuredly been now on the way to England with broken down nerves. We were holding a part of the line where there was much mining activity. I was OC craters. There were over 30 of them. 8 mines were exploded while I was there. These were always accompanied by trench mortars which were the fathers and mothers of all previous ones I have ever seen.

As a support for the war effort and to provide comfort for the troops, schoolchildren collected eggs and sent them to troops recovering in hospital along with letters of support. In 1917, Private J.B. Low, 9th Battalion Gordon Highlanders, was recovering in No. 3 Stationary Hospital, Rouen. In a letter to his schoolgirl pen pal Mary he wrote: 'You may think that you would like to be a man, so that you would have a chance of having a shot at the Germans, if so I would like to say that this is murder not fighting, and its horrible.' Low had been injured at Arras in April, when German shelling had brought a house down on top of him, quite literally. He had been buried alive for a considerable period and was subsequently affected by the experience. In another letter to her he wrote:

> When I was eleven years old I joined the Boys' Brigade, and I can remember the night when I was handed my belt, haversack, and hat, and put them on, and my idea was, that I was of some importance, and I longed to be a soldier, but I find now that I'm a soldier, that I would rather be the boy again, for sham fighting is a great deal different to the real thing.

Low was sent to a Canadian Red Cross Hospital in Buckinghamshire, from which he sent Mary another depressing letter reflecting his emotions:

> Well little friend I am so glad to be in England again, after thirteen weary months in France, away from the hardships, and terrible bloodshed. Oh little friend it was something awful, the sights one saw there was enough to put a lot of men mad, and I only hope I'm not sent back again.

Letters from home were eagerly awaited. Alan Macgregor Wilson recorded in his diary on 30 May 1915: 'I have not yet received any word from home. It is become a serious drain on my patience. Waiting for a piece of Scotland to be sent me conveyed on the pages of a letter.' Corporal Garside echoed this anxiety at the lack of news from home. On 22 June 1916 his diary reads:

> Been right down in hell with worry over Jeanie not writing since 7th June. Began to feel uneasy on Sunday 18th. Getting worse

every day. Imagine all sort of things may have happened. Wrote Mother yesterday and asked her to enquire, have always written Jeanie regularly twice a week and cannot understand her silence, cannot help thinking something terrible has happened. Why does she not write. What with the hard work at all hours of night and day, driving on crowded narrow roads in bad conditions in the dark and without lights and the responsibility of looking after my section then this terrible uncertainty about those at home, I am about done up. If I don't hear something in a few days I shall sure have an accident or go mad.

However, two days later he was full of excitement: 'Heard from Jeanie today. Thank God. All well. Don't care XXX for war as long as they are alright at home.'

Charles Bowman, 9th Battalion Gordon Highlanders, landed in France in late June 1916 and was killed in late August of the same year. In the short period of his service he wrote numerous letters, not only to his wife, but in some instances directly to his children. The letters show not only his concern for the well-being of his family but also his optimism for the future:

24 June
Dear Lizzie and the Bairns,
Owing to the censor I can only say I am writing this somewhere in France. We arrived safely after a long journey and a good passage across. We had a bit of rain last night and the ground was a quagmire. It has cleared up now however and is a fine sunny night. We shifted up country a bit today by train. It is very pretty country very like the lowlands of Scotland with the green fields and trees.

I hope you and the bairns are all well. Jean was just beginning to know me when I had to come away. Now dear I have some duties to do tonight I will stop. With love to you all and kisses.
Ever yours
Dad.

28 June
Dear Lizzie and the Bairns,
I hope this will find you all well as I am glad to say it leaves me. I am getting along all right out here and the weather is warm but we are having a good deal of rain. However it is better than if it was cold. I hope you are all getting on alright. I suppose the schools will be closed by now.

They are a very decent crowd that I am with and as yet we don't have too much hard graft although it isn't just a picnic – the place I am writing this in is newly opened and there is a great crowd of Jocks as the Highland Regiments are called. I may not have the same facilities for writing soon and if I am a day or two in writing don't be alarmed. But you can be assured dear that I will write as often as I can. Do you think you could get a photo taken and send it out if you can manage. I would prize it very much.

I was out in the town which is close to our camp last night but I can't say I was greatly impressed by it, the streets were very rough and dirty with a lot of refuse about them. And most of the inhabitants looked as if they had had a quarrel with soap, although 'Sunlight' is very prominently advertised wherever you go.

I will stop now as it is near closing time [YMCA] with lots of love to you and the bairns. Tell Will and Irvine to write me a few lines and as Jean can't write tell here to send a kiss.
Ever your loving
Dad.

6 July
My Dear Lizzie
I got your letter today and have to thank you very much for the PO which you sent. But, Dear, never you mind sending as we get most of the things we need out here, at least we do where we presently are and you will need all your bobs, I hope you are getting into your usual again. It was rather a hurried separation but we will look forward to meeting again soon and you will just need to buck up and I think you will like staying in Aberdeen. Dear

little Jean never got time to get really acquainted with her daddy but will hope to have a good time together yet in Blighty when we finish of the Allyman. I am keeping OK, and with my short hair (you wouldn't complain of the barber not taking it short enough now) and fierce moustache (what what) I don't look like I used too – you will see by the papers how well the boys are doing out here and it is making Mr German dance a bit. The weather is very warm but it gets chilly at night and there is always the appearance of rain. Now dear I will stop. I am enclosing a letter to the bairns. Excuse the scrawl as I am writing this on my knees.
Ever loving
Chas

6 July
Dear Willie, Irvine and Jean
I hope that this will find you all well and that you are enjoying the Summer weather and getting to the links and the sands every day. I was sorry I did not get spoken to you all when I was passing up King Street but never mind we'll all have some good times yet. I had a note from Miss Ganed and she was telling me that Irvine could play God Save the King on the piano. I was very pleased to hear that. I believe Willie would be a fine player on the Gramophone! Eh Bill – Jeans favourite instrument would I think be a ? sugar whistle. I will be very glad if you boys can spare time to write a few lines to me and if Irvine has any sketches to send them on. Jean can ornament the letter with some of her pictures. Now I will stop and I hope that you will maybe get to Montrose before the end of your holidays.
With love to you all
Your loving Dad

19 July
My Dear Lizzie,
I have been expecting to hear from you every day but have not yet got a letter. You will see by above that we are still in the same place

but in a different division so that possibly if you have written it may have gone astray. I hope you are all keeping well and getting good weather for your holidays.

Did you send the paper about the insurance etc, to Alice. I saw by a paper that they were getting it carried on but some were not getting so much as they thought they should. It is a month today since I left Aberdeen, it looks longer to me but the time will pass and roll on the finish of the war and back to Blighty once more. Now as I am going on parade I will have to stop. Hoping you and the bairns are all keeping well and that you will write soon if you have not done so already.
With love to you all
Chas.

27 July
Dear Lizzie,
I have had no word from you since your letter dated 3rd July more than 3 weeks ago and am very wearied to hear from you. It means so much out here to get a letter. Of course with us shifting so much they may be longer in getting delivered. We are getting good weather and I am keeping all right with the exception of my feet which are rather sore but they will get better through time. There was a hot time out here last night. Our artillery were at it all night and no one at home can imagine the scene. The sky was lit up almost continuously with the flack of the guns and the bursting of the shells. Mr Allyman had got it terribly and if we keep it up they cannot stick it much longer. I hope you are keeping all right and not worrying. How is Jean getting on. She is a dear wee girl. I hope the boys are also keeping all right. They will soon be going back to school. Now dear, I will stop and I will write again at the first opportunity. With fondest love to you and the bairns.
Ever yours
Chas

6 August
Dear Lizzie,
I got your letter yesterday after I had written you and the bairns. I was very pleased to hear you were having a good time at Montrose.

I was very sorry to hear that Willie Edwards had died of wounds after coming through so long a time but there has been nothing like the ramy that is going on just now since the war began and I hope and think that it will finish Mr Allyman before the winter is past.

I think you should send in the paper as it might be the means of you getting a few quid which would be a very handy thing for you. If you could get a house like we had in Dundee or something similar it would be nice but there is the flitting back, that takes some work. With love and kisses to the bairns and yourself.
Ever yours
Dad.

Dear Irvine,
I am writing this to wish you many happy returns on your birthday and hope you will be spared to see many of them and before your next one comes that I will be at home beside you all. You will see by the above address that I have shifted [from the 9th to the 1st Battalion]. We have all got kilts again and were sent up to the front on Saturday. You would have laughed if you had seen us in cattle trucks lying on the floor and sitting with feet hanging out at the door. When we arrived at the end of ou[r] railway journey we had to march all night to get up here and you may be sure we were tired enough. We had a rest all day yesterday and we needed it. We are just at the back of the firing line and the big guns are going night and day. Last night the French were giving the Huns beans but today things are quiet except for a few Jack Johnston's [heavy artillery shells] which the Bosch are sending over to keep us in mind they are there. Now as the man is waiting to take the letters I will stop. I will write you tonight. With love to you all.
Ever your loving
Dad.

Dear Lizzie,
We are getting very warm weather out here in fact we do all our work In shirt sleeves and then it is hot enough. There is one thing we can get a bath every day in a river that is quite near and it is not too deep so that it does not matter whether one can swim or not there is no danger of getting drowned unless you lie down to it.

Did I tell you when we came to this battalion we got new kilts so we are the real MacKay again and not half highlanders as when we left King Street. It looks a long time since we came down that way. It is 6 weeks past Thursday since we left. Now dear I will stop and if I have time before the Post Corporal comes round I will write a line or two to the boys if not I will write soon. With love and kisses to you and the bairns.
Ever your loving
Chas.

On 13 August he wrote: 'If it wasn't for the sound of the guns in the distance one would think we were camping out down in the country at home.'

On 18 August he sent a postcard:

Just a line or two to let you know I am OK we are up in the line having a hot time. Hope you are all keeping well and have benefited by your holiday. Love and kisses to you and the bairns.
Your loving
Dad.

Charles Bowman was killed on 18 August 1916, shortly after sending this final card.

16

The End?

With the coming of the armistice, some, like Captain Patrick Duncan, 4th Battalion Black Watch, were already thinking ahead to the future. He wrote to his brother Bob:

> Did you go to hear Bonar Law's speech? What are your ideas of the latest developments in politics? If there was as much 'action' among politicians as 'talking' things would soon be settled at home. I do not envy the troops in Russia. I never thought we could be beaten in the war but I did not expect such a complete overthrow of Germany, especially about June of this year.

He later wrote to his father on the same subject: 'I quite agree with Bob's views re Asquith's party. What we want now is a strong government who will enforce the law all round.'

Lieutenant E.W. Hancock, serving in East Africa with the Gordon Highlanders, was a patient in the British Base Hospital, Mombasa, when he heard the news of the armistice. He gave a typically subdued reaction: 'Armistice declared with Germany. I don't propose to effervesce over this. Everybody knows what everybody else feels and thinks about it.' Perhaps the last word should go to William Duncan, Scottish Horse, who shared Hancock's feeling of anticlimax and whose thoughts turned to the works of Robert Burns:

When the armistice was announced there was no great flag-waving. We had all had enough. We now had a feeling of quiet satisfaction and relief. We had enough of this bloody, filthy thing called war. There is no glamour. Civilisation? Can the dream of Robbie Burns ever come true when 'Man to man the world ower shall brothers be for aw that'?

Soldiers Quoted

A. Alexander, Royal Scots Fusiliers
C. Alexander, Argyll & Sutherland Highlanders
W.L. Andrews, Black Watch

J. Barber, Black Watch
C.N. Barclay, London Scottish and Scottish Rifles
W. Begbie, Royal Scots
D. Bell, Machine Gun Corps and Tank Corps
I.F. Bell, Gordon Highlanders
I. Bolton, Argyll & Sutherland Highlanders
H. Bowie, Black Watch
C. Bowman, Gordon Highlanders
J. Braid, Black Watch
G.J. Brown, King's Own Scottish Borderers

W. Cameron, Black Watch
W. Cameron, Scottish Horse
J. Campbell, Cameron Highlanders
T. Chamberlain, Cameron Highlanders
A. Cheyne, Gordon Highlanders
H.D. Clark, Argyll & Sutherland Highlanders
N. Collins, Seaforth Highlanders
R.M. Craig, Cameron Highlanders
A. Crerar, Royal Scots Fusiliers
J. Cumming, Morgan Cameron Highlanders
J.C. Cunningham, Argyll & Sutherland Highlanders
W. Cuthill, Black Watch

W.S. Dane, Seaforth Highlanders
D. Dick, Argyll & Sutherland Highlanders
P. Duncan, Black Watch
W. Duncan, Scottish Horse

D. Ferguson, Machine Gun Corps

Corporal Garside, Motor Transport Company
A. Gilmore, Argyll & Sutherland Highlanders
Sergeant Grey, Royal Scots

E. Hakewell-Smith, Royal Scots Fusiliers
E.W. Hancock, Gordon Highlanders
A. Hay, Scottish Horse and Black Watch
J. Hay-Young, Argyll & Sutherland Highlanders

A. Imlah, Gordon Highlanders
W. Imlah, Gordon Highlanders

J. Jack, Black Watch

M.D. Kennedy, Scottish Rifles (Cameronians)

K. Kershaw, Argyll & Sutherland Highlanders

M. Lawson, Duke of Cornwall's Light Infantry
J.R. Leslie, Black Watch
J.B. Low, Gordon Highlanders
J. Lunn, Cameron Highlanders

D. MacDonald, Scottish Rifles (Cameronians)
F.B. Mackenzie, Royal Scots
J.D. Mackie, Argyll & Sutherland Highlanders
I. Maclaren, Black Watch
J.B. MacLean, Scottish Rifles (Cameronians)
J.M. Marshall, Black Watch
H.E. May, Cameron Highlanders
T. McCall, Cameron Highlanders
G.G. McKay, Royal Scots
F. Merton, Royal Scots
A. Mitchell, Black Watch
R.C. Money, Scottish Rifles (Cameronians)
W. Morison, Royal Naval Brigade

W. Nelson, Highland Light Infantry
A. Nicol, Argyll & Sutherland Highlanders

A. Paterson, Highland Light Infantry

R.L. Ramsey, Black Watch
J. Reekie, Black Watch
W. Reid, Royal Scots
A.G. Ritchie, Scottish Rifles (Cameronians)
C.B. Robertson, Argyll & Sutherland Highlanders
R.H.W. Rose, Scottish Rifles (Cameronians)

S. Saunders, Gordon Highlanders
J.G. Scott, Black Watch
V. Silvester, Argyll & Sutherland Highlanders
W. Sorley Brown, King's Own Scottish Borderers
L. Sotheby, Argyll & Sutherland Highlanders, attached Black Watch

A. Thompson, Black Watch
P. Thompson, Argyll & Sutherland Highlanders

M. Thorburn, Black Watch

J. Wallace, King's Own Scottish Borderers
F. Ward, Cameron Highlanders
T. Williamson, Royal Scots Fusiliers
A.M. Wilson, Black Watch
J. Wylie, Black Watch

List of Illustrations

25 Mopping-up party clearing enemy trenches and dugouts. (QOHMC)

26 A caricature of the officers of the 8th Battalion Royal Scots queuing outside their bath house. (RSM)

27 Soldiers of the King's Own Scottish Borderers searching for lice on the beach at Gallipoli. (KOSB)

28 Black Watch on the Western Front searching for lice. (BWA)

29 Steam was the most common method of pest control. (KOSB)

30 Work party carrying equipment through the mud at Beaucourt, November 1916. (QOHMC)

31 King's Own Scottish Borderers using a machine to reload machine-gun belts in a trench at Gallipoli. (KOSB)

32 A work party clearing debris from the Le Sars–Pys road in France, March 1917. (QOHMC)

33 The Scarpe at Blangy, April 1917. (QOHMC)

34 Stores being unloaded in Palestine. (RSM)

35 A transport column in Palestine. (RSM)

36 Troops bivouac for a short rest in Fricourt Wood, June 1917. (QOHMC)

37 The Black Watch at rest. (BWA)

38 Men of the Black Watch at rest before the Battle of Loos. (BWA)

39 Royal Scots church parade in the field. (RSM)

40 Black Watch hold sports while resting at Bailleul, May 1917. (QOHMC)

41 A ration party from the 6th Battalion Cameron Highlanders going up the trenches at Arras, March 1917. (QOHMC)

42 Men of the Black Watch relax in the line. (BWA)

43 King's Own Scottish Borderers filling water bottles from two flat-sided containers. (RSM)

44 Bread being distributed from a field bakehouse. (RSM)

45 Men of the Royal Scots Fusiliers gather round the field kitchen in Krithia Gully, Gallipoli. (KOSB)

46 A river boat on the Tigris which was converted for use by the Red Cross. (KOSB)

47 The liner *Mauritania* was used as a Red Cross hospital ship.

48 Stretcher bearers struggle to carry the injured past waiting Seaforth Highlanders in the narrow front line trench.

49 Officers' dugouts in Palestine. (RSM)

50 The Black Watch on the march. (BWA)

52 Seaforths resting by the side of the road. (QOHMC)

52 Rations being distributed to the carrying parties. Black Watch. (BWA)

53 Watercolour of Royal Scots in trench. (RSM)

54 Route march.

55 Black Watch. (BWA)

56 Walking the plank: the dangers facing work parties. (QOHMC)

Index